DISCARD

Chapter 11
electrocution
photo.

D0778525

VANCOUVER PUBLIC LIBRARY

The borrower is responsible for returning
this book in good condition. Please examine
before taking out and report any damage.
Fines will be charged on items not returned
by closing time on the date due.

Form 15

JUN 29 1992

Sensationalism

and the

New York Press

Columbia History of Urban Life
Kenneth T. Jackson, General Editor

COLUMBIA HISTORY OF URBAN LIFE
Kenneth T. Jackson, GENERAL EDITOR

Sensationalism and the New York Press

JOHN D. STEVENS

Columbia University Press / New York

COLUMBIA UNIVERSITY PRESS

NEW YORK   OXFORD

Copyright © 1991 Columbia University Press

ALL RIGHTS RESERVED

Library of Congress Cataloging-in-Publication Data

Stevens, John D.

Sensationalism and the New York Press / John D. Stevens.

p.   cm.—(Columbia history of urban life)

Includes bibliographical references and index.

ISBN 0-231-07396-8

1. American newspapers—New York (N.Y.)—Political aspects—19th
century.   2. American newspapers—New York (N.Y.)—Political
aspects—20th century.   3. Press and politics—New York (N.Y.)—
History—19th century.   4. Press and politics—New York (N.Y.)—
History—20th century.   5. Sensationalism in journalism.

I. Title.   II. Series.

PN4899.N4S74   1991

071′.471—dc20

90-47144

CIP

Casebound editions of Columbia University Press books
are Smyth-sewn and printed on permanent
and durable acid-free paper

PRINTED IN THE UNITED STATES OF AMERICA

c 10 9 8 7 6 5 4 3 2 1

Contents

JUN 29 1992

Preface

New York City, contrary to what many who reside there think, is *not* the world, nor even the United States. It is anything but "representative." It has been for more than a century and a half, however, the nation's cultural capital. In journalism, as in so much else, the rest of the nation takes its cues from the Big Apple. Some see the city as fact, others as symbol—but nobody can ignore it or what goes on there.

Like so many others, author John Gunther was at once dazzled and repulsed by New York, which he called "the incomparable, the brilliant star city of cities . . . a law unto itself, the Cyclopean paradox, the inferno with no out-of-bounds, the supreme expression of both the miseries and the splendors of contemporary civilization."*

Historians of American journalism, dazzled by presumed political influence, have devoted far more attention to Greeley's *Tribune* than to Bennett's *Herald*, more to the *Times* than to the *Daily News*. Although many more New Yorkers read the *Herald* and the *Daily News*, they were not the people who interested historians. Because archivists shared this same

*John Gunther, *Inside USA* (New York: Harper & Row, 1951), p. 573.

elitist bias, such papers are difficult to study. Some are not even micro-filmed; those that have been are found in few libraries. Related records and manuscripts are almost nonexistent. This work concentrates on the newspapers of New York because their records, while terreibly sketchy, are far more complete than those for papers published elsewhere.

After a survey of sensationalism in earlier eras, we will examine New York City and its innovative newspapers during three pivotal periods. Part 1 focuses on the 1830s, a time when a new breed of penny publishers stepped up the tempo and broadened the appeal of their papers. We will try to see how and why these papers reflected the rapidly changing city.

In Part 2, we will move to the next watershed, the 1880s and 1890s, when Joseph Pulitzer and William Randolph Hearst added illustrations and big headlines to popular content, and attained record circulations. How were these "yellow" papers different from the ones invented sixty years earlier?

In Part 3, we will consider the new breed of pictorial tabloids that appeared in the 1920s. Again, we will compare these papers to earlier ones and set them in the social context of their day. The afterword discusses the supermarket tabloids of the late twentieth century.

In each period, we will be seeking clues about who read these papers and why. Most important, we will see what the papers actually printed as well as what contemporary critics and historians said about them. In each period, we will examine in some detail the coverage of spectacular crimes.

Newspapers—even the slightly scruffy ones—have supported more often than challenged prevailing moral standards. On balance, their continuity is remarkable. Nothing is more consistent than their wretched excess.

Acknowledgments

The author thanks the following for invaluable advice, research materials, and comments on drafts of parts of the book as it progressed: Patricia C. Cohen, Timothy Gilfoyle, Mary Hartman, Kenneth Jackson, Robert Kahan, Marion Marzolf, Harold L. Nelson, John Nerone, Donald Shaw, Mitchell Stephens, William H. Taft, Dwight Teeter, and Betty Winfield. A special thanks to the Gannett Foundation and the Gannett Center for Media Studies for the nine-month fellowship during which I did most of this research. Everette Dennis and the center staff were patient and understanding. I also am grateful for the sabbatical leave granted me by the University of Michigan and for research assistance from the Howard R. Marsh Center for the Study of Journalistic Performance.

My blessings on all librarians, especially those who tend the manuscripts and microforms. Much of this research was done in four fine libraries: Columbia University, the New-York Historical Society, the New York Public Library, and the University of Michigan. Martha Briggs was most helpful during my visit to the Lake Forest College collection.

My research assistant, David Robarge, was invaluable. Like most authors, I sometimes dragooned my wife as a research assistant; as in all matters, I relied heavily on her good sense and advice. Gwen, this book's for you.

Part One

T H E
1830S

1

"The More Things Change . . ."

"Nothing but scandal!"

"Isn't it disgraceful?"

"All that sex and crime stuff is enough to make you sick!"

"Why don't we ever hear about the good things that are going on?"

We could be eavesdropping almost anywhere and anytime in the last 2500 years. Those complaints were aimed at the diurnas of Ancient Rome, the balladeers of the Middle Ages, the broadsides of the fifteenth century, and at newspapers since they emerged in the seventeenth century. We can assume such complaints began as soon as men first learned to talk. They probably told tales—many of them none too nice—about one another. About 4000 years ago, when we learned to manipulate written symbols, we multiplied our tale-telling capacity.

Because scandals fascinate nearly everyone, they epitomize news. When two British journalists set out to record a history of scandals, they decided a scandal fascinates us precisely because we love to see the hypocrite naked before us—the more respectable the victim, the juicier the gossip.[1]

"The public wants to be shocked in order to confirm its own sense of virtue," the British journalists decided, a view that sounds very much like what sociologists call deviance theory. Emile Durkheim and his followers insist it is the deviant individual who challenges, and thus defines, the borders of acceptable behavior. In passing judgment on the deviant, the majority reassures itself about its own current standards. According to this theory, a society of saints would have to punish some to reaffirm majority values.[2] We all glory in seeing the mighty fall.

The author of a history of American political corruption defined scandal as "a moral stumbling," which, if exposed to the public, would discredit the politician.[3] As was emphasized, those standards change, and not always in the direction of liberality. For example, Americans elected as president such acknowledged philanderers and womanizers as James Garfield and Grover Cleveland, but in 1988 rejected candidate Gary Hart.

We are fascinated but simultaneously appalled at our own fascination. Wishing we were more high-minded, we denounce those who convey the scandalous information. "She (or he) is such a gossipmonger," we mutter as we rush to tell someone else. The better-educated always have been chagrined about lowbrow publications that dish up sex, crime, and scandal. But look what happens at the newsstand. Many more Londoners buy the *Sun* and *Mirror* than the eminently respectable *Times;* the *Daily News* and the *Post* outsell the *Times* in New York; the story is the same in France, Italy, Japan, India, and elsewhere.

There is nothing new about the allure of scandal. Oral tales and broadsides of earlier times were even more sensational than today's supermarket tabloids. Audiences have always had an insatiable appetite for real or imagined accounts of disasters, murders, and scandals; perhaps, as Mitchell Stephens suggests, because these interests are tied to a primitive need to be alert to potential threats and potential mates.[4]

WHAT IS SENSATIONALISM?

"Sensationalism" is one of the overly broad and vague "snarl words" denounced by semanticists. In common usage the term is pejorative, a label to categorize and stigmatize subjects we do not like. Sometimes we are offended by the content of the stories, at other times by the way in which they are presented or emphasized. Many times, we simply resent having such unpleasant matters forced on our attention.

Modern dictionaries emphasize the negative motives behind sensationalism. The *Oxford English Dictionary*, for example, talks of its being "calculated to produce a startling impression." *American Heritage Dictionary* says it is content designed to arouse strong reaction by exaggerated or lurid details. The *Random House Dictionary* says sensationalism is intended to produce "a startling or thrilling impression or to excite and please vulgar tastes." On the other hand, *Webster III* and *Funk & Wagnalls Dictionary* ignore intentions and emphasize effects, suggesting it arouses "intense, and usually superficial emotional response" or "gratifies improper curiosity." It is worth noting that *Samuel Johnson's Dictionary* of 1775 carried no negative connotations. To Dr. Johnson, sensationalism meant "perception by means of the senses." (This meaning is retained as a subfield of philosophy.) In the intervening two centuries, the Western intellectual tradition has shown far more respect for knowledge gained through the intellect than through the senses.

Widely used textbooks in journalism history courses equate sensationalism with excess. Frank Luther Mott, the dean of journalism historians, said sensationalism goes too far in appealing to our "fundamental and primitive human desires," while Edwin and Michael Emery define sensationalism as "emphasis on emotion for its own sake."[5] Sensationalism also has been defined as material published strictly for entertainment. Our heritage barely tolerates "mere" entertainment. First Amendment protection for content that entertains came late. Motion pictures were not protected until 1947, and still rank lower on First Amendment priorities than "serious" works, especially those concerned with politics.

Few writers acknowledge the positive side of sensationalism, namely that such accounts offer an alternative to the official view. As Joyce Milton suggested recently, "Indeed it might be argued that the history of the free press is the history of sensationalism."[6]

Much of what is labeled "sensational" is news of crime. No other type of news is of such universal interest. Newspaper accounts emphasizing thrills, horrors, shocks and alarms do not so much inform readers as allow them to share in the feelings of the actors in the real-life Grand Guignol. Display, emphasis, illustrations, and especially writing style are ensnarled in the modern concept of sensationalism, further complicating attempts at definition. Few of us read crime news for information; instead we read about crime in order to confront the dilemmas in our own life and society.[7] For many, reading such stories is a kind of "guilty pleasure." Offended by crime and violence itself, we are uncomfortable with *news* about those subjects. There was plenty of both before there were mass media, as there would be if we had no media to report them. It is easier to "kill the messenger" than to solve the underlying social evils.

George Juergens, in the introduction to his book on Joseph Pulitzer, isolated three dimensions of sensationalism: (1) emphasis on personalities; (2) preference for trivial over significant news, and (3) use of colloquial, personal language.[8] He found that sensational newspapers expanded the human interest story to report gossip and scandal about individuals that had formerly been regarded as private. In doing so, they struck a rich lode of news in crime and everyday happenings. This text adopts Juergens' definition.

There is at least a modicum of sensationalism in any news account intended to grab the reader's attention, so perhaps as Warren Francke has suggested, "the very elements of story-telling are so interwoven with the concept that any narrative treatment of news risks the damning label."[9] The more chatty and breezy its tone, the more likely a piece of prose is to be branded sensational.

Sex and violence are inherent in some stories that are "hard news" and must be covered. Even the calmest newspapers "distort" the reality of crime, in overreporting violent crimes, especially crimes against the person, while underreporting much more frequent property crimes.[10] Although editors say their readers demand crime news, it is worth noting how few potential jurors can recall reading about even the most spectacular local crimes. Although few would deny that the public has a legitimate interest in knowing enough to protect itself and in monitoring its criminal justice system, people of goodwill disagree about where that line should be drawn. Does the publication go out of its way to find and feature bloody and bizarre happenings? Readers turn to certain magazines for gore or titillation but presumably look for something more in their daily newspapers. Even an avid reader of *Playboy* might be offended to find on page three of his daily newspaper a large picture with absolutely no news tie-in of a bare-breasted girl; yet that is precisely what one London paper has been running in every issue for years. It is a matter of expectations.

NEWS HAS ALWAYS BEEN SENSATIONAL

Our survey begins in Ancient Rome and with the first organized agency of news collection in the West. Even then, elitists were accusing the popular media of sensationalism. Roman poets like Juvenal and essayists like Seneca made fun of *Acta Diurna,* the official court publication, which was written by scribes. At first the papyrus copies contained only verbatim accounts of Senate proceedings and official proclamations, but the scribes gradually added what we call "vital statistics"—notes about births, deaths, marriages, and divorces.

Copies were sought so eagerly that several firms competed to provide unofficial newsletters, containing not only the stuff of the *Acta* but also accounts of natural disasters, scandals, and changing alliances among noblemen. The scrolls recorded the triumphs of Roman armies, the murder of Julius Caesar, and the debaucheries of the mad Caligula. Although their circulation was minuscule and certainly limited to the rich and powerful, they prompted Seneca to write in one of his essays: "Is there any woman that blushes at divorce now that certain illustrious and noble ladies reckon their years, not by the number of consuls, but by the number of their husbands, and leave home in order to marry, and marry in order to be divorced? They shrank from this scandal as long as it was rare: now, since every gazette has a divorce case they have learned to do what they used to hear so much about." Or, one might suggest, they learned to do as the Romans did.

Violence, crime, and sex were staples in our folktales and ballads centuries before there were newspapers, but they were seldom censored. In copying the most popular tales, monks often sanitized them.[11] Within a century after its development in the early fifteenth century, printing had spread throughout Europe and into the British Isles, and the pioneer printers retold those same tales in their broadsides and corantos. Because their products were heavily censored everywhere by church and state, early printers avoided touchy political issues. The same British censors who checked every nuance in reports of the Thirty Years War seemed totally unconcerned with romantic and bloody tales.[12] From the sixteenth through the eighteenth centuries, almanacs were by far the most popular reading material in England, in part because they were peppered with astrology, witchcraft, rapes, and hangings.[13] Although during and after the French Revolution both Royalists and Republicans used almanacs to inculcate political ideas most Frenchmen continued to buy the cheap, apolitical versions from peddlers, which almost always included records of longevity and monstrous births.[14]

The British newsbooks abounded with ballads of murders, executions, and bizarre sex. They told of a Scotsman arrested for having sex with his horse, lovers so engaged in a kiss that they fell into a beer vat and drowned, and the man "hanged for Pederasty, in plain English buggery." Several reported the conviction in 1655 of a Kent woman for murdering her husband's mistress, cutting out her vulva and serving it up to her unfaithful husband. One sixteenth-century British news book told how a husband had murdered his sleeping wife by pouring ratsbane and ground glass into her vagina. Although illegal, pornography, most of it focusing on royalty or the clergy, circulated freely in pre-Revolutionary France. In such books Marie Antoinette was painted as a sexual monster, variously accused of being an insatiable nymphomaniac, a masturbator, a lesbian, and a dominatrix.[15]

The established editor, appealing to an elitist audience, has always been quick to denounce the sensationalism in upstart competitors, so it is not surprising to find Joseph Addison, as early as 1709, decrying the scurrility in other London papers.[16] Even in the late twentieth century, few editors of respectable publications speak out in defense of their less-esteemed competitors who test the boundaries of acceptable taste.

Until the late seventeenth century, the government tended to ignore the occasional outcry against sensational content, but it cracked down when large numbers of women became literate and started reading novels.[17] So long as reading had been confined to upper-class males there was little concern about bawdy novels such as *Tom Jones*. British censors reacted only when the relatively tame light novels, read mostly by women, became the best-sellers and the backbone of the new rental libraries.

British printers responded with even more crime stories. During the late seventeenth and early eighteenth centuries a flood of single-page broadsides and pamphlets detailed cases ranging from petty theft to murder, many betraying the admiration of the public for outlaws bold enough and strong enough to become highwaymen and even murderers.[18] Like every storyteller since Scheherezade the pamphleteers often made a good story better, and sometimes invented them out of whole cloth.[19]

Judging from the content of early nineteenth century broadsides such as the *Newgate Calendar,* sold cheaply on the streets and at fairs and public gatherings, Englishmen felt more threatened by thieves and brigands than by murderers. In this series of pamphlets named for London's most notorious prison, even the most hideous crimes were described calmly; often the confession was included, thus converting them into parables.[20] One issue was headlined:

The Full Account and latest Particulars of the Awful, inhuman and barbarous Murder of a female by cutting off her head, arms and legs and burning them.[21]

For the benefit of the many illiterates, broadsides often included crude line drawings and easily memorized verses that capsulized the moral. By referring to perpetrators as "fiends," "monsters" or "maniacs," publishers of broadsides comforted "normal" readers by distancing them from the perpetrators.

Throughout the centuries, literary censorship has focused more on the obscene than on the violent. As one literary critic expressed it:

> Where sex is censored, the substitute is sadism, the literary lynch and increased violence. . . . The popularity of violence is due to the fact that it is the only outlet for fears and inadequacies that is socially acceptable and still open to us. Our literature as a

result is empty of sex and reeking with sadism. . . . Violence and death have saved us from sex. Sex, which is legal in fact, is a crime on paper, while murder—a crime in fact—is on paper the best seller of all time.[22]

Long before there were newspapers, sermons conveyed news in early New England. In a period when all occurrences, especially those out of the ordinary, were clothed in religious, and therefore public, meaning, the public naturally looked for explanations to their ministers. The ministers obliged. More than half the catalogued seventeenth-century sermons were clearly and principally linked to events, often violent or sensational events. Many were delivered at public executions.[23] Thomas Carlyle wrote that in the modern nation, journalists had replaced clergymen as the moral guardians.[24]

The single issue of our first American newspaper, *Publick Occurences Both Foreign and Domestick,* published in Boston in 1695, included accounts of a suicide, sexual dalliances in the French Court, and an Indian massacre. John Campbell established the *Boston News-Letter,* the first successful American newspaper in 1704. Although Campbell published a dull and deferential little weekly, he regularly chronicled such "providences" as storms, fires, drownings, Indian attacks, and weird animals. He filled half an early issue with an account of the hanging of six pirates. Hangings were among the most popular subjects for pamphlets, as well.[25] In the wake of the Revolution, there were so many published accounts of seductions, murders, piracies, and hangings that Fisher Ames, a starchy conservative who seldom approved of anything the *hoi-poloi* did, wrote in 1801: "There seems to be a sort of rivalship among printers, who shall have the most wonders, and the strangest and most horrible crimes." That rivalry has never stopped.

2

New York, Crime, and the Newspapers

What was New York City like during the second quarter of the nineteenth century, this city that gave birth to the new form of American journalism we call the Penny Press? It was vital, vibrant, and violent—a gangly adolescent that had grown too fast for its own good.

First and foremost, it was the center of commerce, handling half the nation's imports and exports. The city's showpieces were the temples of commerce—the New York Custom House, the federal government's principal source of revenues, and the four-story Merchants' Exchange on Wall Street. The city's great harbors pulsed with outbound vessels, many of them laden with cotton; arriving ships brought not only finished goods, but hoards of eager immigrants. Beginning in 1825 the Erie Canal brought from the West another stream of products and people. New York's merchants were renowned for their shrewdness.[1]

Before 1820 the vast majority of Americans identified with the land. but now people were pouring into the cities, and especially into New York. A modest city of 60,000 in 1800, it had swollen to nearly a quarter million by

1830 and would double again by mid-century. Walt Whitman thrived on the city's excitement, especially its port.[2] The wharves, docks, and warehouses hummed with commerce. Carters and drayman clogged the nearby streets. By 1832 more than $100 million in commerce cleared the port; by 1841 New York handled half the nation's imports and exports.[3]

The pace of change was dizzying. Factories, stores, and hotels appeared in a twinkling only to be replaced as quickly by even grander ones. Broadway was where the wealthy shopped, dined, and went to be seen, but almost everyone lived and worked in the area below Washington and Union Squares. Such density made for an inviting market for those who had a product to peddle—like a cheap newspaper.

ON THE DARK SIDE

From ancient times, crime has been associated with the city. Thomas Jefferson wrote from Monticello in 1823 to a friend: "A city life offers you . . . painful objects of vice and wretchedness. New York . . . seems to be a cloacina [anus] of all the depravities of human nature. Here on the contrary, crime is scarcely heard of . . ."[4] In spite of the jeremiads by agrarians, there was little disorder in the cities of early America. It wasn't until the 1830s that municipalities considered crime serious enough to justify the hiring of policemen.

Americans have always been convinced a city's dark streets hide dark deeds.[5] The streets of New York certainly were dark, narrow, and dangerous. Only flickering candles and whale-oil lamps lit most of the city, although the better sections of town had gas street lights. After dark, "policing" was entrusted to about one hundred watchmen who were paid about $1 a night. The historian of New York policing wrote that the men either had other day jobs or could hold no other job. Many were political hacks. Supposedly on the lookout for crime, their incompetence and reluctance to get involved was legendary. "Thus, while the size and responsibilities of the Watch increased, its prestige and efficiency declined."[6]

Nor was crime control much better in the daytime, because the forty appointed marshals spent most of their time serving writs for the courts. The mayor named a commissioner who presided over the sixteen constables, elected from among those willing to run for the low-paying elected posts. The demands for a full-time paid police force had just begun and were realized at the end of the decade.[7]

Although statistics for the period are notoriously poor, crime and disorder apparently were spreading. In the twenty years from 1814 to 1834, the police court docket grew six times as fast as the population, and grand jury indictments suggest a modest but steady increase in criminal activity. Some of the increase can be attributed to better policing and reporting, but diarists and editors also thought crime was out of control. Most indictments were for assaults and petty thefts, but the New York *Herald* reported twenty-three murders during ten months in 1839.[8]

If policing was a problem, fire-fighting was a horror. Most houses and commercial buildings still were wooden, and even buildings with substantial facades had beams of dry timbers. Devastating fires frequently leveled entire blocks while rival volunteer companies stood by helplessly. (It would be another two decades before the city had paid firemen.) The swelling population had overwhelmed all city services; the reluctance of Albany to grant fuller home rule complicated matters further. A gagging stench hung over the slum areas where there were no sewers and little plumbing. Thousands of dray and cab horses dumped tons of manure along the streets daily, and except for the pigs, dogs, and rats, there was no regular garbage disposal.

Because poor people got where they were going on foot, they had to live near their jobs. If they felt like splurging and happened to be headed in the right direction, they might flag down one of the horse-drawn omnibuses, which charged two or three cents. Few of them would have had occasion to ride the new train, which in 1835 extended from lower Manhattan up to Yorkville.

New York City, it seems, has always had a housing shortage, and one not confined to the poor. Merchants and businessmen and their families sometimes spent months or even years in hotels; most unmarried men lived in boarding houses. Transients complained that no matter how many hotels opened none of them had vacant rooms.

Why did all those people keep coming? Primarily for economic opportunity, but for many other reasons as well. Many sought the exciting, magical place they had read about in popular novels. Although highbrow authors and poets painted a far grimmer picture, the ordinary reading fare celebrated the American city as a symbol of progress and growth.[9] Those who could not afford the quarter to buy such novels could obtain copies from lending libraries and reading rooms. Because of public schooling, literacy was fairly widespread by the 1830s.[10]

A RIOTOUS ERA

The city had known riots before, but nothing like the sixteen in 1834 and the thirty-seven the next year. At least 125 people were killed in the riots of the 1830s. The slums festered with poverty, vice, crime, and violence, and the churches and fraternal groups could not meet the burgeoning need for charity. (There was no government welfare, of course.)

Labor unrest sparked some riots, ethnic and religious differences started others. Frequent targets were Abolitionists, free blacks, Catholics, and immigrants. Except for a handful of Spaniards and Portuguese, virtually all the Catholics were Irish. Many Catholics complained of mistreatment by the predominantly Protestant police. Occasionally, a mob would break up a whorehouse or a saloon "for sport." [11] As Paul Gilje suggested, most of these riots represented the clash between the earlier moral economy that celebrated conformity and the new market economy that encouraged individualism and competition. "Given the plebeian penchant for taking grievances into the streets, that clash necessarily involved rioting." [12] Rioting by the lower classes grew more frequent and more violent, confirming the worst fears of conservatives (including most newspaper publishers) about having too much democracy. No newspaper denounced unions more loudly than the city's largest, the *Courier and Enquirer*.

The panic of 1837 that idled one-third of the city's workforce crushed the fledgling efforts to unionize factory workers. The few unions of skilled tradesmen, such as the printers, that survived faced widespread public hostility. Many who sympathized with their demands for higher wages were wary of their calls for free schools and the end of imprisonment for debt. The courts then declared unions illegal conspiracies, and the city hired its first full-time policemen.

Revisionist historians have chipped away at many of the myths about Jacksonian America, asserting that not only was it not an egalitarian age, but that the economic gap between rich and poor actually was widening. Money, more than birth, was coming to determine one's place in society, but economic advancement was harder to achieve than ever. [13]

Foreign visitors were impressed by the widespread interest in politics. Although the elites retained tight control of the nominating process, nearly all adult white males could vote. After the death of the old Federalist party of John Adams and Alexander Hamilton and the splintering of Jefferson's party, Andrew Jackson was elected president in 1828 and again in 1832. In spite of periodic panics, the economy boomed during his presidency. One of the great problems—almost impossible for us to believe today—was what to do with the federal *surplus*. The tariff was the major source of government funds. The soundness of the dollar depended on imports paid for by the flow of cotton through New York to the mills of England. [14]

Because of the high birthrate and unprecedented immigration, the nation's population tripled between 1790 and 1830. [15] Newcomers, most of them Irish or German, seemed to emerge from the lower decks of every arriving vessel. During the 1820s and 1830s, 35,000 came each year. Unlike the Germans, many of whom could afford to push on to the inland farm lands, most of the Irish arrived penniless and looked for work at the cities where they disembarked. By 1850, one-fourth the residents of New York City were Irish-born, and the parents of many others had fled the potato famines. Their fierce loyalty to their church and their homeland offended their neighbors; so did their rowdiness and their drinking—not necessarily in that order.[16] Unable to afford liquor and tobacco in their homeland, many of them tried to make up for lost time. For the first time they could afford newspapers, too.

Eager to work, Pat and Mike found the dirtiest, heaviest, lowest paying jobs. With their broad backs, they built America's cities and railroads, shoveled its coal and loaded its ships. Bridget and Theresa washed, cooked, and mopped floors in private homes and hotels. Although these lasses had a reputation for being "saucy" and awkward, they were also good-natured and honest.[17] To many Americans, the Irish seemed the fulfillment of their nightmares about a permanent working class. If the Paddies seemed a special curse to those attempting to organize labor unions, they were a blessing to Tammany Hall, maintaining itself for decades on Irish votes. An immigrant gained full voting rights five years after his arrival. This political influence infuriated Phillip Hone, a staunch Whig, who wrote in his diary: "These Irishmen, strangers among us, without a feeling of patriotism or affection in common with American citizens, decide the elections in the city of New York."[18] Such political antipathy underlay the riots that accompanied the city election in the spring of 1834. Although most elections included a certain amount of hooliganism, this time at least one man died in the three days of clashes between Whig mobs and Irish Democrats.[19]

Many Protestants, fed unending rumors about papist plots, really believed the Irish were all spies and agents for the Pope.[20] Nativist mobs burned Catholic convents and churches and beat Irishmen on the streets. The police court dockets are filled with Irish names, some the attackers and some the victims. During the 1850s, nativist political parties did well in New York and other Eastern states. From the beginning, the Irish did not get along with the blacks, with whom they competed for jobs and housing. Irish-Americans led a violent race riot in July, 1834.[21] A quarter-century later many Irishmen rioted against the Civil War draft; others who donned the blue made it clear that they were not fighting to free the slaves.

THE ESTABLISHED NEWSPAPERS

Because newspapers had always been for elites, an increase in the city's population did not automatically mean more circulation. The typical daily, geared to the interests of commercial and professional men, sold only 1200 copies in 1830.[22] Most still were scissor-and-pastepot operations, the smaller papers copying from their big city cousins. Free postal service for exchange copies encouraged the practice. During the 1820s, the nascent political parties took advantage of the provision to set up party papers throughout the country that would copy their editorials from the flagship papers in Washington.

As the decade of the thirties opened, the nation supported 65 dailies and 650 weeklies; ten years later the numbers had doubled. There is no evidence to support Tocqueville's assertion that American newspapers in 1831–32 devoted three-fourths of their space to advertisements.[23] Probably none carried as much as half ads and most of them far less. Circulations grew impressively. The largest paper in New York, the *Courier and Enquirer,* claimed in 1836 a circulation of 6000, still small compared with the leading London or Paris papers. Many American bankers and merchants looked on their $10-a-year subscription as a sort of cachet. (Although almost all copies circulated by annual subscription, it was possible to pick up single copies at the offices and a few other places for six cents.)[24] The worker had little reason to invest any of his dollar-a-day salary in a paper devoted to elite politics and mercantile affairs anyway.

Of course the commercial dailies stressed mercantile news, but it was an era in which economic issues like the tariff and the national bank were at the vortex of politics. In addition to political intelligence, the publishers carried lists of commodity prices, ship sailings, commercial or legal notices and ads for wholesalers. Their readers paid handsomely for information useful in their jobs. Gossip they picked up from their peers at the Merchant's Exchange and in their clubs. They knew little, and cared less, about what the common folks were doing. By the definition of their readers, the six-cent papers had a great deal of "news."[25]

These papers seldom sent out reporters, instead reprinting items from one another. They delighted in printing lists, whether of out-of-towners registered at hotels or arriving by steamer, or of governmental appointments—even military promotions. Sporadically they also printed minutes of the city council and other official agencies. Such information was easy to collect and seldom offended anyone. A few papers had long employed legislative correspondents (James Gordon Bennett at one time had been

Washington correspondent for the *Courier and Enquirer*) and the practice spread until by 1840, almost all the New York papers published letters from their correspondents in Albany and Washington.

These papers did not ignore crimes—they would devote an inch or two to murders, suicides and the like—but they left the details to the weekly story papers, penny pamphlets and broadsides. As late as 1824, the *Niles' Weekly Register* noted that the nation's criminals were not found in the newspapers, but in the "street literature"—the ballads and almanacs.[26] The American papers paid less attention to crime than the British. Trial verdicts were summarized in a sentence or two after the verdict was returned.[27] But even before the appearance of the penny papers, the mercantile papers published short items under such headings as "Awful Murder," "Drowning," "Another Fire," or "Melancholy Event," the last meaning a suicide. They never seemed to miss a steamship explosion. Many of their items were reprinted from other papers, sometimes with credit given and sometimes without.

Even a paper as staid as the *Journal of Commerce*, whose publisher refused even to collect news on the Sabbath,[28] was not above an occasional entertaining item. Here is one published in 1831, two years *before* penny papers entered the scene:

> **COMMUNICATION—A visitor from the country returned early last evening to his lodgings from the school of morality, quite satisfied in his lesson and quite elated that he had bethought himself to leave his money at the bar—happy when he went out, having only one dollar in his pocketbook, which was taken from his inner pocket by some scholar of older standing. It was at the Park School [a reference to the Park Theater, a notorious hangout for whores], or at that in Chatham St., this deponent sayeth not. He had lost but a dollar and a half, he said, including the half dollar for a pit ticket, which he reckoned was lost money.[29]**

Presses dictated an unvarying four-page format but gradually accommodated larger page sizes, some growing to three feet by two feet, or four feet wide when spread out on the library table or counter. No wonder they were called "blanket sheets." Amid long columns of commercial notices were letters from abroad and political treatises, usually denouncing some outrage by the Jacksonians.

The owner of a newspaper, by then usually called a publisher, worked alongside a couple of clerk-bookkeepers and two or three editors. As small-scale and primitive as this arrangement sounds, it represented an advance from an earlier era when the proprietor was the printer. Now such work was contracted to a totally separate shop or to a partner whose sole concern was the mechanical production.

As we will see in the next chapter, the traditional papers soon faced a new kind of journalistic competition in the penny press.

3

A Press for the Masses (Sort of)

he idea of cheap publishing was in the air. In the 1830s, as Merle Curti pointed out, publishers were wooing the common man and his wife.[1] Watching newly literate masses devour the easy-to-read religious tracts, almanacs, and workers' papers, commercial publishers on both sides of the Atlantic adapted the same technological advances to print first cheap books and then newspapers. While vital, such mechanical improvements hardly "preordained" the penny press.[2] In fact, the first penny papers were firmly established before steam power was harnessed to the printing press.

During 1830 there were at least two attempts to publish low-cost dailies in the United States. The Boston *Daily Evening Transcript* succeeded, but the Philadelphia *Cent* did not. The "cheap newspaper"[3] did not appear in New York until the first day of 1833. Horace Greeley's two-cent *Morning Post* fell victim to underfinancing and bad weather in less than a week. Nine months later, Benjamin Day introduced his New York *Sun,* the real beginning of the Penny Press.

One of the remarkable coincidences of journalism history is the way that key mechanical changes have coincided with times of increased social demands for information; examples abound, from antiquity to the invention of movable type and beyond.[4] The craft of printing became in the early nineteenth century the first mass production industry. A London paper had added steam power to the cylinder press in 1814, but until papers broadened their appeal they had little need for the added speed and capacity. It was logical, therefore, that Day should in 1835 be one of the first Americans to install a steam press. The penny papers appeared at the perfect time to exploit the improvements in printing. James Gordon Bennett planned from the beginning to add steam presses as soon as he could afford them.

Day was one of the last of the old breed. He earned more from job printing than from his newspaper. Active for some years among those agitating for workingmen's rights, he absorbed some of that radicalism.[5] With the aid of a compositor and a printer's devil, he ran off copies of his first four-page, 8-by-11-inch paper on a hand press. In addition to short original items, that initial issue included items copies from the six-cent papers, including his reports from the police court. Like its larger rivals the *Sun* published ship sailings, business notices, commodity prices, deaths, and marriages. Historians have stressed the differences in content between the penny and mercantile papers rather than the similarities.[6] Even the *Sun*'s smaller size was not *that* new; although most were short-lived, there apparently had been several attempts every year to set up small papers in New York.[7] An item in 1832 in the biweekly *Working Man's Advocate* claimed such newspapers were "catching on everywhere" to serve readers who could not cope with the mammoth traditional dailies.[8] The *Advocate,* itself, began publication in 1830 as a four-column 12-by-20-incher and was a stablemate of the daily *Evening Sentinel.* Although the *Advocate* lived up to its name, in that era of scissors-and-pastepot journalism it took many news accounts from six-cent papers. Many Americans, including New Yorkers, still relied more on weekly and biweekly newspapers than on dailies.

Day, like his penny rivals, made much of his political independence, but he meant freedom from party subsidies, not from expressing partisan opinions. He considered himself a good "Jacksonian,'" and so did the publishers of the *Transcript* and the *Herald.* Of a decidedly more conservative persuasion were two later cheap papers, Horace Greeley's *Tribune* and Henry Raymond's *Times.* Greeley established his whiggish *Tribune* in 1841 as an alternative to what he saw as gutter journalism. In his first issues he attacked the *Sun* for immoral ads and the *Herald* for too much crime. During the next four decades he propounded his views on a remarkable range of topics. Although Greeley decried immoral and degrading police reports and "loathsome details" of crimes, the *Tribune*'s first real circulation boom came with its extensive coverage of a murder.[9]

Even if, as Schiller and Saxton have argued, publishers deliberately emphasized crime news as a means of exposing the corruption, cruelty, and class bias of the criminal justice system,[10] it leaves open the question of what readers made of the stories. Like audiences since antiquity, they may have enjoyed the sensations and ignored the subtle messages.

Within a year Day's circulation was 8000, the largest in the city, and he kept the promise made in his first issue to enlarge the *Sun*. He could publish many more items in his new 12-by-18-inch format, but still far less than the commercial blanket sheets. Within a few years, there were cheap papers in most cities with enough literate wage earners. On the Continent and in England the same democratizing forces were broadening both the franchise and the reading public. *La Presse* debuted in Paris in 1836 and with its mixture of politics and gossip was an immediate success. In England, the weekly "pauper press" called its products "magazines" in order to evade the tax on newspapers, but like their American cousins, were heavy on crime, sex, and violence. The largest of these sold twice as many copies as the *Times* of London and frequently were quoted in the American penny papers.[11]

WHO READ THE PENNY PRESS?

Although an Englishman who visited in 1837 thought the American newspapers "dreadfully licentious," he was impressed that "cabmen, boatmen, tapsters, oysterwomen, porters" all read and commented on the daily news.[12] He may have been watching them read penny papers.

Because almost no business records of early nineteenth-century newspapers survive, we will never know who bought and read the penny papers, but we can make some reasonable guesses. The traditional answer is that they were "urban workingmen." In today's usage this term conjures up a factory worker or a ditch digger, but in the early nineteenth century included laborers, small merchants, retail tradesmen, and clerks.[13] Given the levels of literacy, many of the readers must have worn white collars. Thousands of literate and ambitious clerks, bookkeepers, and junior partners lived and worked within a few blocks of the waterfront. Each year they accounted for a higher share of the city's workforce; already they comprised as much as one-third.[14] These people who stamped, indexed, filed, and sold were the likely bedrock of the penny press circulation. These workers (a few of them women) had to be literate and, at least as important, had the reading habit. Junior clerks, who earned less than $100 a year could hardly afford $10 for an annual subscription to a commercial daily (in which they would have found little of interest anyway), but some of them read ethnic and labor weekly papers.[15] This new white collar worker had some extra coppers for theaters, sporting events (not to mention sporting houses), and penny papers.[16]

There is no reason to think that wives were less literate or less interested in reading than their wage-earning husbands. The novels favored by women, like the cheap papers, stressed tales of derring-do and dalliances. In spite of domestic chores, they were more likely than their husbands to find a spare moment to read. Many men left for work and returned to their dim homes in the dark. Penny papers courted women readers. In its first issue, the *New Era* assured the city's seamstresses that they had a new friend. The *Herald* publisher boasted of his large sale among women, adding "I have the generous, the liberal, the lively, the intelligent public with me, especially all the ladies."[17] There were brief attempts in both 1834 and 1836 to publish penny papers specifically for women. Immigrants, on the other hand, probably bought few penny papers. The Germans had their own thriving press and the Irish were too poor.[18]

At least as important to its success as the one-cent price was the *Sun*'s method of distribution. Because working people seldom ventured more than a few blocks, Day sold copies where they lived, worked, and shopped. This was another idea borrowed from London, where for several years papers had been employing young toughs to deliver their papers to subscribers and to sell additional copies on the streets. The *Sun* did the same. Even in New York it was not a radical idea, since mercantile papers sold as many as 100 copies a day at the docks and in Wall Street. While the six-cent papers relied primarily on annual subscription and the penny papers on single-copy sales, it is important to remember that they all bragged about their new *subscribers*. In 1835, the *Sun* reported that subscribers accounted for 16,000 of its 19,000 sales.[19] That probably meant regular customers of newsboys rather than those who paid in advance by the month.

Although at first Day paid his hawkers a weekly salary of $2, he soon dropped the salary and began selling them a dozen copies for nine cents. The newsboys (and there may have been some girls) were drawn from among the hordes of children, often abandoned by their parents, who lived by their wits on the streets. Even before Horatio Alger, the newsboy became the symbol of hard work and self-reliance in sentimental fiction. When ambitious youths began making $5 a week (half what *Sun* printers were earning), some adults joined in, one of whom was soon earning $13 a week. Other men began brokering routes—buying the copies and then hiring youngsters to do the legwork.[20]

Obviously it was to the advantage of the carrier to develop a reliable list of regulars, and that in turn stabilized the press run. Advertisers certainly liked knowing how many copies of their ad would be read. Not incidentally, the penny papers also began demanding cash in advance from advertisers. The cash distribution system ended those twin plagues of journalism, no-pay and slow-pay subscribers and advertisers.

Newspapers became products that had to be sold, had to prove their utility not only to readers but to advertisers. From the first issue of *Publick Occurrences,* American newspapers had always carried a few ads, including those advertising the services of artisans and craftsmen.[21] Now local retailers and makers of elixers and patent medicines joined banks, shippers, and insurance companies in placing notices, many of which ran for a year or more unchanged. Many six-cent papers refused ads for theaters, lotteries, or Sunday events; however, the penny papers, needing revenue to replace the lost political subsidies, could not be so choosy. Schudson hailed this broadened advertising base as another form of democratization.[22]

POLICE COURT NEWS

Day was not breaking new journalistic ground when he featured news from the police and lower courts. London papers such as the *Morning Herald* had been doing it for some time, and even the staid New York six-centers used police items once in a while, but the *Sun* really emphasized them.

Although not a facile writer himself, Day hired George Wisner, who had a concise and sprightly style, at $4 a week to cover the police courts. Within weeks Wisner had become Day's editor and partner and hired as his court reporter William H. Attree.[23] By 4 A.M., Attree was seated in the dingy courtroom, listening to the travails of those headed for (as he liked to write) "durance vile." From the weft and warp of the human dramas enacted before him, he spun morality tales, often mimicking the brogues of those accused. The *Sun*'s reporter related, with obvious gusto, a tale of wife-swapping in which *all* the participants complained of being short-changed. He quoted an attorney defending an alleged seducer as saying his client could not be guilty because he was too ugly, poor, and foolish for any woman to take seriously.[24]

Although his accounts often dripped with bathos, it was easy to detect the sniff of disapproval in his brief stories. Here are two examples:

> **Jane Dunn, an incorrigible old vagrant and rum head was ordered to the penitentiary for six months.[25]**

> **Sally Kip, a black Amazon of the Five Points[26] was tried for petit larceny, stealing from Charles**

> Welch, a silver watch and appendages and money,
> amounting to $23. Kemp was holding a dalliance
> with Sally at her rookery in the Points, during
> which Sally, with a slightness of hand in which
> long practice had made her proficient, extracted
> the property.[27]

Day soon had penny imitators. The *Transcript,* and to a lesser degree, the *Man,* stressed the same brevity and mockery in reporting on the wife beaters, drunks, bawds, and brawlers.[28] The *Herald,* after its establishment went even further, as this example, published on—of all days—St. Patrick's Day, 1836, indicates:

> POLICE, Wednesday—Theresa Melionas, an
> ill-looking haggard, dissipated creature, about
> 30 years of age, one of those degraded wretches
> who infest the parlieus of the Five Points, was
> brought up under the following circumstances:
> Floyd T. Roscoe, a simple, thick-headed, long-
> sided Yankee, from the land of Cannan, not Ca-
> naan of old, but new Cannan in Connecticut,
> made affidavit that as he was passing along
> Anthony at Orange street, he felt the temptation
> to drink come very strong over him, and seeing
> the door of a shop open, through which he saw
> visions of brandy, whiskey, and gin, he suffered
> himself to be led astray and entered—But it
> proved to be a perfect den of iniquity. He slaked
> his parching thirst with a "pen-north of red eye,"
> had deposited the money therefor, and was on
> the eve of departing and repenting, when the fair
> prisoner, in gentle accents murmured "Won't you
> treat?"
> Mr. Roscoe was *un gallant uomo,* he could
> not, he would not refuse a request so trifling; a
> request made by such fine lips, and backed by
> such beautiful eyes. Besides, the cost was only
> one cent. He acceeded—the fair one drank, he
> pulled some money from its hiding place to set-
> tle the bill, when lo; the fair one proved that she
> was false as fair—she knocked the money from
> his hand, among which was a five dollar gold
> piece and a half dollar. Miss Theresa and a

woman who chanced to come in on the moment, grabbed them and made off, and he, finding it impossible to regain his money by fair means, resorted to foul ones, and most ungallantly had her esconrted to the Police Office.

On her examination, she gave herself such a bad character that the sitting magistrate deemed it advisable to send her for 6 months to the Penitentiary at Bellevue, which course after a little reflection, he adopted and she was forthwith despatched.

Mr. Roscoe arrived here in a sloop with a cargo of calves, of which he had sold the greater part, and the money lost was a portion of the proceeds.

Margaret Norris, a wretched, drunken, dissipated being, disgracing the very name of female, was brought up yesterday afternoon by a couple of citizens who had the misfortune to know her, and then requested that she might be provided for, as she was a habitual drunkard, and in the frequent practice of insulting every person who chances to pass when she is under the effects of liquor.

She felt very eloquent, and holding on to the rail, begged permission of this "Honrable Honor," and the "Jontlemen of the Jury," to "plade" her own cause. Her request was granted, and it would have puzzled the most skillful stenographer to have kept pace with her tongue. She talked about justice, honesty, sobriety, and mercy, but her forte was "vartu." Upon her possession of that inestimable virtue in large quantities she chiefly prided herself, and dwelt long and energetically upon the proper use of it. The unfeeling magistrate, while she was thus employed, was busily engaged in making out her commitment, and it being finished, he cut her oration short by ordering an officer to take her over to Bridewell.[29]

One journalist of the day complained about this class bias: "That an innocent man, because he is poor and defenceless, may be caricatured, and consigned to the infamy of a day, and even to the loss of employment, is of little consequence. The people must be amused . . ."[30] Harriet Martineau, that intrepid English traveler, was appalled during her visit of 1834–36 by the prevalence of such stories in the American press. She was disgusted by the "jocose tone of their police reports, where crimes are treated as entertainments and misery as a jest." She declared American newspapers as hopeless as American novels.[31] Unlike foreign visitors, who were offended by the nosiness of Americans, editors of cheap papers were determined to give readers what they wanted.[32] That included publishing the names of all the accused, the rich as well as the poor. That policy earned the *Sun*'s Attree at least one beating.[33] The penny papers chided judges who showed favoritism for the well-to-do. In a period when those in the working class were convinced they did not get a fair shake from the judicial system, the penny papers helped keep the judges and juries honest.[34] The *Sun* chastized the *Transcript* in 1834 for what it considered shabby police court reporting.[35]

OTHER CONTENT

Day did not avoid all political news, but for him it was just one more category that competed for attention with other subjects. In the city election of 1834 his paper merely ran a list of all the candidates without endorsing anyone. In the late twentieth century, newspapers often do not endorse, but such indifference was startling in the 1830s. Although Day insisted that every editor had a "high duty" to speak out on public issues, he seldom did so.[36]

His primary purpose was to entertain, and probably no story illustrated that better than the "moon hoax." The publication of that series in 1835 made the *Sun* the talk of the town and far beyond. This series purported to be an account of recent astronomical discoveries at the Cape of Good Hope, authored by Sir John F. W. Herschell and reprinted from a Scottish scientific journal. Actually it was written by Day's reporter, Richard Adams Locke. The first installment appeared August 25, 1835, and filled three columns. In describing a powerful telescope Locke introduced scientific terms. Before the series had run its 11,000-word course, he even described the batlike inhabitants.[37] Readers snatched up every available copy, and on both sides of the Atlantic, newspapers quoted from the stories. Many scientists were taken in as was the sophisticated Philip Hone. Novelist Edgar Allan Poe, whose own fictional series about lunar discoveries was appearing at the time in the *Southern Literary Messenger,* wrote that the moon hoax series firmly established the penny paper system.[38]

Although some six-cent papers, such as the *Courier and Enquirer,* were taken in (one claimed it had received more details from Sir John that it would publish soon), others were more cautious. Three days after declaring the discoveries important, the *Evening Post* joined the *Commercial Advertiser*'s conclusion that the stories were fakes.[39] In James Gordon Bennett's first account, he praised the "superb drollery" of the author, whose identity he revealed, but he grew indignant when the *Sun* continued the deception.[40] With its press running day and night in a futile attempt to keep up with the demand, the *Sun* had little incentive to hurry; when it finally confessed, nobody seemed upset. Nonetheless, the penny papers, recognizing they had to operate within the broad conventions of newspapering, published few more hoaxes. They understood, if only instinctively, that readers would resent being fooled too often.[41] Too many hoaxes would cost them their credibility, as would too much "daring" of any kind.

Crime news was still news, as was news of divorces, something the six-cent papers eschewed. Sometimes the *Sun* resorted to the mocking tone and verbatim report style it used for criminal cases. For example:

GIVING A DIVORCE—Yesterday morning a little curly-pated fellow by the name of John Lawler was called up on a charge of kicking over the mead-stand of Mary Lawler, alias Miss Donohue, alias Mrs. Donohue.

MAGISTRATE: (to the complainant) Mrs. Donohue, what were the circumstances of the affair?

COMPLAINANT: You will be so good, sir, if you please, as to call me Miss Donohue. It is my maiden name and I wish no other.

MAG: Very good. Miss Donohue, how came he to kick over your stand and break your bottles and glasses?

COMP: Aye, yes, now. I like that better. Every virtuous woman should be called by her own right and proper name.

MAG: Well, let's hear your story. Do you know the boy?

COMP: The boy, did you say? Indade, sir, divil a bit o'boy is here about the baste, nor man neither, barring he drinks brandy like a fish. (loud laughter)

MAG: Did you ever see him before?

COMP: Indade, I guess I did. Many years ago

> he was my husband, but your honor sees, I gave
> him a divorce. That is, ye see, I gave him a bit of
> paper stating that I would live with him no longer.
> (Laughter)
>   PRISONER: It's no sich thing, yer honor. She
> used to go off with other men, so I sold her for a
> gill of rum.[42]

The mercantile papers responded to the soaring circulations of the penny papers by beefing up their reports from Wall Street, Albany, and Washington. The *Courier and Enquirer* added a series of humorous political letters from "Major Jack Downing." Most increased their attention to books, plays, and even horse racing. The *Express* and *Telegraph* began publishing both morning and afternoon editions. Several purchased new presses and used larger and blacker typefaces. But, in a Democratic city, the older papers clung to their staunchly Whiggish political and economic views.

Whether out of genuine moral outrage or jealousy, other editors denounced the corrupting influence of the stories and advertisements in the penny papers. They gloated when Day lost a libel suit, and the *Sun* admitted to "some 25 to 30 suits" a year.[43] Unlike later times, trials were quick, the penalties light, and appeals almost unknown. Beginning in late 1835 Phillip Hone frequently lashed out in his diary at "the penny papers and the two-penny public of our slander-loving city."[44] Meanwhile the penny papers kept right on printing tales about courts, courtiers, and courtesans. As Emery and Emery observed, "This tapping of a new, much-neglected public started with a wave of sensationalism."[45]

By 1840 the *Herald* and the *Sun* sold more copies than the nine surviving mercantile papers combined. But the columns of the six-centers still bulged with advertising. Day was no longer in the newspaper business. Plagued by imitators, lawsuits, and especially the Panic of 1837, he sold the *Sun* to his brother-in-law in June 1837 for $40,000.[46] As Saxton pointed out:

> The larger the circulation, the greater the irreducible costs. Aside from printers and reporters the *Sun* now carried engineers, firemen, mechanics, bookkeepers and salesmen on its payroll. Entire outfits of type wore out every few months. Such costs were irreducible because more circulation was the source of financial success. Unfortunately for Day, however, circulation, although necessary to success, by no means assured it. Expanding circulation generated a diminishing portion of gross revenue. What produced revenue was advertising, which varied directly with circulation, but varied also with the cycle of boom and depression that characterized capitalist growth in the nineteenth century.[47]

Penny papers took hold and flourished only in the larger seaboard cities
—New York, Boston, Baltimore, and Philadelphia. In New York in 1830,
one resident in sixteen read a daily paper; twenty years later it was one in
five. Elsewhere newspapers evolved slowly throughout the antebellum
period, seemingly indifferent to the journalistic "revolution" in New York.[48]

Although not revolutionary, the cheap papers were an evolutionary
milestone. By redefining the standards of content, distribution, page size,
and cost, they captured a class of readers that never before had read daily
papers.[49]

4

Bennett and His Damned *Herald*

May 6, 1835 was a warm and sunny spring day in New York City. Few among the city's quarter-million residents knew or cared that a new daily newspaper called the *Herald* had been born. They already could choose from among a dozen dailies and even more weeklies and semiweeklies.

In his mansion up on Broadway, Phillip Hone took no note of the event in his detailed diary. The aristocratic former mayor had not even gone downtown where the newsboys hawked the new tabloid-sized paper. In a few months he would be fulminating about the "infamous" New York *Herald*. Nor did the new paper draw much notice from those at the other end of the social scale. After twelve hours of hoisting, digging, or loading, even those laborers who could read were more inclined to spend a spare penny on grog than on a newspaper.

Newspapermen are always aware of a new rival but are reluctant to acknowledge it in print. There was bad blood between Bennett and James Watson Webb, his former boss. The 2000 blueblood readers of the city's premiere commercial paper, the *Courier and Enquirer*, would not have cared anyway. Benjamin Day saw no reason to give his potential rival any free publicity.

Down in his dingy basement office on Ann Street, James Gordon Bennett had little time for reflection. He had written and edited the whole of the first issue of the *Herald* himself, and now he was hard at work on the second. He had invested his entire savings of $500 in furnishing the office and in retaining a job printer. The street urchins he had rounded up did not sell many copies of the tiny four-page sheet, even at a penny. Passersby thought it ugly, nearly as ugly as its gangly and raw-boned publisher. His close-set hazel eyes were crooked, as was his long nose. He looked older than his forty years.

Most of the first page of the first *Herald* was devoted to a history of Matthias the Prophet, an infamous fraud. Following a short publisher's note in which Bennett promised "Our only guide shall be good, sound, practical commonsense, applicable to the business and bosoms of men engaged in everyday life," the rest of page two was filled with foreign notes and "Theatre Chit-Chat." Page three exhorted the mechanics of the city to worry more about getting work and fair wages and less about politics. (This would be a familiar theme.) The *Herald* promised its police court notes would be more tasteful than those in the *Sun*. To illustrate, Bennett reprinted some recent *Sun* items, a clever way to include some police court items on a day when Bennett had no time to go to court. A few marriages and deaths were listed. The back page included some doggerel. Ads and paid notices filled about half of pages three and four.

Those who plunked down their pennies (probably mostly clerks, book-keepers, and other white collar toilers) hardly could have realized they were holding in their ink-stained fingers the harbinger of the modern commercial newspaper. Before long it would become the largest and most influential American newspaper and would retain that position throughout most of the nineteenth century.

APPEALING OR APPALLING?

Bennett already had fifteen years of solid reporting experience. Although most of his attention had been to politics and business, he had covered at least one murder trial.[1] Both as a writer and as a publisher, Bennett left Day in the shade. Day was first a printer, and only incidentally a newspaperman. Bennett was first, last, and always a journalist. Well-educated in his native Scotland, he had never earned his living with his hands. Recognizing that he would have to wrest readers from the *Sun* and the *Transcript*, he also had his eye on a better-heeled audience. In battling the full-sized morning dailies, Bennett had a trump card—his own unsurpassed knowl-edge of finance. He began running detailed analyses of financial markets and his was among the first newspapers to publish up-to-date stock prices and bankruptcies. In his money columns (the first one appeared May 11, less than a week after he started the *Herald*) readers learned for the first time what went on in the back rooms of mercantile houses and the stock exchange. The columns were written in plain language, intended for nonspecialists. These columns provided an excuse to many respectable people to read the *Herald*. (Once they had a copy they may have read beyond the money news.) Although it seemed nearly everyone at that time was dabbling in stocks and western lands, Bennett insisted he was not. Certainly most of the other newspaper publishers in the city were. It is difficult to believe the claims of an anonymous pamphleteer who insisted that decent folks bought the *Herald* only to laugh at it.[2] French composer Claude Debussy once defended a contemporary, ridiculed because his mu-sic "pleased young milliners." He might have been writing of Bennett when he suggested:

> His brethren could not really forgive this power of pleasing which strictly speaking is a gift. . . . Make no mistake: this is a delightful kind of fame, the secret envy of many of those great purists, who can only warm their hands at the somewhat pallid flame of the approbation of the elect.[3]

Bennett was at once an intensely private and public man. It was not that he was hiding much; it was that especially in the early years he had almost no existence outside his newspaper. The detailed accounts, the sometimes tasteless remarks, the strident editorials *were* Bennett. His paper spoke for no party or faction, but only for Bennett.[4] A contemporary journalist wrote that Bennett arose early and after a long day of gathering and editing news, sat up late, keeping his own accounts and posting his own books.[5] Even a fire that destroyed the print shop hardly slowed him. After missing two weeks, he found a new printer and in a paid ad in the *Sun* announced his resumption.

Like Day, Bennett considered himself a good Jacksonian Democrat (years later he said he had been a "rampant Jackson blockhead")[6] but now wanted no part of political subsidies. He still resented not being properly rewarded for his propaganda work for Jackson in 1828. Jacksonians could be ruthless in disciplining an editor who bolted.[7] Taking his chances in the marketplace, Bennett insisted on cash in advance from advertisers and from the boys he hired to sell his paper on the streets. Because choice corners were overrun with peddlers of everything from fruits to shoelaces; it was not a job for sissies.

In its editorials, the *Herald* decried party and factional politics, but the proprietor never tired of playing them. As the election of 1836 approached, Bennett wrote that he didn't know or care who the Democrats nominated for President.[8] In truth, he always cared a great deal and worked behind the scenes for candidates, occasionally even for those outside the Democratic party ranks. In the antebellum years, he endorsed William Henry Harrison, Zachary Taylor and John C. Fremont over Democratic rivals for the White House. In city politics he usually backed whichever party was out of power (usually the Whigs or their close relatives), having long since given up on the incumbent mayors. In statewide races, though, he seldom backed Whigs, Republicans, or Fusionists, in part because of his dislike for their Abolitionist bent.[9] Almost every day for thirty years, *Herald* readers were reminded that politicians were spoilsmen, thieves, or worse, but at the same time Bennett was angling shamelessly to win a diplomatic post for himself.[10] Although he was close to President James Buchanan, he never was appointed. It is difficult to imagine anyone less cut out to be a diplomat. By 1856, Bennett was boasting that the nation's course was set by the independent press, not a handful of politicians.[11]

Throughout his long career, Bennett was a jingoist and sword-rattler. His tireless boasts about American destiny to rule the entire Western Hemisphere worried Spanish, French, and British diplomats. Because the *Herald* circulated far more copies in Europe than any other American newspaper, his rash words were often mistaken for American policy.[12]

In spite of his readership, Bennett showed little sympathy for unions and none at all for strikes. In the riotous summer of 1836, he wrote: "These trade unionists should be stopped now."[13] Ironically, strikers often bought small ads in the penny papers to enlist public support, and some employers then bought space to counter the union claims.[14]

On one subject Bennett's views coincided with those of labor leaders: immigration had to be checked. He was convinced the new immigrants were of inferior stock and would dilute the aryan stock. In the city election of 1844, he endorsed the victorious Native American Republican party, but he was never as virulently nativist as many New York contemporaries.[15] On the other hand, he was a Negrophobe. He considered blacks inherently inferior and better off under benevolent slave owners than on their own. He considered the attempts to free slaves on Caribbean islands as unmitigated disasters. He had scorn for the Free Blacks he saw in the city and absolutely no use for "nigger-loving" politicians.[16]

Nor did Bennett care much for women's rights. In noting that two women had graduated from a Mississippi school, he asked: "Can they cook a beefsteak or make a pudding?"[17] Bennett later ridiculed suffrage leaders and treated the entire women's rights issue as a joke. In his unrelenting praise of female beauty and delicacy, as in so many other areas, he reflected a very Southern attitude.

While opposing divorce and infidelity, the *Herald* published all the juicy details of divorces and scandals.[18] Not long before he introduced his own Sunday edition, Bennett denounced the *Sunday News*. New Yorkers "cannot, and ought not and will not" tolerate a Sunday newspaper, he asserted, applauding the arrest of newsboys for bothering those on their way to church.[19]

Although Bennett wrote that each morning he exposed the "deep guilt that is encrusting over society,"[20] the early *Herald* probably was, as one historian observed, "the most sensational, salacious and sardonic newspaper in the whole world."[21] The *Herald* conveyed lasciviousness without publishing profanities. (Like other papers, it even resorted to "d———d" in direct quotes.) In reporting the trial of a book publisher for obscenity, the reporter interrupted his verbatim account of the testimony to write: "Here occurs a passage too indecent for our columns, but the pious believers in these stories can find it at full length in the volume itself."[22] An anonymous pamphleteer was correct in charging that Bennett never missed a chance to insert sexual innuendo.[23] What other justification was there for such saucy "brighteners" as this?

> **A young lady ... was caught in the shower on Broadway. All the shops were so crowded that there was no place for shelter. She had no umbrella, and not wishing to have her brand new hat ruined, she threw her frock, as she thought, over it. In her haste to preserve the hat, she did not observe how many garments she had raised, and she cut rather an odd figure promenading.[24]**

Bennett at least deserves credit for his willingness to stay with a story, like Scheherazade, spinning and elaborating it for days on end. He did not settle for the official version but made inquiries of his own. That may have been his greatest innovation. He demonstrated this in his coverage of the Great Fire of December 1835. Even in that day when fires were a commonplace, that conflagration, which destroyed more than 400 buildings, was in a class by itself. So was Bennett's reporting of it. All the papers reported the fire, of course, but Bennett for *seven consecutive issues* carried long, first-person narratives, based on his walks through the decimated area; he even published maps and a sketch of the burned-out Merchants' Exchange.[25] It marked one of the first times any daily newspaper illustrated a news story. No English newspaper would do so for another seven years.[26] Furthermore, he moved the main news story to the front page. The boulevard papers of Paris had done that but not American or British newspapers. For them the biggest news stories went on page two. Bennett decided the best story deserved the best exposure.[27] Other papers were slow to follow his lead, and even he was inconsistent about the practice. He also emphasized speedy newsgathering. He tried harbor boats, pigeons, and express riders. Later he pioneered in using the telegraph.[28] He was among the first American editors to hire correspondents to mail reports from Europe. Since for most of the nineteenth century the *Herald* printed more news than any other paper, Bennett might be forgiven his exuberant boast that the *Herald* was "the great organ of social life, the prime element of civilization, the channel through which native talent, native genius, and native power may bubble up daily."[29]

On January 30, 1836, Bennett gained his first grudging notice in the diary of Phillip Hone. Had Bennett known, this would have amused him. Hone wrote:

> There is an ill-looking, squinting man called Bennett . . . who is editor of the *Herald,* one of the penny papers which are hawked about the streets by a gang of troublesome, ragged boys, and in which scandal is retailed to all who delight in it at that moderate price.[30]

Clearly Bennett had made a mark—to some a stain—on the city, but no one could have guessed the attention he would draw in the next few months with his coverage of the Maria Monk disclosures and the Robinson-Jewett murder case.

EXPOSING A HOAX

Bennett's skepticism served him well in handling one of the most celebrated incidents of 1836, the publication of the confessions of a girl, calling herself Maria Monk, who claimed to have escaped captivity and sexual debauchery in a monastery in Montreal. Within a few weeks, her *Awful Disclosures* sold 12,000 copies. She told of her education and conversion to Catholicism, her decision to become a nun, and what she found out went on in a monastery. Told by the Mother Superior that she must obey, unquestioningly, the priests' orders, she soon found this meant satisfying their carnal lusts. Uncooperative nuns were murdered, buried in the basement beside their strangled babies. She had fled to spare her own unborn child that fate.

The book's amazing success can only be understood within the charged nativist atmosphere. Anti-Catholic propaganda had a long history, but in the 1830s it turned from disputes about theology to attacks on papist immorality. Popish plots were reported everywhere, some as outlandish as a scheme to move the Vatican to the trans-Mississippi West. As the leading historian of the campaign put it: "Nativist propagandists were learning the lessons that sensationalism had far more appeal for the average American than sober arguments."[31]

No-Popery works depicted convents as brothels to which innocent Protestant girls were lured. Nativists focused their wrath on the Ursuline Convent because several daughters of wealthy Bostonians had gone there and its Mother Superior had taken pen to refute charges of the convent's immorality. When an irate mob burned that convent in 1831, religious journals of all persuasions denounced the action; so did the commercial papers. But much of the public treated those brought to trial and acquitted as heroes.[32] One European visitor said his hosts told him the primary motivation for the attack was not so much bigotry as just plain curiosity about what went on behind the high gray walls.[33] His American hosts may, however, have been trying to put the best reading on the event. Almost before the flames had died at the convent, two Catholic newspapers were founded.

All of this set the stage for the appearance of Maria Monk's book which, except for *Uncle Tom's Cabin*, probably sold more copies than any book in pre–Civil War America. By 1860, there had been twelve authorized printings and at least as many bootleg editions, with a combined circulation of perhaps 500,000. Not only the nativist papers, but many of those published by Protestant denominations, praised *Awful Disclosures*.[34] The *Sun* was among her journalistic champions. That alone almost guaranteed that the *Herald* would take the opposite position.

Bennett hesitated, claiming to weigh his opinion. Rather than sitting around like other editors and pondering the religious doctrines, he went to see the lady, to judge her at first hand. Bennett was a practicing Catholic, but that had no apparent effect on his evaluation. No editor of the day was harsher in his denouncements of the Pope. In his first-person account appearing in the *Herald* on March 1, he described going to her hotel room, in the company of several believers, and listening as she described her experiences. Maria, he wrote, was pretty and wore her hair in ringlets, topped by "a narrow straw bonnet of the fashion." Bennett did not transcribe the interview in the question-and-answer format, probably because, as he wrote, he asked no questions "for I know very well you never can get the truth out of any woman in questions to her."

> **Maria, however, is very plausible and tells a straight story. If her book is all invention, she has a wonderful imagination. I do not think,**

however, that I am more of a believer than ever.
I don't know what to think about it. She may, and
she may not, tell the truth—the whole truth. It
may be embellished ... but I hardly can believe
that the atrocities she relates of the priests are
credible. Men will not commit more villainy than
is necessary to gratify their passions.[35]

Bennett's growing suspicions were confirmed when the girl's mother admitted her ne'er-do-well daughter had never been near a convent. One of the clergymen who brought her to New York later admitted he had written the book. There was a falling out among the sponsors (one group even produced another "nun" from the same convent and tried without much success to repeat the bonanza that had been Maria), and they ended up suing one another over copyright claims.

Bennett sniped at her long after the story faded from public view, inserting paragraphs about her promenading on Broadway, her visits to the *Sun* office and her denunciations of the committee investigating her charges. In August, he pronounced her exposed as "a common prostitute," and published two installments of a parody of her book, daring Maria and her lawyers to sue for libel.[36]

Apparently, Maria reaped little profit from the book or its 1837 sequel. She later bore another child out of wedlock and this time did not try to blame a priest. Years later she was arrested as a prostitute and died in prison. Even after the exposures her books continued to sell. One edition reappeared during the 1960 presidential election and probably circulates in some anti-Catholic circles to this day.[37] As Henry Steele Commager observed, "Intolerance has always been an index of the things men thought important and certain."[38]

BACKLASH AND CHANGE

The Robinson-Jewett murder case of 1836, discussed in the next chapter, set the *Herald* on firm financial ground, but it also drew the wrath of those who considered the coverage excessive and salacious. Two years after founding his paper, Bennett estimated his own wealth at $100,000, and by the 1850s his annual profits were $50,000, probably more money than any other newspaperman in the world.[39]

Bennett learned that names made enemies as well as news. At a time when most respectable people did not want their names in any newspaper, much less a despicable sheet like the *Herald,* Bennett ran lists of marriages, deaths, and revelers at society dinners and balls. The *Herald* pioneered in listing arriving passengers from ships and new registrants at hotels, practices quickly adopted by other papers. It is well to keep in mind the observation nearly a century later by sociologist Robert Park in his famous essay on "The Natural History of the Newspaper." His final paragraph:

> The real reason that the ordinary newspaper accounts of incidents of ordinary life are so sensational is because we know so little of human life that we are not able to interpret the events of life when we read them. It is safe to say that when anything shocks us, we do not understand it.[40]

Many New Yorkers during this period of religious revivalism already resented the *Herald*'s anticlerical tone. Established churches were competing vigorously for members, especially among those who had left their church-going traditions back home when they moved to New York.[41] Many of those people read the *Herald*'s frequent denunciations of church hierarchies. Bennett raised many hackles when he accused the Catholic bishop of luxuriating in Saratoga Springs while his clergy labored among the dying during an epidemic in New York slums.[42]

In spite of the growing criticism the *Herald*'s circulation continued upward, even if one allows for some exaggeration in his claim in mid-1836 that he sold 12,000 copies a day. He threatened to fire any carrier who charged a premium, as many reportedly were doing. With his new steam-powered press, he soon claimed a daily circulation of 40,000, almost certainly an exaggeration. He said advertisers were begging for space.[43] Bennett insisted the ads were an interesting part of the paper and encouraged advertisers to change them frequently. In 1847 he began requiring changes at least every other day.[44]

Bennett seemed to believe that when he doubled his price to two cents in August 1836 he purchased a more respectable audience. He claimed more women subscribed to the *Herald* than to all other papers in town.[45] The paper maintained its price for the next twenty-six years, until forced upward by Civil War inflation.

Although frequently critical of municipal leaders, he was a consistent civic booster. If New York was not already the greatest city in the world, it soon would be.[46] He championed home rule for the city and charter improvements. Bennett decried imprisonment for debt and opposed monopolies. He published many exposés of corruption and mismanagement, especially among the police and judges.[47]

At the peak of the Robinson trial he claimed the *Herald* sold 20,000, about twice his normal sale. Like all circulation claims of the era, this is probably an exaggeration.[48] Almost immediately, he stepped up his assaults on the "lowly" penny papers, charging that the bulk of their readers were "loafers." The *Herald* dropped the one-liners in the police court column and scolded the *Sun* for not following suit. A few weeks later, Bennett held all court and police news from an issue in order to make space for the text of the president's address, a demonstration of his new-found "respectability."[49]

To encourage a flow of quality material in the fall of 1836, Bennett offered several cash prizes for poems and essays in several categories. For the best essay on women, he doubled the prize to $40. The winners began appearing in December.[50]

The *Herald* published sports items, mostly about horse races. Accounts were brief and irregular. Horse racing was legalized in New York in 1821, and several tracks operated in and around the city. Racing was still a rich man's sport, but trotting less so. There was considerable interest in intersectional and international match races in the 1830s.[51]

A new penny paper, the *New Era,* entered the New York field that same fall. One of its two editors was Locke, the author of the *Sun's* "moon hoax" of the year before. When the new (and short-lived) paper termed Bennett a "disreputable and universally execrated scribbler" and a "degraded, knavish, horse-whipped, bribed, mendacious and miserable poltroon," he gleefully reprinted the attacks.[52]

The *Sun* still led the *Herald* in circulation, so of course Bennett relished in Day's conviction for tampering with a packet addressed to the *Courier and Enquirer.* The packet contained the text of a presidential address and had been forwarded by the *Courier's* Washington correspondent. From the time of the indictment in August until the trial, conviction, and fine in October, Bennett seldom missed a chance to refer to Day as "thief."[53] He also delighted in reporting that a woman charged Locke with seduction and that the *New Era* was suing the *Sun* for libel.[54] Bennett reported the bitter falling out in early 1837 between the editors of the *Sun* and the *New Era.* Day called the editor of the *New Era* a "pitiable wanderer from the path of sobriety and honesty," which was returned with a charge that Day was a "villain of the deepest turpitude." Bennett shook his finger at both the "dirty penny vehicles."[55]

His front-page boasts were frequent and overblown, but he was close to the truth of his paper's success when we wrote:

I have entered the hearts of the people—I
have shown them their own sentiments—I have
put down their own living feelings on paper—I

> have created a passion for reading the *Herald*
> among all classes.[56]

When to flaunt decorum he printed words like "legs" and "petticoats," it gave rival editors the opportunity to express outrage and helped bring on the so-called "moral war" in 1840. It went beyond an attempt to get readers and advertisers to boycott the *Herald,* and even urged hotels not to rent rooms to those carrying a copy. One target of protesters was the *Herald's* thinly disguised ads for patent medicines, quack doctors, prostitutes, and abortionists. Madame Restell, New York's best-known abortionist, advertised regularly in both the *Sun* and the *Herald.* She was the wife of a *Herald* printer. Apparently readers understood the euphemisms in her ads and those of other abortionists about "female irregularity" or "suppression of the menses." Her advertising dollars may have bought Bennett's support. As late as March 1839, the *Herald* denounced her "filthy" advertisements; but three months later, after receiving a sizable contract, the paper published an elaborate puff piece. A year after that, Bennett not only defended running her ads but suggested critics were jealous because they were not getting their share. Her ads disappeared quietly after May 1845. Neither the *Sun* nor the *Herald* reported her conviction in 1846. She spent a year in prison, but in 1848 resumed her business and her ads. The *Herald* carried ads for abortionists until well after the Civil War.[57]

Bennett became concerned as the *Herald's* circulation fell from 17,000 to 12,000 and some advertisers pulled out. Publishers of the mercantile papers were delighted, of course, but by their failure to attack other penny papers acknowledged the *Herald's* influence. Certainly not all who opposed him were prudes; Bennett had plenty of enemies among religious, political, and social leaders. The paper provided politicians a convenient whipping boy. Like other moral wars, this was prompted by the status anxiety of an established elite.[58]

As if to flaunt his vulgarity, Bennett announced his own engagement on the front page in the purplest of prose. It was perhaps the ultimate example of what Schudson termed self-advertisement.[59] At forty-five, Bennett was several years older than his attractive Irish wife, who soon wearied of the abuse hurled at him by other editors and fled to France with James Jr. Papa visited only occasionally.[60]

Prudently, Bennett toned down his columns, regaining readers with superior coverage of the Mexican War and later of the Civil War. Long after he turned over the day to day news operation to Frederic Hudson, Bennett still spent long days (and nights) in the office and made the policy decisions. Hudson was the highest paid editor in America. The *Herald's* salaries generally were the highest and its equipment the best in the business.

REAL "FIGHTING EDITORS"

Editors of the day were ready to back up their editorial lambastings of one another with fists, cudgels, and horse whips. James Watson Webb of the *Courier and Enquirer* pummeled Bennett three different times.[61]

Three days after detailing his former boss's stock market dealings (he allegedly had profited from insider information) the rival pummeled Bennett with his cane. In the next morning's *Herald* Bennett laughed off the attack, claiming Webb hit him from behind. "After I was down, he continued his brutal attack" and then cursed Bennett "in a blustering, impudent manner." Bennett's promised such villainry would never cow the *Herald*.[62] With the encounter the talk of the town, the *Herald* sold many extra copies.

A few weeks later, Bennett dared him to try it again, and Webb took him up on the challenge. Bennett reported that Webb again won the physical contest, but that he fought with the "brutal and demoniac desperation characteristic of a fury."[63] When in July Bennett learned that another newspaper was preparing a journalistic attack on Webb, he protested, insisting, "Col. Webb is our property." A few days later he published a report of his third, and apparently final, caning by Webb.[64]

Chuckling about the low comedy of these encounters, the *Sun* called Bennett "a notorious vagabond" and a "common flogging property."[65] But Bennett continued to twit Webb, charging in October that he lacked "ballast, judgment, and sound discretion."[66] By then Webb must have wearied of the street fights, for there is no report of a reprisal. Webb mentioned in his newspaper a street brawl with William Leggett, an *Evening Post* editor, but never the three encounters with Bennett.[67]

In other encounters, a Wall Street broker came after Bennett with a whip, a disappointed Tammany office-seeker with his fists. After the manager of a theater and his friends ransacked the *Herald* office, Bennett complained "Civilization is yet defaced with traits of barbarism." Bennett had no takers when he posted a reward for information about the identity of six ruffians who on another occasion assaulted him in his own office.[68] Given the riotous times, it is a wonder someone did not kill Bennett; certainly there were attempts. A bomb left for him in 1852 was discovered before it went off. Two young Republican zealots bungled a plot to murder him during the Civil War.[69]

By 1866, when Bennett turned over the *Herald* to his playboy son and namesake, he had published the paper for thirty years, and during most of that time it was the nation's largest. He claimed 77,000 by 1860, a figure unmatched even by the European papers. While the old man lived out his last years as a recluse in his uptown mansion, "Jamie" surprised almost everyone by making the paper even more dominant and more profitable. His decade of direct control ended dramatically in 1877, when during a dignified New Year's party in the home of his fiancée he disgraced himself by urinating in the fireplace. Some accounts insist it was in the grand piano or an ornate vase, but the result was the same. The next day the brother of his ex-fiancée (for by then she was that) beat him up in public. From then on Jamie ran the paper mostly from Paris. Immense profits from the *Herald* supported his yachting and other amusements.

Most historians, like most of their own contemporaries, have denounced both Bennetts for catering to the basest instincts of readers and for trivializing the newspaper. Although a few credit James Gordon Bennett Sr. with "inventing" news (whatever *that* means!) his real innovation was going beyond the official sources and following up on a story. Nowhere was that better illustrated than in the *Herald*'s coverage of the Robinson-Jewett murder case.

5

The Robinson–Jewett Case

The Robinson–Jewett murder case of 1836 was a landmark in American journalism history, the first time newspapers really exploited a crime story. Its coverage of the case made the upstart *Herald* the city's dominant newspaper, a position it would retain for half a century.

The facts of the case can be stated briefly. Helen (Ellen in some accounts) Jewett, a strikingly beautiful twenty-three-year-old prostitute, was found bludgeoned to death early one Sunday morning in a burning bed in one of the city's most elegant bordellos. Apparently the murderer had set the fire to cover his tracks, and the smoke had aroused the madam. A watchmen found a cape, immediately identified by the madam and other girls as belonging to Richard Robinson, one of Helen's "regulars." A hatchet was found in the backyard. The nineteen-year-old Robinson was arrested in his room, a mile away.[1] Robinson, a handsome youth, employed as a clerk in a nearby mercantile firm, admitted visiting the house but insisted that when he departed, Jewett was alive and well. He was jailed and the next day charged with the murder.

We have the word not only of Bennett and other journalists that the murder excited wide interest, but also a similar statement from the son of a leading attorney and socialite. George Templeton Strong, then a sophomore at Columbia University, recorded in his diary on April 12, "Everyone was talking about the case." He even rode past the murder site and caught a glimpse of the proprieter.[2]

Prostitutes often met with violent deaths. Twenty girls had perished in the twenty-two brothels in a single block during the preceding three months.[3] Such incidents seldom produced court trials. Of the handful of murder or manslaughter trials heard each year in the city only three or four a month were recorded in the New York newspapers.[4] London papers published far more crime news. As early as 1823, they had such lavish coverage of the murder trial of John Thurtell, a gentleman gambler, that his attorneys blamed his conviction on the publicity.[5] Detailed accounts of crimes and trials were staples of even the most respected London papers by the 1830s. New York papers were about to catch up.

It is tempting but misleading to credit the unprecedented interest in the Robinson–Jewett case solely to newspaper hype. Bennett recognized in it the classic elements of a mystery: an exotic setting, handsome victim and accused, illicit sex, a brutal murder—even a burning bed.[6] Crime novels of the day equated illicit sex with homicide. Writers, like doctors and ministers, were especially obsessed with the "wages of sin theme."[7]

Bennett set out to provide the doubt that would round out the mystery. He knew many young clerks and bookkeepers thought Robinson was being prosecuted more for his lifestyle than for his alleged crime and there was an even wider distrust of the criminal justice system.[8] By casting doubt on Robinson's accusers he would kindle those resentments.

THE OLDEST PROFESSION

Prostitution had been in the limelight, thanks to the well-publicized activities of four major antivice reform groups. Clergymen finally acknowledged the existence of prostitution. Even the stodgy six-cent dailies discussed the furor set off by one group's claim that there were 10,000 full-time and a like number of part-time harlots in the city. The figures seem exaggerated. If true, nearly one out of three females of marriageable age performed sex for pay. The same report suggested half the city's males, married and unmarried, patronized the painted ladies.[9] Editors joined civic leaders in denouncing the estimates as far too high, but they were equally skeptical of the city's official estimate of only 1,438 prostitutes.[10]

Regardless of the figure, men agreed prostitution needed to be discussed—at least by men. In 1834, a grand jury declared a tract on the subject a public nuisance because it might offend women, and in 1836 (less than six months after the Robinson trial, during which prostitution had been widely discussed), the *Herald* expressed outrage that a women's reform group published a report on prostitution. Bennett insisted it was a subject no decent woman should even contemplate.[11] The legal system did not seem to want to deal with it either. The watchmen and magistrates looked the other way unless a cheated customer or a bothered neighbor complained. If a girl was charged, it was as a vagrant; if an owner was charged with operating a disorderly house, it was for doing exactly that—allowing the brothel to become a public nuisance. That usually meant its noise and fights had spilled out into the streets.[12]

By the 1830s, there were well-defined classes of prostitutes. The youngest, most attractive, and most refined courtesans like Helen Jewett worked in the dozen or so elegant parlor houses, concentrated west of Broadway, where six to twelve girls rented rooms.[13] Some reportedly cleared $100 or more a week at a time when a domestic servant or a laborer was fortunate to earn $8.

Bennett devoted nearly the whole of his front page of April 11 to the MOST ATROCIOUS MURDER.

> **Our city was disgraced on Sunday by one of the most foul and premeditated murders that ever fell to our lot to record. The following are the circumstances as ascertained on the spot:**
>
> **Richard P. Robinson, the alleged perpetrator of this most horrid deed, had, for some time been in the habit of keeping (as it is called) a girl named Ellen Jewett, who has for a long time resided at no. 41 Thomas street in the house kept by Rosina Townsend.**
>
> **Having, as he suspected, some cause for jealousy, he went to the house on Saturday night as appears, with the intention of murdering her, for he carried a hatchet with him. On going into her room, quite late at night, he mentioned his suspicions, and expressed a determination to quit her, and demanded his watch and miniature together with some letters that were in her possession. She refused to give them up, and he**

then drew from beneath his cloak the hatchet, and inflicted upon her head three blows, either of which must have proved fatal, as the bone was cleft to the extent of three inches in each place.

She died without a struggle, and the cold-blooded villain deliberately threw off his cloak, cast the lifeless body upon the bed and set fire to that. He then ran downstairs unperceived by any person, went out of the back door and escaped in that manner.

In a short time Mrs. Townsend was aroused by the smell of smoke—she rushed upstairs and saw the bed on fire and the mangled body of the unfortunate girl upon it. She ran down, raised the alarm, and the watchman rushing to the spot, rescued the body and preserved the house from being consumed.

Robinson's cloak was in the room, and at once they suspected the murderer. Mr. Noble, the assistant Captain of the Watch, instantly went and aroused Mr. Brink. They received such information as the horror-stricken inmates could afford them, and processed on their search. On Sunday morning, at seven o'clock, Robinson was arrested in bed at his boarding house, no. 42 Day street, and brought at once to the house where had been committed the foul deed.

On seeing the body, he exhibited no signs of emotion, but gazed around and on the victim cooly and calmly.

The Coroner was summoned, a Jury formed, and on patient examination of the testimony, they returned a verdict that "she came to her death by blows upon the head inflicted with a hatchet, by Richard B. Robinson."

Robinson is a native of one of the Eastern states, aged 19, and remarkably handsome and intelligent, and has been for some time past, in the employ of Joseph Hoxie, 101 Maiden Lane. But his conduct upon this occasion, must stamp

him as a villain too black a die for mortal. Of his
intentions there can be no doubt, for he took the
hatchet with him ...

FOLLOWING UP

On that Monday, all the city's papers detailed the murder but only the
Herald published the story on the front page or went beyond the facts
disclosed in the coroner's hearing.[14] Bennett himself went to the bordello
(he would return twice more in the next few days) and described the scene
and the corpse for his readers:

> The countenance was calm and passionless.
> Not the slightest appearance of emotion was
> there. One arm lay over her bosom—the other
> was inverted and hanging over her head. The left
> side down to the waist, where the fire had
> touched, was bronzed like an antique statue. For
> a few moments I was lost in admiration of this
> extraordinary sight—a beautiful female corpse
> —that surpassed the finest statue of antiquity. I
> was recalled to her bloody destiny by seeing the
> dreadful bloody gashes on the right temple, which
> must have caused instantaneous dissolution. ...
> What a melancholy sight for beauty, wit and
> talent, for it is said she possessed all, to come
> to such a fatal end![15]

Failing to grasp the potential reader interest, the other two penny
papers carried only sporadic short stories on the case until it came to trial
in June.

Although in his first story Bennett said the murderer was "no doubt"
Robinson, within a few days he was referring to Robinson as an "innocent
boy." The *Times* called the evidence against Robinson "overwhelming," but
the *Herald* asked why, if that was so, the police barred the press from the
inquiry. Bennett suggested they were afraid to expose the brothel's other
customers on that fatal night. "There is a story afloat that a certain married
man, a merchant downtown, who was caught in that night's haul, begged
the watchman to let him off and even offered a $1,000 bribe." Bennett
suggested Jewett had been killed, either out of jealousy or to rob her, by
the madam or one of the other girls. He hinted at a conspiracy to frame the

clerk.[16] To Bennett, the evidence seemed too neat, the proceedings too swift.

Bennett determined to pump the story for all it was worth—and it was worth plenty. He claimed that during the first ten days of the Jewett story, the *Herald*'s circulation rose from less than 4000 to about 15,000, and that only his limited press capacity kept it from climbing still higher.[17] Thanks to his enterprise, Bennett alone could reveal that the victim's real name was decidedly unromantic: Dorcas Doyen. Raised in a good family in Maine, she got pregnant, was betrayed by her lover and turned out by her family. She soon headed for the big city to trade on her raven-haired beauty. She had worked in several brothels and was a familiar promenader on Broadway near City Hall.[18]

Three times Bennett visited the murder scene, apparently the only journalist to do so. In those days of one or two-man staffs, an editor seldom ventured outside the office. An anonymous pamphleteer later likened Bennett's visits to those of "a vampire or a carrion bird."[19] On his first visit to the yellow house on Thomas Street, Bennett reported that a guard allowed him to enter, and when someone asked why, the guard responded. "He is an editor on public duty."[20] That was not an idea widely shared at the time, but Bennett gloried in it. After his second visit he described Jewett's deserted room, and on the third, he conducted his famous interview with the proprietress, Mrs. Townsend. This woman with a "dark devil of an eye, and a slight emaciation in the contour of her visage" told Bennett she had recognized Robinson, a frequent caller. Bennett wondered who would end up with Helen's expensive jewelry and clothing.[21]

Bennett seemed to take ghoulish glee in describing the bordello that had been "the pride of the gay, young reprobates from one end of the Union to the other." He wrote in his most purplish prose, "Behind the pile of elegant buildings was a garden decorated with elegant arbors, picturesque retreats, evergreens, flowers, and all the beauties of the vegetable world. Under the bright, shining moon, climbing up the dark blue heaven, during soft summer months, these arbors would be filled with . . . champagne, pineapples, and pretty *filles de joie*, talking, chattering, singing, and throwing out all the blandishments their talents could muster."[22]

Bennett hung the story on every peg he could find. He reported that Jewett's bedside table held a slim book of verse by that most tragic of all poets, Lord Byron, and a copy of the *Knickerbocker* magazine, the city's toniest monthly, thus establishing not only her solemnity but her refinement. Bennett never mentioned that an article in the same issue of the *Knickerbocker* ridiculed the trivia being published in the penny press.[23]

Not only did the *Sun* and the *Transcript* drop the story during the six weeks between the arrest and trial, both accused the *Herald* of being bribed by Robinson's friends, a charge that haunted Bennett to his grave.[24] Most six-cent papers published nothing during that period but did hire stenographers to report the proceedings when the trial went to court.[25] While other papers ignored the accused murderer, the *Herald* published something nearly every day, even if it was only that he was popular with his jailers or that he spent a lot of time reading novels and smoking cigars.[26] Several commercial artists sold renderings of both Robinson and Jewett, but not even the *Herald* published any portraits.

The *Sun* asked how any clerk could afford to patronize Mrs. Townsend's expensive house.[27] Robinson later admitted he had done it by robbing his employer's till. When the *Sun* published extracts from Robinson's diary, the *Herald* charged the police had illegally leaked the material to poison public opinion. The *Sun* even published an obviously burlesque love letter from Bennett to Jewett.[28]

Soon Bennett was blaming society for the crime. "The question new before the public involves more than the guilt of one person. . . . It involves the guilt of a system of society—the wickedness of a state of morals—the atrocity of permitting establishments of such infamy to be erected in every public and fashionable place in our city."[29] Ministers based their sermons on the case, and one historian considers this linkage of crime with societal ills as a step toward real political reporting.[30] Although he wrote frequently about the "morbid excitement" about the case, his many critics insisted Bennett was more concerned with profits than pieties.

THE "FIRST" INTERVIEW

Standard journalism histories credit this interview with Rosina Townsend, published in the *Herald* on April 17, as the first journalistic interview. Scholars have uncovered earlier published examples but none with the impact of Bennett's reports from the Thomas Street brothel. Mitchell Stephens was closer to the mark in citing the Townsend interview as an early example of enterprise reporting. He wrote that while other reporters may have nosed around a crime scene, Bennett's efforts "stood out for their visibility, their manifest commercial success and their timing."[31]

In the midst of a story that filled three columns, Bennett included the text of thirteen short questions and answers, similar to that in many published court transcripts. Together, they accounted for less than one-half column. The real point of the story was to denounce the *Sun* for its biased coverage against Robinson.

Q. Did you hear no other noise previous to the knocking of the young man you let in?

> **A.** I think I heard a noise and said who's there, but received no answer.
> **Q.** How did you know that the person you let in was Frank [the alias Robinson used at the house]?
> **A.** He gave his name.
> **Q.** Did you see his face?
> **A.** No—his cloak was held up over his face. I saw nothing but his eyes as he passed me—he had on a hat and cloak.

Here, Bennett was asking about what she saw on her last visit to Jewett's room:

> **Q.** What was he (Robinson) doing?
> **A.** He was lying on his left side, with his head resting on his arm in the bed, the sheet thrown over him, and something in his other hand.
> **Q.** What was that?
> **A.** I can't say.
> **Q.** Was it a book?
> **A.** I think it was—either a book or a paper. I saw his face.
> **Q.** What did he say?
> **A.** Nothing. Helen said to me, "Rosina, as you have not been well, will you take a glass of champagne with us?"[32]

Because Bennett, an unblushing self-promoter, never claimed that interview was anything unusual and because the other papers ignored it, it seems reasonable to conclude it was not a journalistic milestone. Bennett's true contribution to journalistic history was his persistence in covering a topic. All early interviews were with social outcasts such as Mrs. Townsend; among the upper crust, it was considered bad form even to have one's name printed in a newspaper, which accounts for the outrage when the *Herald* published guest lists from balls and banquets and why clergymen resented so strongly his accounts of their annual meetings.[33]

THE TRIAL AND ITS WAKE

When the trial opened on June 1 the eminently respectable Ogden Edwards was presiding. He had just fined the leaders of the tailors' union for "conspiring" to resist wage cuts.[34] The grandson of theologian Jonathan Edwards and cousin of Aaron Burr, Edwards was a former Whig legislator and candidate for governor. After many years as a surrogate, he had been named circuit judge in 1820.[35] Handbills posted throughout the city had called for a mass demonstration at the time he was to sentence the tailors, but that had been delayed by the Robinson trial.[36] Except for the *Evening Post* every daily in town sent a reporter, as did more than thirty out-of-town papers. No trial had ever attracted reporters from so many American papers. Most papers devoted five to six columns to the transcripts of the testimony on the first two days. Predictably the *Herald* put the story on page one but so did others.

Among those fighting for seats in the courtroom was the aristocratic Philip Hone, who reported in his diary:

> I perceived in court a strong predilection in favor of the prisoner. He is young, good looking, and supported by influential friends. Sitting between his counsel and Mr. Hoxie, his employer (who does not abandon his protege in the hour of adversity), he certainly looks as little like a murderer as any person I ever saw. These are good reasons for public sympathy, but there are others, less benevolent. There appears to be a fellow-felling in the audience; I was surrounded by young men, about his own age, apparently clerks like him, who appeared to be thoroughly initiated into the arcana of such houses. . . . They knew the wretched female inmates as they were brought up to testify, and joked with each other in a manner illy comporting with the solemnity of the occasion.[37]

The clerks sported distinctive "Robinson caps" to show their support. Like Robinson, they enjoyed the new freedoms of the city, and their employers and elders feared where that might lead. Why couldn't these young fellows spend their time in the library established in 1820 by the Mercantile Library Association or at the Association of Merchant Clerks under the auspices of the Chamber of Commerce instead of saloons and brothels? The preamble to the library association's constitution made its goals clear:

> In a large and populous city, with excitements to pleasure surrounding them on every side, and hurried on by the warmth of early years, too many have sacrificed their health and their characters at the shrine of dissipation and run the giddy round of error before they have beheld the dawning of manhood. Our object is to oppose an obstacle to the inroads of these moral fires and to guard

ourselves against their contaminating influence. The end we have in view is intellectual improvement.[38]

Of an estimated 4000 clerks, 200 joined. Robinson was not among them. Nor did the same merchants have any more success with a reading room for sailors in port that promised to exclude "all works of an immoral or irreligious tendency." It hardly seems surprising that many young sailors or clerks looked beyond reading rooms to quench their "moral fires."

Bennett soon was strutting like a peacock, boasting of his soaring circulation (he claimed it reached 20,000, almost certainly an exaggeration) and begging for more carrier boys to meet the demand. Newspapers in Philadelphia, Boston and Albany reprinted the *Herald* stories, often without attribution. Bennett defended his sensational style:

> **Instead of relating the recent awful tragedy of Ellen Jewett as a dull police report, we made it the starting point to open a full view upon the burdens of society—the hinge of a course of mental action calculated to benefit the age—the opening scene of a great democratic drama, that is yet to be completed by the trial of Robinson, a drama that will, if properly conducted, bring about a reformation—a revolution—a total revolution in the present state of society and morals.[39]**

During the week of testimony Mrs. Townsend, her boarders, and the watchmen stuck to their versions of what happened the night of the murder. Robinson's attorneys kept several incriminating letters from being admitted into evidence and by all accounts, "out-lawyered" the prosecution. Although Robinson never took the stand he maintained that a friend borrowed his cloak long before the fatal night. He had brought the ax, but not on that night, to Helen, who wanted to chop kindling. A friend testified Robinson had spent the late hours of that night in his store.[40] There was conflicting testimony about aliases and disguises, but the marks on his trousers that apparently came from the newly whitewashed fence behind the bawdyhouse never really were explained. The case really turned on the testimony of the madam and her girls. The defense attorneys impugned their reliability and apparently convinced the jury, who after five days of testimony—lengthy by the standards of the day—required only fifteen minutes to acquit Robinson.[41]

At the decision, the courtroom exploded with cheers, in which Bennett probably joined. Within hours, the *Times,* the *Transcript,* and the *Herald* were on the streets with extras, reprinting their trial stories of recent days.

Bennett tempered his joy with a stern demand that the real murderer must now be found "and the first step in this great duty is the instant arrest of every man, married or single, who was caught in the arms of love and licentiousness in that house of infamy, on the awful night of the 9th of April last. . . . Let the whole inmates, male and female, permanent and temporary, be put under instant arrest. Let Rosina Townsend be caged at once." The *Herald* demanded justice for the "pale and ghastly spirit of Ellen Jewett."[42]

Most readers must have recognized this for what it was: the self-interested cry of a journalist who wanted to keep alive the best story of his career. The case was never reopened and the murder never solved.

Both the *Sun* and the *Transcript* groused that skillful lawyers had carried the day but that in the court of public opinion Robinson stood convicted. According to Hone the verdict appalled most of the city's respectable citizens. Both he and Strong believed the rumors about bribed jurors.[43] The *Evening Post* heaved a sigh of relief at being able to get back to more important and tasteful news.[44] Less than a week after the trial George Templeton Strong purchased a cheaply printed account of Robinson's life from a street hawker.[45]

Bennett was like a bulldog, refusing to let go of the story. In a dramatic follow-up, he visited Robinson's former cell. The crayon drawings of Miss Jewett and verses from Byron that covered its walls reconfirmed his belief that such a man would not kill.[46] He managed at least a mention of the case nine times in July and at least once a week for the next year.

The *Sun* repeated its belief about Robinson's guilt in the course of covering the unrelated larceny trial of his former roommate.[47] In late July, the *Sun* demanded that the case be reopened and the names released of all the men taken in the raid on the murder night. The *Times,* on the other hand, praised the district attorney for not calling witnesses whose testimony would have added nothing to the case but embarrassment for their families.[48] In Boston, the *Times,* which had devoted twelve of its sixteen news columns to the opening day of the trial, wrote: "The New York papers, for the want of something more important to feed the morbid appetite of the public, are all striving to outdo each other in horrible surmises relative to the late Thomas street murder."[49]

The Robinson–Jewett case was rehashed for years in pamphlets and in at least two thinly disguised novels.[50] It was burlesqued in an 1837 melodrama entitled, *The Hatchet of Horror; or, the Massacred Mermaid.* Robinson and Jewett were represented in a wax works exhibit that toured the nation in 1840.

The case struck some deep chords and lent itself to parables, but so did many others that never captured public fancy. One historian concluded that

Robinson and Jewett embodied the "submerged sexual tensions of ante-bellum America." He represented the innocent young man unable to resist the temptations of the wicked city, she the new sexually and financially independent woman. Jewett capitalized on the new public nature of sex, but at the same time, her tragic death reinforced the equation of the loss of virginity with degradation and death.[51] Less than a month after the trial, a reform magazine claimed that because of all the publicity, the bawdy houses had more recruits than ever.[52]

Although for the rest of his career Bennett exploited every lurid crime, he never topped his success with the Robinson–Jewett case. Papers on both sides of the Atlantic soon were carrying longer and more detailed crime reports.[53] For Day, the case signaled the beginning of his end as a journalist. Within two years, Day would get out of the newspaper business. The *Transcript* failed during the financial panic. Bennett would dominate New York journalism for decades to come.

Richard Robinson fled to Texas, changed his name and lived a long and apparently blameless life. Did he actually murder Helen Jewett? Probably. At least no other reasonable suspect turned up. Was he proven guilty "beyond a reasonable doubt" in court? Definitely not, whether through desultory police work, inept prosecution or perjured testimony.

The *Sun* reported that Mrs. Townsend opened another brothel in Phila-delphia but apparently later returned to New York.[54] The superstitious insist the ghost of an unsolved murder victim hovers forever at the fatal site. If so, Helen Jewett's spirit inhabits an office building, a stone's throw from the Federal Plaza.

Part Two

THE
1890S

6

Gilded-Age New York and Its Newspapers

As the nineteenth century closed, even more corporations moved their headquarters to New York. Their desire to be near the hub of communications and finance increased the city's domination of American commerce, business, and the arts. The population of Manhattan alone was nearly 2 million and the same number lived in the other boroughs. Of all the cities in the western world, only London was larger.[1]

Since the Civil War the United States had been transformed from a sprawling landscape of 3000 square miles dotted with a few isolated towns and cities into a real nation. Railroads had made it all possible, but it was the cities that maintained it. They had to be built and then supplied.[2] It was the period, as Arthur Schlesinger observed, in which urban values first came to dominate American thinking. "In its confines were focused all the new economic forces: the vast accumulations of capital, the business and financial institutions, the spreading railway yards, the gaunt smoky mills, the white-collar middle classes, the motley wage-earning population. By the same token the city inevitably became the generating center for social and intellectual progress."[3] Uncle Sam, a business figure, triumphed as the national symbol over Brother Jonathan, once the embodiment of rural folk wisdom. Materialism was equated with morality in the social gospel of the day.

Certainly New York was the epitome of all that during the so-called Gilded Age. The soaring cost of Manhattan real estate steadily reduced the amount of space even the wealthiest residents could call their own. For those living in the opulent mansions on Fifth Avenue, it may have been the Gay Nineties, but well over half of New Yorkers resided in tenements or, worse yet, in the lean-tos and shanties along the alleys. The typical brick tenement, five or six stories high, housed dozens of families. In one area, the density was nearly 1000 per block, similar to that in Bombay.[4] In the 1890s a leading American architect proclaimed New York too crowded for the construction of really livable apartments; most builders were not much interested in quality, anyway.[5] Thousands caught in the Panic of 1893 and its aftermath could afford no housing at all. "There has never been a time in our history when work was so abundant, or when wages were as high," said President Benjamin Harrison in his last message to Congress in December 1892. A year later, 500 banks had failed, 16,000 businesses had declared bankruptcy and two to three million people were out of work. In New York the police estimated 70,000 were unemployed and another 20,000 homeless. As wages and prices dropped, the panic broadened into a depression. After a temporary recovery, there was another decline in 1896. The economy improved then but as the new century began, four out of five Americans lived on the margin of subsistence, with few workers earning as much as $18 a week.[6]

As the Treasury's once healthy gold reserves shrank, everyone pointed to someone else as the culprit. President Cleveland blamed Republican tariff reformers; the Republicans put the onus on what they saw as Cleveland's inept monetary policies, and the Populists thought it was the gold standard coupled with plain old corporate greed. There were more fundamental causes, all largely beyond the control of any political party: (1) the inadequate American banking system was overextended, (2) many industries had expanded beyond demand, (3) a worldwide glut of agricultural products depressed farm prices, and (4) scandals had disrupted the European money market.[7] There were serious recessions in fourteen of the final twenty-five years of the century.

In spite of the hard times, New York City was moving quickly in two directions—northward and upward. Except for ethnic ghettos, the entire southern part of Manhattan was now devoted to business and finance, while most manufacturing plants had moved from the island. With the expansion of the streetcar and elevated railroads, a worker no longer had to live within walking distance of his job. Both homes and businesses pushed uptown. Steel-frame construction and the elevator made possible the skyscrapers, which by the end of the century reached twenty-nine stories. The newspapers advertised their status and profitability with taller and grander buildings along Park Row.

Despite the occasional engine that jumped the tracks, passengers flocked to the noisy, but rapid elevated railroads. Horse-drawn vehicles still ruled the streets below. In addition to all the carts and wagons, twelve separate horsecar companies ran twenty-one routes through New York. The horsecars were notoriously slow and uncomfortable. As if the 15,000 horses and their droppings did not pose hazards enough, the pedestrian now had to dodge bicyclists. Sewers often overflowed, and after a shower mud and waste covered Broadway.

Difficult as it was, city life also offered excitement and produced its own effects. As Gunther Barth wrote:

> Most people accepted the heterogeniety of their world as an integral component of their lives. No single culture dominated their activities outside their living quarters. The give and take of daily chores, the mingling of people in the crowded streets, the parks and theaters, shops and factories, exposed them to a multitude of different influences. Over the years these encounters eroded old loyalties. From the chaos emerged the experience of living with the various elements of a new, diverse culture. The awareness of others produced an urban identity that stamped members of heterogeneous groups as city people.[8]

The entertainment industry centered on Union Square at Fourteenth Street. Many of the songs heard at Tony Pastor's and other nearby music halls were played and sung in parlors across the nation, thanks to the dozens of music publishers whose offices were in the neighborhood. "After the Ball," the biggest hit of the nineties, sold a remarkable five million copies. Its verse tells the story of a child who asks an old man why he has no children. He replies that he once caught his sweetheart kissing another man at a dance. Refusing to listen to her explanation, he never could forgive her. Years later he learned the man was her brother. By then the woman was dead.[9] However bathetic it sounds today, the song really got to Victorian audiences.

Comedians were also music hall favorites. Audiences never seemed to tire of some skits. For example, DeWolfe Hopper began reciting "Casey at the Bat" in 1888 and did it the rest of his life. Many acts were ethnic, and the Irish were often the butt of the jokes.

If nothing else, the city *was* brighter. By the end of the century most downtown streets and retail establishments boasted incandescent lighting. So did most of the four dozen theaters lining the Rialto along Broadway from Madison Square to Forty-Second Street. More important for publishers, better home lighting extended the hours for reading.[10]

Great webs of telephone and electric wires hovered over the business district, while garish signs and posters plastered buildings and fences. Whether the city really was uglier, noisier, and dirtier than ever is debatable, but residents and visitors alike thought that it was. Planners rhapsodized about the city's neat grid of streets, but British novelist Rudyard Kipling found fault even with that. "This is not a city in the sense in which we understand the word, we who have grown up amid the charm of irregular cities which grew as the trees do, slowly, with the variety, the picturesque character of natural things. This is a table of contents of unique character, arranged for convenient handling."[11]

By almost any measure, crime had outpaced population in recent decades. By the 1890s, there were about 2000 felony convictions a year in the city, half of them for burglary and theft. There also were about thirty convictions a year for manslaughter and murder.[12] The city's 40,000 prostitutes were seldom bothered by the nation's foremost police force. (The changing attitude toward sex among "nice girls" is captured in the title of one of the most popular songs: "She's Is More to Be Pitied Than Censured.")[13] An 1894 investigation verified widescale corruption among "New York's Finest."[14] By then the Irish cop had become a stock comic character in popular stories and plays. Although New York had long since replaced the disreputable volunteer companies with professional firefighters, the city was still plagued by blazes, many of them now the result of arsonists to collect insurance. Fire codes were still primitive and unenforced. Most of the buildings were wooden, and the ladders and fire hoses were too short to reach their upper stories.

Although it was a period of fierce party politics, most New Yorkers were skeptical that any government—national, state, or local—could solve their social problems. Robert Wiebe called it a period of "intense partisanship and massive political indifference."[15] Republicans controlled the national government, but Tammany Hall had shaken off the muck of the Tweed scandals and again ran New York City. Many of those who worked in the city no longer cared, because after work they joined the great nightly exodus to the other boroughs (and it took more than a charter for Brooklynites to think of themselves as "New Yorkers") or for the suburbs beyond.

CHANGING WORKFORCE, CHANGING WORKPLACE

The 1870 Census showed that women filled only 4 percent of office jobs in corporate offices and retail establishments in the United States; thirty years later they filled 77 percent. An inner sanctum of the American male not only had been penetrated but overrun. Typing schools were founded and public schools added "commercial" classes to meet the continuing demand.[16]

Behind sales counters, the trend was the same. Although London and Paris were developing huge stores at about the same time, it was in New York that the first full-scale department stores emerged. They not only openly displayed an eye-dazzling variety of goods but provided well-appointed lounges decorated with paintings for the enjoyment of women shoppers. As Barth observed, "The department store made the new phenomenen of a feminine public possible." These new stores were designed to pamper women shoppers, who emerged as directors of family consumption. Shopping, not merely buying, became an end itself. The department stores and the art of shopping grew up together. As Michael Schudson put it, "Indeed, the department stores made themselves great stages. People thought of the stores as social centers and dressed up to go shopping.[17] In his novel, *Sister Carrie,* set at about this time in Chicago, Theodore Dreiser described his heroine's first visit to a department store:

> Carrie passed along the busy aisles, much affected by the remarkable display of trinkets, dress goods, stationary and jewelry. Each separate counter was a show place of dazzling interest and attraction. She could not help feeling the claim of each trinket and valuable upon her personally, and yet she did not stop. There was nothing there which she could not have used—nothing which she did not long to own.[18]

To meet their growing need for educated employees, the firms and stores turned to women, who by then far outnumbered men in high school graduating classes. Women comprised 80 percent of the workforce at Macy's. Many customers liked female clerks, especially in the ready-to-wear sections. Although the clerks were subject to strict rules, often being required to stay on their feet for ten or more hours, the work was more dignified than waiting tables or domestic service. Even with sales commissions, few earned more than $5; "Christmas help" received half that. As many as one-third of the clerks resorted to prostitution to survive.[19]

At the same time the percentage of workers engaged in strictly blue

collar jobs decreased steadily. As always the most recent immigrants—
now Italians, Greeks, Russians, and Poles—filled the "grunt jobs," and
many of their wives and children found work in the sweat shops of the
garment district. The unskilled laborer put in long, back-breaking hours and
barely made ends meet. More than half the factory workers were recent
immigrants. Two-thirds of recent immigrants had remained in New York,
New Jersey, Pennsylvania, and New England. The flourishing foreign-
language press helped to cushion their cultural shock.

Many Americans, scared of losing their jobs and their social standing,
demanded immigration restrictions. Organized labor led the demands. Although stronger than they were earlier in the century, unions' gains had
been slow and were nearly wiped out in the Panics of 1873 and 1893. The
eight-hour day was at the heart of many of the more than 8000 strikes
during the 1890s, but since only 5 percent of workers belonged to unions
such tactics had a limited effect. In recent bloody strikes the public had
shown them little sympathy because as one historian observed, "the anar-
chy of labor was deemed more reprehensible than the despotism of capital."[20] At the turn of the century the American Federation of Labor counted
only a half-million members. The much smaller Knights of Labor was more
radical and linked in the public mind with anarchist violence.[21]

Efficiency was the by-word of the day in business. The great attention
to statistics and record-keeping came at the same time that baseball, a
sport glorying in percentages and records, became the undisputed National
Game. Business efficiency was enhanced by such inventions as the time
clock, cash register, mimeograph and adding machine. These inventions,
coupled with the advances in transportation and communication, spurred
the development of large and decentralized industries. Retailers concentrated on quick sales and rapid turnover of inventories.

Printing, too, whirled in the maelstrom of change. Linotype machines
speeded type setting; presses grew larger and faster and paper made from
wood pulp cut the cost of that essential by nearly 90 percent. New pro-
cesses allowed multicolumn headlines and illustrations. Big drawings changed
the look of the front pages. Newspapers were on the verge of color
printing. The half-tone photographs would follow. But those who produced
the words got some help, too—from the fountain pen, the typewriter, and
the telephone. As Neil Harris wrote, "The typewriter and the telephone,
both novelties at the 1876 Centennial in Philadelphia, playthings fondled by
visiting royalty and gawked at by curious crowds, revolutionized in twenty
years the pace at which Americans gathered and reviewed information."[22]

The telegraph had been around for decades, but newspapers made much
greater use of it. The Atlantic Cable had reduced from days to minutes the
time it took to receive messages from Europe. By the 1880s the Associated

Press was the dominant American news agency, thanks mostly to its exclusive arrangement with Western Union. The AP, in turn, was dominated by its member papers in New York City.[23]

POPULAR PASTIMES AND STODGY NEWSPAPERS

Americans liked their reading light and simple. Best-seller lists were dominated by potboiler romances in which simple, virtuous Americans triumphed over evil foreigners.[24] That theme had long been popular on the stage. Although a few naturalist authors such as William Dean Howells wrote more honestly about sex, most still bowed to Victorian prudery. "All the same," one recent writer noted, "there's plenty of evidence that the mere mention of sex didn't bother many Victorians at all. Millions bought marriage manuals that were as sexually explicit as manuals available today."[25]

By the turn of the century, nine out of ten adult Americans could write their names, and probably even more could read. Still, the average adult had only five years of schooling. Only the well-to-do owned bound books, but for the common folk there were lending libraries and many kinds of cheap, unbound reading materials. Far more people read almanacs, weekly story papers and dime (and then nickel) novels, all heavy on crime and scandal, than read daily newspapers. But in a sprawling metropolis these forms could not provide a substitute for old-fashioned gossip. The daily newspaper could and did.

The once-strong public opposition to Sunday editions had disappeared during the Civil War when there was a demand for news of the conflict seven days a week. New York dailies now had their largest sales on Sunday. That was the only day city dwellers had for leisure and explains why baseball crowds were largest on the Sabbath.

Baseball was well-organized by the 1880s, with professionals playing under contract to franchised teams. Many of the teams had direct ties to local political bosses. Rules and schedules had been regularized. "There is no game now in vogue the theory of which is more simple that that of baseball," wrote Henry Chadwick, the leading baseball journalist of the day, "and hence its attraction for the masses."[26] Promoters cracked down on beer, gambling, and profanity in an effort to attract women to the stands. Many of them did come, although old photos nearly always show far more men than women. Sunday baseball was permitted by one professional league but banned by the other. Because Brooklyn, like many cities, had ordinances forbidding Sunday games, its entry in the Players' Association played out of town every Sunday.[27]

By 1890, some 250 American newspapers had Sunday editions, nearly a threefold increase in a decade. Sports news received lavish space in the Sunday editions of the newspapers. Put together early in the week, they were filled with features stories and illustrations. *The Forum* said the Sunday newspaper "rivals the pulpit in directing life, reaching people and forming public opinion."[28]

Daily newspapers also adjusted to the working-day schedule of its readers. More and more editions were published in the afternoon, so that workers could purchase them on the way home. By 1890, twice as many American dailies were published in the afternoon as in the morning. A decade later the ratio was three to one.[29]

THE ESTABLISHED NEWSPAPERS

In the early 1880s the *Herald* and the *Sun* were the kings of the newspaper hill. Their circulations were about the same, but the *Herald* carried far more advertising, so much so that its first two pages carried nothing but commercial announcements. The other significant dailies were the *Tribune,* the *Evening Post,* and the *Times,* all in the doldrums following the deaths of powerful publishers. Bennett was especially uncomfortable in sharing the New York Associated Press cartel with Jay Gould, the Western Union boss who was publisher of the decrepit *World.*[30] Among the journalistic also-rans were some descendants of the old mercantile blanket sheets and many special-interest weeklies. The post–Civil War era was one of journalistic calm many observers mistook for the established norm. They soon were to be rudely awakened.

The four large New York dailies all reflected their owners. The rakish James Gordon Bennett, Jr. ruled the *Herald* from Paris, visiting New York only occasionally. He devoted much of his attention to yachting and preferred being addressed as "Commodore." His *Herald* bore little resemblance to the paper to which his father gave birth in 1835. It was conservative on most issues and handsomely printed. Priced at five cents, it offered more news and illustrations than any daily in town; more important, it carried far more ads.[31] The paper had drawn worldwide notice by sending reporter Henry Stanley in 1871 to rescue the missionary David Livingstone in the jungles of Africa. (Upon reaching him, Stanley learned the good doctor had no desire to leave.) In 1893 Bennett's attorney said he was worth "at least $4.5 million."[32]

Under Charles A. Dana the *Sun* was the best-written and best-edited paper in the nation, the office to which every writer aspired. Its scope was limited, however, because it had never expanded beyond four pages, its publisher hoping that eventually all ads could be eliminated.[33] Copies sold for two cents. Until his death, Horace Greeley *had been* the *Tribune.* Founded in 1841 as a penny paper, the *Tribune* had followed Greeley in and out of nearly every fad of the nineteenth century. Lately it had become the staid voice of liberal Republicans. Like the *Times,* it sold for four cents. The *Times* had slipped badly since its Tweed Ring exposures of the 1870s but soon would rebound under Adolph Ochs.

All these newspapers were big businesses, in many ways indistinguishable from other industries and subject to the same economic imperatives. Gunther Barth suggests they were models of the new, complex institutions in the big city.[34] Any corporate management seeks to control the extraction, production, and distribution of his product. A large company could buy raw materials (such as newsprint and ink) cheaper and had an easier time borrowing money to buy the newest equipment. No less than the producers of sewing machines or typewriters or the refiners of steel or oil, the big newspapers enhanced their competitive edge by capitalizing on technological advances.[35]

In the classic pattern of all industries, the big papers gobbled up weaker competitors and hired away the best people from the others. By the late nineteenth century, New York papers employed thousands of men and women (hundreds in the newsrooms alone). They pooled their news-gathering efforts primarily to eliminate or cripple potential competitors, and like executives in other businesses, banded together in national and state associations. By standardizing their products and the tasks of their workers publishers were able to turn out low-cost items for a mass market. One measure of newspaper profitability was their selling price. The *Sun* sold for $168,000 in 1868, the nearly bankrupt *Times* for more than $1 million in 1893, at a time when a trade journal said none of its healthy Park Row neighbors could be purchased for less than $5 million.[36] Thanks to the upsurge in advertising revenues (ten times as much in 1900 as thirty years earlier) and the dramatic drop in the price of newsprint, most newspapers were prospering.[37]

Because display ads flowed in from the new department stores, and classified ads filled several pages, the papers could offer for a few cents daily editions of ten and twelve pages and Sunday papers twice that size. In the 1880s ads filled less than one-third of a metropolitan newspaper's space, by 1900 one-half. That was the period when advertising agencies became significant. With advertising paying most of the newspaper's bills, the reader's pennies became essentially a fee to qualify him for the advertiser's attention. In short, the press had become an adjunct of the marketing system.

That change troubled many both inside and outside journalism. Was the *only* obligation now to the advertiser? Was the newspaper no longer to serve as a watchdog, protecting the rights of individuals? This debate prompted the formation of city, state, and finally national associations. At their meetings, however, they spent more time talking about ad contracts and newsprint prices than about social responsibility.[38] Prominent journalists continued the debate in trade journals and popular magazines, often focusing on the resort to sensational content to lure large audiences. Critics called it pandering; defenders said they were just giving the public what it was willing to pay for. They followed the lead of a few sporting journals and paid more attention to baseball scores and horse race results.

In most papers the editorials were bland until election time. Then the editorial writers grew sure about their heroes and villains. Reporters, on the other hand, were supposed to be factual. To avoid judgments, news writers hid behind attribution, which led almost inevitably to a reliance on official sources.[39] Many editors and reporters, especially the increasing number of college graduates, retained their idealistic visions. Outright hoaxes were out of fashion, but in his autobiography Lincoln Steffens admitted faking a story that set off a "crime wave." As a police reporter for the *Evening Post* he overheard detectives talking about a series of burglaries and reported it as an exclusive. Immediately every editor, including his own, pressured their reporters for more such stories. There were hundreds of such petty crimes every day, but reporters usually ignored them; now they described every one. Frightened readers thought New York was awash in burglaries. The crime wave subsided a few days later when the papers again ignored most of them.[40]

In 1884, New York reporters were paid $15 to $25 a week. Many in other cities were still on "space rates," paid only for their words that were actually published. By 1900 the best-paid New York reporters earned $60, about the same as compositors.[41] The idealists aspired to positions on the New York morning papers. Readers *subscribed* to a morning paper but merely *purchased* the *Tribune* or the *Telegram* from a newsstand, depending on which had the most arresting headlines and illustrations.

With several dull dailies getting rich by doing little more than accepting the advertising that fell in their laps, New York journalism was ready for new publishers to shake up the scene. From St. Louis and San Francisco came such men. In succeeding chapters we will examine the phenomenon of yellow journalism, especially in the two New York newspapers with which the term is forever associated. After looking at Joseph Pulitzer's *World* in the period before William Randolph Hearst bought the *Journal,* we will compare the journalistic style of the Yellow Kids.

7

Pulitzer Shows the Way

On December 10, 1890, the gleaming new home of the New York *World* was dedicated on Park Row, across the street from City Hall. At twenty stories, it was the tallest building in the city, and its golden dome was visible from far out in the harbor. The building was a fitting monument to Joseph Pulitzer's rapid rise to the pinnacle of New York journalism. Had he ever visited the executive suite, Pulitzer quite literally could have looked down on the hated *Sun,* which had been so hostile. Down the street were the quarters of the *Times* and the *Tribune.* Young Bennett eschewed the skyscraper contest, settling his *Herald* three years later into a three-story terra-cotta building on Broadway (near the present site of Macy's).

Ten-year-old Joseph Pulitzer Jr., in a sailor suit, represented the family because the day before, on doctor's orders, his father had sailed away on his yacht. Although he had relinquished direct control of the paper in 1886 and had announced his formal retirement earlier in 1890, Pulitzer still oversaw every detail of the building and of the paper. At forty-three, he was nearly blind and a nervous wreck; soon he would be unable to bear even the slightest noise.[1]

Although he published the *Post-Dispatch* in St. Louis from 1878 on,[2] his active involvement with New York journalism lasted only three years, cut short in 1886 by his deteriorating health. After that he visited the *World* office only three times. He spent the last two decades of his tormented life firing off cables second-guessing (and sometimes firing) editors from his soundproof yacht. He died in 1911.

Within five years of the dedication of its Park Row headquarters, the *World*'s position as the leader of New York and American journalism was under attack from both flanks. William Randolph Hearst's *Journal* was going for the downscale audience and Adolph Ochs' *Times* for the upscale. The *Times* was the voice of enlightened conservatism. Even the *Times*' slogan ("All the News That's Fit to Print") emphasized decency, and it attracted thousands who would have blushed to be caught reading one of the yellow papers. Unlike publishers of earlier mercantile dailies, Ochs was not ashamed to promote his paper. He deliberately priced the *Times* to compete with the yellows.[3]

It is tempting to overstate the originality of Joseph Pulitzer's contributions to journalism. The truth is that he invented almost nothing, but by adapting and demonstrating so many techniques he set new standards for the business. Certainly he was not the first to exploit sensational news or to gear content to appeal to women. Others had printed drawings and photos. It was Pulitzer's success with all these approaches in the early 1880s that prompted imitation by other publishers. As Juergens put it, he "led the profession in fashioning a new style for the dowdy American newspaper."[4]

Pulitzer excused his use of sensational stories and layouts as his way of drawing readers so that he could inform and influence them. Contemporaries doubted this self-serving rationale, but historians have tended to accept it. In the history books Pulitzer towers above his contemporaries, like his building, his shortcomings excused and his stated good intentions accepted at face value. In a 1934 poll, editors gave him more votes as the outstanding American journalist than all the others combined.[5] He probably would capture the same honor today, if for no other reason than having his name attached to journalism's most cherished prizes and to the journalism school at Columbia University.

The term "sensational" was applied in the public prints to newspaper journalism as early as 1869 and became quite common in the journals of the 1890s. Edwin Godkin was especially appalled by the financial bonanza the New York *Herald* had found with its low-brow approach. He was not alone in taking offense at "keyhole journalism." Others decried the emphasis on crime and the low moral tone, especially the "seductive art," especially in the Sunday papers.[6]

PULITZER INVADES NEW YORK

Financier Jay Gould had picked up the struggling *World* in 1881 as part of a larger business deal but soon grew tired of losing money on it. He was deeply involved in running the Western Union and other lucrative interests, and by then had already exploited fully the advantages that came with a seat on the board of the New York Associated Press. He sold Pulitzer the *World* in early 1883 for $346,000; although it included a coveted AP franchise, most Park Row insiders thought the price too high.[6] The paper was on its uppers, having lost circulation and influence under the shady Gould. Shortly before he purchased the paper, one of its editors told Pulitzer it was losing about $1,000 a month and would need to double its daily circulation to 30,000 to break even.[7]

In congratulating Pulitzer on his purchase, a Boston editor told him he should have no problem routing the dull dailies in New York. "You are in a wonderful field and you ought to move all America."[8] With the exception of the *Herald,* the New York morning dailies were in a rut. A generation of great editors had died off, and their successors had not found their voices. Allen Churchill, a colorful if sometimes overzealous historian, wrote that Pulitzer entered confident that all New York journalism needed was a heavy dose of sensationalism. He quotes one of the publisher's intimates as saying "Such sensations were as plentiful as mushrooms, but were being trampled underfoot unnoticed by the editors of the sedate old-fogey newspapers, who thought a bit of snappy personal repartee on the editorial page was a humdinger and that pictures were degrading, if not actually improper."[9]

Pulitzer immediately streamlined the makeup, actually reducing slightly the size of headline type but adding more decks to the one-column headlines. Technical limitations that prevented the printing of multicolumn headlines and illustrations would soon be overcome.

Within a week, Pulitzer had put his stamp on the content, as well as the look, of the *World.* Backed by the top staffers he brought from St. Louis, Pulitzer sent reporters in pursuit of crime, sensation, and disaster stories, and told them to write in a racier narrative style. The headline writers went for punchier verbs and alliteration.

In his first issue, the front-page lead story described a dynamite attack by Haitian rebels that left 400 dead and wounded. Editors at other papers found the wire story far less compelling. Other stories on the page described a fatal bolt of lightning, a jailhouse wedding, and a condemned killer's last night. (The killer refused to listen to a priest.) The inside pages carried similar stories. The lead editorial sounded a theme that would be repeated frequently as it denounced the plutocracy of Park Avenue. Although it stopped far short of endorsing class warfare, many readers no doubt thought the editorial radical.

Hangings apparently had as much reader appeal as ever, since **SCREAMING FOR MERCY** was the headline the next day over a full-column account of the last moments of the unrepentent murderer. The front page also detailed a society divorce case and a barroom brawl. A civil service scandal was exposed in the third issue, the local staff's first real enterprise story. There was no follow-up on it. The day's longest feature, for which there was no news peg, described human sacrifices performed by religious fanatics. On the fourth day the *World* was hitting its gory stride, serving up a killer tornado in Kansas, a boy killed when his pony fell on him, a smallpox scare, and a miscegenation case on Long Island. On May 15, there was another story on the tornado **(DEATH RIDES THE BLAST)** and the execution of yet another convict. Also chronicled in the first issues were a murder, a lynching, a suicide, several robberies and muggings, and for good measure, a grave robbery.[10]

LOVE AND COLD POISON drew readers to a story of a man who poisoned his sweetheart when he discovered she was penniless. A "plagiarism scandal" at Yale made the front page. Inside was the usual assortment of holdups, beatings, and fracases. Pulitzer finished his first full week with a fairly decorous front page, featuring an account of a congressman found not guilty of murder. There was also the first of many front-page denunciations of Tammany Hall. (Throughout his career Pulitzer remained an anti-Tammany Democrat.) Inside pages, however, sparkled with such headlines as **WHILE THE HUSBANDS WERE AWAY, MONSTERS FROM THE DEEP** and **A MYSTERIOUS FEMALE PRISONER.**[11] Most were in large type above short wire stories.

Each front page that first week gave prominent display to three stories, at least two of which focused on crime, sex, violence, and divorce. This was true for twenty-three of the first thirty days, and on nine of those days, all three top stories were of that sensational type. The pattern did not change much in succeeding months.

How was the *World* of the 1880s different from the penny papers of a half-century earlier? Its pages were more than twice as large and contained six columns. Pulitzer printed eight or ten of these larger pages to Bennett's four small ones. There were more illustrations and many more ads. He had a veritable army of reporters and editors at his command. Unlike the Penny Press editors, he could select from among the far wider menu served up by the wire services, much of it focused on violent or freak events. Court stories no longer were grouped under a single heading but ran throughout the paper.

Within another week, the opening of the Brooklyn Bridge provided the *World* with its first really big story. The engineering marvel of the day, the bridge was the source of tremendous civic pride, hailed by some as the "Eighth Wonder of the World." It was destined to quicken the fusion of the nation's first and fourth largest cities into a single metropolis.

Embarrassed that the previous owners of the paper had opposed the construction, Pulitzer went all out to celebrate the event. (The *Herald*'s was the only discordant voice in the chorus of praise; Bennett was offended that the dedication coincided with Queen Victoria's birthday.)[12] Several days before the opening Pulitzer published a four-column illustration of the bridge on page one and another of the same size on the day of the dedication.[13] For all the extravagance (artists charged dearly for such woodcuts), a threatened printers' strike almost kept the *World* from appearing on the day when 150,000 pedestrians and 1800 vehicles crossed the structure.[14]

A week later, crowds took advantage of a balmy Decoration Day to promenade on the new span. By late afternoon, more than 2000 people jammed the bridge. Trouble began when the crowd pressing up a narrow staircase to the promenade deck at the Manhattan approach collided with the people descending from the tower. Apparently a woman lost her footing, and her screams caused a panic that killed twelve and injured hundreds.

All the papers devoted many columns to the story and the subsequent demands for improved security and to the resulting lawsuits.[15] The *World* headlined its account, which ran to about six columns, **BAPTIZED IN BLOOD**. Pulitzer defied prevailing journalistic practice by running this, his lead story, in the right-hand column of page one; the accepted practice was to run the biggest story down the left. He continued the policy on most days thereafter. The *Herald*'s slightly longer story was headlined **CRUSHED TO DEATH**. Both included several sidebar accounts on survivors' experiences. The other papers provided equally lengthy accounts, the *Sun* apologizing for printing such "melancholy accounts."[16] This, however, was one of those inherently violent stories that had to be covered, so the detailed and graphic accounts cannot be classified as "wretched excess."

During those first few weeks, the *World* increased its front-page attention to sensational news from about one-third of the space to more than one-half. Headlines for the month included **MOTHER'S AWFUL CRIME, WITHERED BRIDAL BOUQUET, A MERCIFUL MURDER,** and **VICTIM OF HIS PASSION**.[17] With such stories, the *World* circulation climbed to nearly 40,000 within three months.[18] Pulitzer earned the undying enmity of Dana and other publishers by printing in 1884 the records showing the underassessment on their plants.[19]

From the beginning, then, Pulitzer demonstrated three of the characteristics historian Frank Luther Mott considered keys to the *World*'s success: the emphasis on interesting, lively and exciting news; the bold editorial page; and lots of cartoons and illustrations. The others (stunts and crusades to attract attention, a strong promotion and sales campaign, and "ears" on either side of the nameplate) would soon follow.[20]

Pulitzer reshuffled the staff, firing and reassigning holdovers and summoning more of his trusted aides from St. Louis. The most notable of them was John Cockerill, for eight years the paper's main editor.[21] Pulitzer's enthusiasm for editors was usually short-lived. A parade of incompetents followed Cockerill, their already difficult tasks compounded by the publisher's penchant for assigning overlapping authority to executives. Designed to keep them on their toes, the practice instead often paralyzed them. Pulitzer also kept close tabs on the operation back in St. Louis.[22]

Although his salaries seldom matched those at the *Herald,* he assembled a top-notch staff. In 1884, the *World* paid reporters fifty cents an hour and $7.50 a column for what was printed. The citywide average was $15 to $20 a week, but in most other cities reporters still were paid only a space rate.[23]

Pulitzer's journalistic targets were the respected *Sun* and the profitable *Herald.* Within a year, his morning edition of the *World* was selling 100,000 copies, mostly on newsstands and at street corners. Unfortunately, we do not know *which* street corners; if such detailed records existed we could be more confident in describing its readership.

One of his incentives for invading New York had been the *Sun*'s unreliability as the only Democratic voice among the morning papers. True to form, the *Sun* quarreled with Democratic leaders and turned its back on Cleveland in 1884. Almost one-third of its readers deserted to the *World.* As its circulation plummeted to 85,000 the *Sun* stopped publishing its figures.[24] Along the way Charles A. Dana, the *Sun* editor, began ridiculing Pulitzer in print, frequently with anti-semitic overtones.[25] Pulitzer certainly was not the only publisher to writhe under Dana's acidic barbs. Dana had treated Horace Greeley even more harshly.[26]

OVERTAKING THE *HERALD*

The *Herald* played into Pulitzer's hands by joining the *Times* in a price cut. Bennett even purchased full-page ads in the *World* to announce his new two-cent newstand price.[27] Instead of adding thousands of readers, the

Herald watched retail advertisers move their accounts to the dominant *World*. Pulitzer responded by adding pages to both the daily and Sunday editions. To add to the *Herald*'s woes, news dealers, whose profit had been reduced, refused to sell the *Herald*. Bennett then had to organize his own expensive sales force.[28] The *Herald* was never again a serious challenger for circulation leadership.[29]

The *World* claimed an average daily circulation of 400,000 for 1893.[30] Circulation of the morning edition declined after Hearst's invasion in 1895, but increases in evening and Sunday sales took up most of the slack. By 1898, the *World* was selling one-third of its daily copies and nearly half its 600,000 Sunday copies outside the New York metropolitan area.[31] But, as we have seen, the key to profits was advertising, not circulation. In addition to many display ads, the *World*'s "wants" sometimes filled an entire section on Sundays. By 1893, the *World* was publishing nearly 100,000 ads a month. In 1886, the *World* charged ten cents a line per day for all "Positions Wanted" notices except for those looking for menial jobs, charwomen, laundresses, waitresses, and seamstresses, who paid only five cents. The highest charge, forty-five cents, was for notices placed by clairvoyants.[32]

According to Swanberg, Pulitzer "was reaching for people who normally never read newspapers . . . the city's teeming settlements of Irish, Germans, Jews and Italians whom the existing editorial establishment ignored."[33] If that is so, few of his crusades reflected any blatantly ethnic appeal. In one exception the *World* led a petition drive on behalf of Irish home rule.[34] Even more than had Bennett a half-century earlier, the *World* built its circulation on the clerks, secretaries, and salespeople, who by then constituted about half the city's workforce. So different from Bennett's day, nearly all the native-born had some schooling and at least rudimentary literacy. Most immigrants read their foreign-language papers but longed for the day when they could carry home a "regular" paper, a proclamation that they had really become Americanized.

The *World* never tired of declaring itself the organ of the working man,[35] but its position in labor disputes was moderate. The paper applauded negotiations but denounced violence as in the Haymarket Riot of 1886 when it supported wage and hour demands by the street car drivers but condemned the rioting.[36] Six years later came the Homestead strike, in which locked-out steelworkers repulsed the arrival of 300 Pinkerton agents hired to protect the plant. Ten died in the twelve-hour battle, and the governor called out 8000 militia. Pulitzer was so upset with the *World* editorial, which seemed to endorse the workers' use of force, that he fired the writer.[37]

In one of its 1884 crusades, the *World* focused on the plight of women workers, many of whom eked out an existence in unheated tenements on a few cents a day. Reporter Elizabeth Cochrane (Nellie Bly) experienced first-hand the plight of women employees in a box factory.[38] In later series she described the deceptive practices of employment agencies and the horrendous conditions in asylums, hospitals, and prisons. Another *World* reporter exposed an opium den that operated openly a few blocks from the main police station.[39] Shortly after a mine tragedy, a team of *World* staffers described the bleak lives of coal miners, both on and off their jobs.[40]

THE *WORLD'S* EDITORIAL PAGE

Donald Seitz, one of Pulitzer's long-time editors, insisted that to Pulitzer, the editorial page *was* the paper.[41] Certainly, he was far more interested in ideas than had been his predecessor in sensationalism, James Gordon Bennett, Sr. Taking Pulitzer at his word that the lowbrow content was simply the honey to attract the readers who would stay and savor his editorials, it was a questionable strategy. That vinegary vulgarity repulsed the same respectable citizens who might have read, and perhaps even heeded, the lofty opinions on page six. Pulitzer said repeatedly that he wanted to address a public and not a select committee, but his prized editorial page may not have been read by either. It is unconvincing to show its power by pointing out that nine of the ten planks in his original editorial platform were soon put into effect.[42] The paper urged:

1. **Taxing luxuries**
2. **Taxing inheritances**
3. **Taxing large incomes**
4. **Taxing monopolies**
5. **Taxing privileged corporations**
6. **Levying a tariff for revenue**
7. **Reforming civil service**
8. **Punishing corrupt office holders**
9. **Punishing vote buying**
10. **Punishing employers who coerce their employees in elections**

All except the tariff were enacted, but as the *World* wrote at the time it announced the list, "This is a popular platform." The first five would not cost most *World* readers anything. Captains of industry already were under attack from many quarters. States already regulated railroads. Reformers had advocated the last five for years, so it would take more evidence than anyone has produced to suggest that the *World caused* any of them. Generally, the *World* was a cautious champion of reform.[43]

The *World* could hardly boast of the influence of its political editorials because in local and national elections the paper supported a long string of losers. Pulitzer was obsessed with Democratic Party politics and played key roles in the rise, fall, and revival of Grover Cleveland and of many state and local politicians. Pulitzer himself served four uneventful months in the United States House of Representatives. He recognized that not all readers shared his enthusiasm, and wrote in an 1899 memo to his editors: "I forbid more than one article on national politics any day."[44] Even Juergens, an author who gives Pulitzer every benefit of the doubt, concedes, "In a sense, every *World* editorial was written with one eye on circulation . . ."[45]

One of his most successful crusades was to raise the funds to construct a base for the Statue of Liberty. France had sent the huge statue as a symbol of friendship, but it languished for several years awaiting a pedestal. The arm with the torch had stood in Madison Square park, and many people doubted that the whole statue ever would be erected. In May 1885, the *World* said that since the statue was a gift from the French people to the American people, the people and not the government should build the base. An immigrant from Hungary himself,[46] Pulitzer felt strongly that a statue should greet newcomers as they arrived in the harbor. Eight months later, the *World* had collected the necessary $100,000, mostly in small donations, some as small as a nickel.[47] The statue and its pedestal were dedicated October 28, 1886.

THE *WORLD'S* NEWS COLUMNS

To at least one historian, the *World's* pages "presented a curious, intellectually piebald appearance to the reader, as Pulitzer cast his net for both serious and light-minded buyers. [The editors] had a genius for provocative headlining that drew attention irresistibly to the story and made the paper hard to put down."[48] Most readers seemed untroubled and adjusted to its Jekyll-and-Hyde nature. Swanberg saw in the *World's* ambiguity a reflection of Pulitzer's own internal struggle between reformer and salesman.[49]

Probably the *World's* most celebrated stunt was sending Nellie Bly around the world to see if she could best the record claimed in Jules Verne's celebrated novel, *Around the World in Eighty Days*. The *World* covered her progress almost every day. She completed her journey in 72 days, and the French author wired his congratulations.[50]

Only rarely did the *World's* writing match the literary standards of the *Sun*. Although its lead sentences were often clumsy and its stories rambling, the *World* sometimes used sensationalism to back up its editorial positions. After fighting against use of the electric chair for executions, the

World sent a reporter to cover the first one at Sing Sing in 1890. He conveyed the horror of ax-murderer William Kemmler's final moments:

> The current had been passing through his body for fifteen seconds when the electrode at the head was removed. Suddenly the breast heaved. There was a straining at the straps which bound him, a purplish foam covered the lips and was spattered over the leather head band. The man was alive. Warden, physicians, everybody lost their wits. There was a startled cry for the current to be turned on again. Signals, only half understood, were given to those in the next room at the switchboard. When they knew what had happened, they were prompt to act, and the switch-handle could be heard as it was pulled back and forth, breaking the deadly current into jets. The rigor of death came on the instant. An odor of burning flesh and singed hair filled the room. For a moment a blue flame played about the base of the victim's spine. One of the witnesses nearly fell to the floor. Another lost control of his stomach. Cold perspiration beaded every face. This time the electricity flowed four minutes. Kemmler was dead. Part of his brain had been baked hard. Some of the blood in his head had been turned into charcoal. The flesh at the small of his back was black with fire.[51]

Like other papers of the day, the *World* published many interviews. The form had come a long way since Bennett's stilted Q-and-A with the madam in the Robinson–Jewett case. Newspapers now routinely interviewed persons from all social stations. For a Christmas feature, the *World* sent a reporter to interview prominent inmates in the state prison.[52] Most socialites were pleased to see themselves quoted. Pulitzer urged his reporters to go anywhere and ask anything to get a story and insisted published interviews include personal details and descriptions.[53] When in 1886 the *Evening Post* criticized the *World* for interviewing guests at Grover Cleveland's wedding in such detail, the paper responded, "The President is public property."[54]

The papers still loved to catch a minister in sin or a blueblood in financial trouble. It was front-page news when a Lutheran minister was forced to resign his pulpit amid charges of "uncomely conduct."[55] **A VANDERBILT IN**

DEBT, shouted a front-page headline in 1891. The story concerned "the favorite granddaughter" of the late Commodore. Three years before she had eloped with a coachman and moved to Tarrytown, where before departing for parts unknown she ran up a few hundred dollars in grocery bills. In a similar vein was the *World*'s account of the elopement of the daughter of a millionaire Detroit manufacturer with another coachman. Even when they were not in the news, the wealthy were still fair game. In 1892 the *World* and *Herald* competed to see which could count the most millionaires. The *World* listed 3045, but the *Tribune* turned up 4047.[56]

PULITZER ON SENSATIONALISM

The personality and crime stories that had been considered sensational in the penny papers of the 1830s were commonplace a half-century later. By the late nineteenth century newspapers were criticized more for display and writing style than for substance.[57] Pulitzer did not shrink from either charge. He said the colloquial writing style drew the mass audience he wanted to address. Pulitzer likened the *World*'s flashy layouts to the showroom windows in department stores. Like them, his front pages were to attract the customer inside, perhaps even to the editorial page.

Pulitzer loved illustrations and in 1884 defended their increased use: "We are very proud of our pictures. We observe that the populace appreciates them and that there is always an extra demand for the *World* when it is illuminated, so to speak. A great many people in the world require to be educated through the eye."[58] The *Herald* was running more drawings than the *World*. Because it took so much time to produce illustrations they could be used only in feature stories. A favorite device, particularly in the *Sunday World,* which Pulitzer admitted was used as "a laboratory to test ideas,"[59] was to publish a dozen or more one-column drawings in a feature on the city's leading attorneys, bankers, merchants, chefs, hotel clerks, or beautiful women. Another device was to publish sketches of familiar buildings, parks and street scenes.

Pulitzer longed to illustrate news accounts as well. That became feasible when he hired an artist who overnight could make a drawing from a photograph. His handiwork appeared each morning on the right side of page one.[60] The *World* later used front-page cartoons in its vicious campaign attacks on Republican James Blaine. One authority credits the *World*'s cartoon of October 30, 1884, showing Blaine presiding over a plutocratic dinner at Delmonico's as the moment when editorial cartoons "came of age."[61]

Contemporary journalists considered the *World* to be sensational even before Hearst entered the scene. In praising the work of an editor in 1893, *The Journalist* wrote that he "has enough of the sensational in him to satisfy even the *World.*"[62] Some complaints focused on the sexual and scandalous content, as well. Later the same year, the magazine complained:

> **The sensationalism of the average daily pa-
> per has, no doubt, created an appetite for things
> abnormal. A subscriber to a paper who has had
> a daily sensation dished up to him every morning
> resents it if that paper should fall short in its
> supply. . . . Certain journals, having developed in
> their readers a taste for blood in order to interest
> them, it must be necessary to provide fresh new
> abattoirs in which they may daily revel.[63]**

When a critic announced that his three-month survey of items in the leading New York papers showed that only 39 percent met his definition of "worthwhile," Pulitzer thought that was a good average, better than for most sermons, novels, or works of art. He readily agreed with a minister who said newspapers published what the public wanted to read.[64] Pulitzer never denied that boosting sales was the primary reason for including sex and scandal in the paper, but he warned frequently against vulgarity. The *World* ran many articles (all illustrated, of course) about nude models but chastized the *Tribune* for its detailed verbal description of an assault on a six-year-old girl by two boys only slightly older.[65] Pulitzer assured readers in late 1884, "The *World* certainly does not seek to make a specialty of crime" but went on to say there was much wickedness in the world.[66] At times, the *World* could be quite prim, as when it decried plunging necklines at the opera house.[67] When Pulitzer tired of reading about Lily Langtry's many love affairs, he ordered the stories halted.[68]

Pulitzer wrote:

> **The complaint of the "low moral tone of the
> press" is common but very unjust. A newspaper
> relates the events of the day. It does not manu-
> facture its record of corruptions and crimes, but
> tells of them as they occur. If it failed to do so it
> would be an unfaithful chronicler. . . . Let those
> who are startled by it blame the people who are
> before the mirror, and not the mirror, which only
> reflects their features and actions.[69]**

GENDER-SPECIFIC NEWS

To attract and hold women readers, Pulitzer relied primarily on general interest news, convinced that stories of ill-starred romances, disasters, or murders appealed at least as much to women as to men. He also recognized the need to appeal to and flatter readers of the fair sex. Articles frequently insisted American women were smarter and more beautiful than Europeans.[70] Its etiquette column advised on such arcane topics as how to place finger bowls and word calling cards. The paper also kept them apprised of fashionable wear at lawn parties and seaside resorts and how to furnish their parlors—assuming they had a parlor, of course. Weddings and social events of the rich were covered in great detail. The headline of a long story about an upcoming society cotillion asked:

Are you going to a ball?
And, If So, Do you Want A
Fancy Dress for the Occasion?[71]

Although it seems unlikely that many *World* readers were on the invited list, Juergens pointed to the Cinderella qualities of such seeming irrelevancies: "Although most of the women who read the newspaper might be lucky to purchase a dress every third autumn, and when they did it was for use rather than style, this made them all the more avid to partake at least vicariously of a world they could never join."[72]

The Sunday paper carried columns of news about women's clubs. To help advertisers reach both wives and women wage earners, the *World* pioneered with a Sunday section designed expressly for women. The women's pages were heavy on fashion, beauty, and etiquette and reinforced traditional ideas about the feminine role. The society department was staffed largely by women on a free-lance basis, but at about this time, newspapers, including the *World,* began hiring women reporters for general news beats as well. Nellie Bly was among the most famous.

About once a week a daily edition included a labeled column on page one of telegraph news and gossip aimed at distaff readers. A typical story described how difficult it was for the wife of the governor of Kentucky to crusade against bourbon.[73] Local features stressed the unusual, such as the growing popularity of bowling.[74]

As with most reforms, the *World* was cautious on the changing role of women. Its lower- and middle-class readership was fairly traditional on such matters. One way the *World* steered clear of feminist controversies was by publishing a column of advice letters, by and to other readers. This kind of "agony column" eliminated the need for the paper to take sides and was widely copied by other newspapers.[75] Although Pulitzer personally opposed women's suffrage his entire life,[76] he also recognized that women had become an economic force.

To attract and hold male readers, the *World* beefed up its coverage of popular (as opposed to rich men's) sports, especially professional baseball and prize fighting (still illegal in New York and many other locales.) John L. Sullivan, the heavyweight champion from 1882 to 1892, was America's first real sports celebrity. The public was as interested in what he did outside as inside the ring.[77] The *World* and other papers sent reporters not only to cover his fights but also to interview him on all sorts of subjects. The *World*'s sports department had plenty of space, with its own pages during the week and a separate section on Sundays. The *World* was neither the first nor the last paper to publish detailed accounts of fights on the front page and condemnations of their brutality on the editorial page.

The baseball writers incorporated statistics long before other reporters. Schoolkids who swore they could not understand long division could calculate Cap Anson's batting average to the third decimal point. The *World* reporters were shameless partisans, boosting local teams and stars. Baseball stars sold tickets to the games, and stories about them sold newspapers. In a confidential memo in 1898, an editor advised Pulitzer that the end of the baseball season meant a drop of 5000 copies a day.[78] Gunther Barth stresses that sports—and news stories about sports—taught the public the importance of rules, rationality, and teamwork.[79] Baseball was widely hailed for its democratic ideals, with most players and fans drawn from the lower middle classes.[80] In reporting upon "gentlemanly" sports such as horse racing and yachting, the paper adopted a more detached tone.

Pulitzer's immediate challenge was only a few blocks away in the offices of the *Journal*. The arrival of William Randolph Hearst would trigger the fiercest battle for circulation in American history.

8

With Skirts Higher and Higher

Two years after being expelled from Harvard (allegedly for presenting his professors with chamber pots adorned with their own likenesses), the young William Randolph Hearst outlined in a letter to his father his plans to reshape the San Francisco *Examiner*, which his father had acquired almost by accident. Senator Hearst was never able to deny his son anything. Willie dumped half a million dollars in the effort, but that was pocket money for the Hearsts, whose fortune rested on the Comstock Lode and the Union Pacific Railroad. Within two years he transformed the paper into a profit maker and he used every trick of sensationalism in the process.

William Randolph Hearst had entered Harvard in 1883, the same year Pulitzer bought the *World*. Now at age thirty-two, he felt ready to tackle New York and Pulitzer. In October 1895, his agents found that the *Times,* the *Recorder,* the *Morning Advertiser* and the *Journal* were all for sale.[1] He purchased the *Morning Journal* for a mere $180,000 from, of all people, Joseph Pulitzer's brother Albert.[2] Under Albert, the paper had sunk to a

level not much above several "subliterary" weeklies and biweeklies that
served up backstairs gossip and cheap fiction.[3]

Hearst entered the New York newspaper scene shouting, banging cym-
bals, and tossing around money. As heir to untold millions, he was prepared
to lose money for a long time. His mother advanced him $7.5 million for his
New York venture, one-third of which went into a publicity campaign. He
blanketed the city with posters and bought ads in other newspapers. He
also sent trucks emblazoned with his paper's name into the ghettos with
free ice, coffee, food, and medical supplies. Although Pulitzer already had
done those things, Hearst did them on a far grander scale. He also boldly
copied the *World*'s features and even its makeup. As Pulitzer had done
earlier, he imported editors and top reporters from his former paper.[4]

Hearst immediately challenged Pulitzer on size and price. The *World*
was publishing ten or twelve pages and charging two cents, so Hearst
priced his paper at one cent and offered sixteen pages. As the "ears" on
either side of the masthead kept pointing out, "You Can't Get More Than
the News; You Can't Pay Less Than One Cent." The only other penny
dailies were the *Star,* the *Recorder,* the *Morning Advertiser* and the *Sunday
Mercury,* none of them with much influence. The other dailies charged
three or four cents. Hearst also offered lower ad rates. Pulitzer underesti-
mated the newcomer's tenacity and the depth of his pockets. Within a year,
the *Journal* sold about 150,000 copies a day, only 35,000 less than the
World.[5]

As we did with the *World,* we will examine the early issues of the
Journal under its new publisher. Hearst devoted most of his first front page
and two inside pages to the marriage of an English duke to a Vanderbilt.
Royal weddings always have fascinated readers, and the Vanderbilts were
the American equivalent. Like the *World* of the same date, the *Journal*
published on its front page a huge drawing of the altar scene.[6] Stories
hinted the American bride might be marrying beneath her station. Both *Life*
and *Harper's Weekly* proclaimed it the social event of the season. Prompted
by such stories about their lifestyles, the wealthy demanded civil laws to
protect their privacy. Most states eventually would enact such legislation.

The *Journal*'s front pages looked very much like the *World*'s. Both
papers topped major stories in columns one, three, five, and seven with
single-column headlines of several decks. Shorter stories and single-column
drawings were stacked in the even-numbered columns. The snippets of
foreign news focused on war and violence.

The New York papers were not the only ones using more and shorter
stories. Hazel Dicken-Garcia found the trend in large papers across the
nation. They also copied the yellow papers in terms of the sometimes
contrived effort to impart a sense of drama in each story. "Even headlines

that were mere labels—as many were—included some element of drama (suspense, humor or punning) intended to hook readers," she concluded. She found few remnants of the idea-centered emphasis which earlier had dominated newspapers.[7]

Both papers lavished front-page attention on a yacht race and a society horse show, but the tone of the stories was "rich folks are funny." An English yachtsman was depicted as a sore loser for accusing the American sailors of cheating. The *Journal* devoted two full pages to the opening of the horse show, including several drawings of the gowns seen in the loges. The *World* coverage included a cartoon suggesting the show was to display women's fashions, not horses. In the same vein, the *Journal* devoted two full pages to the opening night of the Metropolitan Opera with sketches of the wealthy patrons, not of the singers.[8] There was far more attention in both papers to society weddings during that week than to sex or violence. Both published long front-page stories about a death in a saloon brawl, but the *Journal* writer waxed more poetic over the victim.[9]

Both papers saved their most lurid stuff for the Sunday editions. That was the only day on which many workingmen had the leisure to pursue reading. The first 28-page Sunday *Journal* sold for three cents, two cents less than but only half the size of the Sunday *World*. The front pages of both included follow-ups on a death in a saloon murder and again featured society weddings. The *Journal* detailed the barbarities of the Turks, a subject of unfailing interest to editors. Both published similar eight-page feature and women's supplements. The *Journal* offered bicycles to those who identified celebrities from their baby portraits.[10] In subsequent weeks, the *Journal* supplement assumed the heavy emphasis on pseudoscience and medical "miracles" that became its trademark.[11]

SUNDAY SUPPLEMENTS

Week by week, the more bizarre stories were grouped in the *Journal*'s Sunday supplement. Sample heads from the first year:

HE HICCOUGHED FOR FIVE DAYS
WHITE WOMAN AMONG CANNIBALS
SNAKES AND THEIR GODS
PRETTY ANNETTE'S GAUZY SILK BATHING SUITS
DEATH'S BEST FRIEND: A GENIUS HAS CONCEIVED PLAN FOR A MACHINE THAT WILL KILL EVERYBODY IN SIGHT
THE FRIGHTFUL DREAMS OF A MORPHINE FIEND
PHOTOGRAPHING THE UNKNOWN DEAD
WERE THEY THE FOOTPRINTS OF GIANTS?

FALL FASHIONS IN UNDERCLOTHES
STOLE THE PASTOR'S BAPTISMAL TROUSERS
THE MAN WITH THE MUSICAL STOMACH
DROP DEAD AND HAVE YOURSELF PLATED

Several features on sea serpents indicated the public was as interested in them as they had been in the days of broadsides and news books. Gharish drawings accompanied most articles. For example, the artwork for a story about cruelty practiced by a primitive tribe showed a prisoner being catapulted into a den of vipers. Drawn from above, it showed the terrified man dropping into the pit of writhing reptiles. The supplement evolved into *The American Weekly,* which, while written by Hearst staffers and inserted into Sunday editions, was always thought of as an independent magazine. Later the supplement was sold to papers outside the Hearst chain, as well. Merrill Goddard, after being lured from the *World,* edited the supplement for nearly forty years.[12] The first issues were printed as sixteen standard-sized pages and carried no advertising.[13] He blue-penciled salacious phrases and double entendres. Goddard, like Pulitzer, contended that all great stories were inherently sensational and that scandals and crimes provided readers with vital object lessons.

The *World*'s Sunday feature section was no less bizarre. It, too, told of terrible Turks **(BLOODTHIRSTY SULTAN)** and sea monsters **(GREATEST OF ALL LOST TREASURES GUARDED BY FIERCE MONSTER EELS)** "Science" articles included "Missing Link Found at Last," "The Microbe of Handshaking," and "A New Jersey Rip Van Winkle." Hardly an issue lacked one or two crime stories, under such titles as "New York's Vast Training School for Vice and Vulgarity," which described Coney Island. In more serious articles, the *Journal* supplement exposed obsolete army rifles and defenseless naval ports, unsafe trolley cars and brutal prison conditions. It also printed fiction by Rudyard Kipling, Stephen Crane, and Arthur Conan Doyle.

SLUGGING IT OUT DAILY

Hearst raided every newsroom in town, luring the best men with salaries that proved irresistible to many including a man he hired as editor-in-chief an hour after meeting him. Willis J. Abbot, later editor of the *Christian Science Monitor,* said it took a while for him to realize that titles meant nothing and that Hearst would always be his own editor. Abbot thought that Hearst paid little attention to the editorial page, treating it with "tolerant contempt."[14] Hearst once awarded cash prizes to school children who wrote the best advice for the mayor on how to run the city. The winners were published as editorials in the *Journal.*

By the 1890s a wire service had become a necessity for a metropolitan paper. Since the paper Hearst bought did not come with an Associated Press franchise and since Pulitzer was sure to blackball his application, he subscribed to the United Press wire at the very moment the two services were locked in a money-losing struggle to the death. UP (not related to the later service bearing the same name) collapsed in 1897, forcing Hearst to organize his own news and feature services. [15]

Like the *World*, the *Journal* crusaded more often on the front page. Less than a month after Hearst took over, the paper fought for a woman who had been falsely arrested, taking credit for attaining writs for her release and devoting a banner headline and a half-page illustration to her "liberation." [16] The paper exposed experiments on cats in Cornell University laboratories. [17] Hearst started a subscription fund to aid the neediest and spearheaded an effort to send slum children to fresh-air summer camps. The whole nation was singing the new hit, "Sidewalks of New York," in 1896 but plenty of kids were eager to escape those same sizzling sidewalks. Each fall there were also many stories about overcrowded classrooms that prevented poor children from attending public schools, still a troubling situation thirty years later.

If the Hearst of that era was consistent on any issue it was support for municipal ownership of utilities. With some justification, he took credit for blocking private takeovers of trolley, light, and gas franchises. [18] Certainly that was a popular position among the working class, but it was also supported by many businessmen. As one historian put it:

> Leaders to be effective had to have followers, and jounalists had to have readers who could be persuaded. Generally the crusaders for municipal ownership pictured themselves as relying on the "people" and it would be folly to deny that Hearst's sensational journalism had more positive influence in the crowded sections of New York City than in the homes of tycoons. But businessmen also had a stake in efficient municipal services and in low prices for them. [19]

It was extremely rare for one paper and not the other to report a crime; usually the coverage was quite similar. Both used large headlines and diagrams on page one to report a diamond robbery from a Manhattan apartment. Sometimes, though, their emphasis was different. For example, in an 1896 murder, the *Journal* headline noted that the young woman had been strangled with her stocking, while the *World* never mentioned any hosiery. [20]

The *Journal* several times used undercover tactics to attain a feminine perspective. One female *Journal* reporter wrote of her experiences waiting tables in a honky-tonk, while another described the bloodlust of a manhunt in New Jersey for a child molester.[21] Such stories prompted a Texas editor to complain that the *Journal*'s news columns often inspired him "with a wish to use a toothbrush on my brains."[22]

Meanwhile, Hearst was pressed to find time for the more conventional use of a toothbrush. He was often still in the *Journal* office at 4 A.M. when the reporters started showing up to start the next day's cycle.[23] A long-time associate called him "the hardest working human being I ever knew," and cartoonist James Swinnerton said the young Hearst "killed off secretaries" who tried to stay up with him.[24] His lifelong passion was the theater. He often absented himself from the office for a few hours to attend musicals and plays and to watch the same shows burlesqued at Weber and Fields Music Hall at Twenty-Ninth and Broadway.[25] Sometimes he watched the vaudeville at Keith's theater. After seeing his escort home, he would return to the office.

PULITZER MISCALCULATES

In January 1896, after Hearst hired away his entire Sunday staff, Pulitzer was goaded into what he later conceded was his worst business decision. He cut the cover price of the morning *World* to a penny. The tactic worked no better for the *World* than it had a decade earlier for the *Herald,* when young Bennett cut his price to "bury" Pulitzer. By the end of 1897, the *Journal* circulation climbed to 350,000, and the *World* editors heard footsteps. By early 1898 a trade journal wrote: "The *World* staggers blindly in the wake of the *Journal,* imitating all its faults and none of its virtues."[26]

A columnist in the *Daily Telegraph* estimated that before Hearst's arrival, the *World* had been clearing $1 million a year; two years later it was barely breaking even. Hearst, he figured, was spending $6 million a year on his paper, about twice what Pulitzer was willing to invest. The *Journal* was still losing money but acquiring reliable advertisers.[27] A confidential memo from a *World* editor to Pulitzer confirmed the *Journal*'s unrelenting gains in both circulation and advertising; however, at the end of 1898 the *Journal* still was losing $2,000 a week.[28] Hearst lavished even more money on additional pages, features, and promotions such as a bicycle race. He inserted copies of sheet music, cookbooks, and dress patterns. Pulitzer, a multimillionaire by then, frantically switched editors. The other papers scrambled to compete, a few even reducing their page sizes a bit to appeal to the ever-increasing number of commuters. Newspaper salaries went up all over town.[29]

Hearst even beat Pulitzer at his favorite game of presidential politics,

Courtesy of the New-York Historical Society, New York City

Front page of Bennett's "damn" *Herald,* April 11, 1836. "Most Atrocious Murder" — an account of the Robinson-Jewett case begins in the left column.

Courtesy of *American Heritage,* New York City

This fierce attack on yellow journalism appeared in *Life* in 1898.

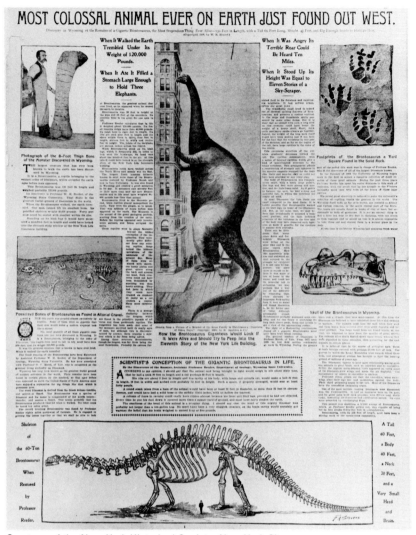

Courtesy of the New-York Historical Society, New York City

Illustrated scientific article by William Randolph Hearst in the *New York Journal and Advertiser,* December 11, 1898.

Courtesy of the New-York Historical Society, New York City

The World, Tribune, and Times buildings on Park Row in New York about 1900. City Hall is to the left.

ONLY A STEPPING-STONE

"THERE IS NO DOUBT THAT HEARST WILL BE ELECTED PRESIDENT OF THE UNITED STATES IF HE LIVES"

Courtesy of *American Heritage,* New York City

Caricature of Hearst's ambitions, *Harper's Weekly,* October 27, 1906

Courtesy of *American Heritage,* New York City

The New York *Graphic* specialized in composites: here Enrico Caruso hails the arrival of Rudolph Valentino in Heaven.

''The Antics of Arabella'' was a popular feature in the *Graphic.*

Courtesy of *American Heritage,* New York City

Homebound city workers read screaming headlines about the Sacco-Vanzetti case.

gaining many readers by his vigorous support of William Jennings Bryan in 1896. Although Pulitzer disliked William McKinley, he also hated free silver, so it took him a long time to endorse the Great Commoner. In the meantime, the *Journal* bombarded readers with caricatures of Mark Hanna and lists of plutocrats backing the Republican candidate. Hearst set up a "political education" fund and matched the dollars contributed by readers. This $40,000 effort was Bryan's largest campaign contribution. An overwhelming majority of the Eastern press supported McKinley. Five million Americans read papers that printed plated matter and readyprint provided by the Republican party.[30] For months, Bryan stumped the country while McKinley sat on his front porch in Ohio. In November, McKinley was not the only winner because Hearst had become a key man in Democratic circles and later would use that as leverage for his own political ambitions.

Hearst joined in lawsuits against monopolistic corporations and if there were two Pulitzers, the reformer and the salesmen, there were also two Hearsts, the patrician and the vulgarian. Always the lord of the manor, Hearst's code insisted upon generosity toward those who served him. In interviews and letters, a host of his former associates testified to his unselfishness, loyalty, and public spiritedness. Hearst was not a sophisticated man, and he made no apology for publishing newspapers aimed at the Great Unwashed. *The Journalist* meant it as a compliment when it wrote in 1896 that the *Journal* was printing "less freakishness," but Hearst made no apologies for the *Journal*'s emphasis on entertainment. He observed that "the public is even more fond of entertainment that it is of information."[31]

ILLUSTRATIONS

An article in *Scientific American* in 1878 praised photography as a new way to see. Photography was not really *that* new, but it was finally out of the laboratory and into the public arena. Photo portrait studios sprang up everywhere, but newspapers held back. The photos of the Crimean War carried in a British publication are probably the first spot news photos, but they had to be translated by artisans into woodcuts. The New York *Daily Graphic* was the first American newspaper to print a photo without that intermediate step in 1880. Although by 1890 newspapers had at their command the technology to publish photos, they were slow to utilize the dry plates, flash, and improved lens. Hearst and Pulitzer both sent illustrators as well as photographers to record the Cuban insurrection.

Hobbyists were much more enthusiastic, and snapshots were a national fad. Daniel Boorstin wrote:

Photography took the first giant step toward documenting the repeatable experience. This it did by transcending language and literature so that anybody without even needing to be literate could observe at will the moment of experience for future repetition.[32]

The *Journal* printed a halftone illustration of a beautiful girl in 1896, but it was another year before any newspaper published a photo on a high-speed rotary press. The *Journal* and the *World* were among just a handful of papers to use photos before 1900. Woodcuts were safe and photos untried, and staff artists who produced the woodcuts enlisted the pressmen in attempts to bar the introduction of photos into the papers.[33] Photojournalism was really born as a servant to yellow journalism and took decades to outlive that sullied reputation.

Even at the age of ten, Hearst had been fascinated with cameras, snapping pictures all over Europe.[34] He never outgrew this love of photos. In 1936, when a German photographer broke his ironclad rule against taking pictures of him with his long-time mistress, Marion Davies, he did not get angry; instead he wanted to know how he could photograph in such low light. That is when he learned about Leica cameras and fast film, both of which he soon ordered to be used at all his own papers.[35] Only days before his death, Hearst was delighted with the gift of a new Polaroid camera. "He was as interested in it as a kid," his son reported.[36]

Like his rival at the *World,* Hearst recognized the power of a front-page illustration not only to draw more readers but also to move them. Although most readers of the yellow press probably had several years of schooling, others were newly arrived from abroad and still had difficulties with English. Illustrations spoke a universal language. Even those with more education did not yet know that pictures could distort reality. In those days, people still thought they could believe what they saw. At the *Journal* Hearst spent more time going over the artwork than the editorials. He hired the best cartoonists and was the first publisher to pay them well and to print their names. "He was always a cartoon enthusiast," recalled Harry Hershfield.[37] In 1898, the color presses printed cookbooks and dress pattern sections for the Sunday editions.

EVENING AND SUNDAY EDITIONS

On September 26, 1896, Hearst launched an evening edition to compete with the *Evening World.* He hired Arthur Brisbane away from the *World* to edit his new paper. The evening edition looked more like it had been dumped out than laid out, with headlines and illustrations seemingly going in all directions. Veteran journalists shook their heads; in fact, nobody liked it except the readers. Hearst pegged Brisbane's salary to circulation gains, and within two months the *Evening Journal* passed the *Evening World,* and Brisbane became the highest paid journalist in America, a position he held for most of his long career with Hearst. Swanberg characterized Brisbane as "a skilled workhorse, to whom the Chief's word was law."[38] Eventually the *Evening Journal* issued five editions daily, the earliest hitting the streets at 7:30 A.M. The *World* followed suit. Because both papers stole stories from one another, the editors often withheld exclusives from the first couple of editions.[39]

Sunday editions provided sections to appeal to audiences that advertisers wanted to reach. Women were plied with more fashions, society gossip, advice to the lovelorn, and homemaking hints. The men were told more about baseball, college football, horse racing, and prize fights. There also was considerable space devoted to reviews of plays, music halls, and books.

The *Sunday World* began the first regular comic section in 1896, the *Journal* the first full-colored comic section four years later.[40] When it became clear that the "funnies" were a hit with adults as well as children, the comics pages became another battleground in the circulation war. Richard Outcault originated the first popular character, the Yellow Kid, for Pulitzer. Predictably, Hearst hired Outcault away. Pulitzer then did something uncharacteristic and offered the cartoonist even more money. Before Outcault could respond, Hearst upped his salary again. Pulitzer then commissioned another artist to draw a panel very similar to Outcault's, and both papers had their Yellow Kids.[41] In both versions, the setting was an alley in a slum, where the ragamuffins pounded on one another while their dogs, cats, and parrots shrieked. The humor was no more broad than the vaudeville acts of the day and in the same way often drew their laughs from ethnic caricatures. It was another twenty years before black-and-white cartoons made their way into daily editions.

Like the showgirls then scandalizing Paris with the can-can, the *Journal* and the *World* hoisted their skirts and kicked higher and higher as they competed for attention. In 1897 both the *Sun* and the *World* reduced the price of their evening editions to one cent to match the *Journal.* By then *World* executives were meeting with their counterparts at the *Journal* to set prices and coordinate business strategies, collusion that today's courts certainly would interpret as violating antitrust laws. Don Seitz often represented the *World* and reported in great detail to the absent Joseph Pulitzer. Seitz told his boss in 1898 that the two papers were working out a uniform policy on reimbursing agents for unsold copies and on jointly raising certain advertising rates. They had agreed to limit daily editions to ten pages and to cut down on promotional posters. [42]

But the course of collusion never did run smooth. When the *Journal* had difficulty transferring the Associated Press contract from the decrepit *Morning Advertiser*, which Hearst bought for that very purpose, *Journal* representatives blamed the *World* and threatened to end their agreements. Organized as a cooperative, the preeminent wire service allowed any member to blackball any new local applicant. Seitz denied any role in the matter. [43]

Sunday editions were outselling daily editions by a healthy margin even before the development of color printing. By 1890, more than half the households in New York City read a Sunday paper. The New York *Recorder* beat out both the *Journal* and the *World* in the race to install a four-color printing press. That is about the only distinction that can be claimed for the paper, which for five years was backed by Duke cigaret money. Its four-color illustration of a society wedding on April 16, 1893, created a sensation while the *World* was installing its color presses and Hearst was still in San Francisco. Vexed by technical problems, the *Recorder* printed in full color again only rarely. After seven months of trial runs, The *World* published its first four-color photo (of St. Patrick's Cathedral) November 19, 1893. Pulitzer was so disgusted with the quality that he shut down the color experiments for nearly a year. By late 1894, a trade journal reported that the "latest social fad" was to visit the pressrooms of the *World* and the *Herald* to view the huge color presses in action. Hearst's *Journal* first printed color on October 17, 1896. [44] Soon the presses of both the *World* and the *Journal* would spew yellow, a development traced in the next chapter.

9

Yellow, Yellow, Everywhere

We all know that William Randolph Hearst caused the Spanish-American War. Thanks to the war, he and Joseph Pulitzer sold so many copies of their yellow journals that they made fortunes. In one of the few lapses in his otherwise upright career, Pulitzer lowered himself to Hearst's level in order to survive. Hearst cabled one of his correspondents in Cuba, "You furnish the pictures and I'll furnish the war." As with so much of our folk knowledge, there is little or no evidence for any of this.

Hearst never really grew up. He got his kicks by watching his *Journal* reporters outwit the police, the military, or the opposition press. (Later he also reveled in collecting movie stars, mansions, and more statues than he could uncrate, but that is not part of our story.) Before turning to "his" war, we will examine the climate of cutthroat competition between the *Journal* and the *World*. The deliberate exploitation and exaggeration of events in Cuba was the natural, perhaps inevitable, result of spiraling competition between two rich and egotistical publishers. In those days publishers made their own decisions without answering to stockholders or boards of directors.

One fine June day in 1897, a dismembered male corpse wrapped in an oilcloth washed up on the bank of the East River. The *Journal* devoted virtually its entire front page to the grisly discovery, including four large drawings and a $1,000 reward offer for clues. The *World* led page one with the story and jumped another seven columns to an inside page.[1] For a week, more recovered body parts were assembled at the morgue. However, there was no head. A *journal* reporter overheard two men in a bar mention that one of the "rubbers" had not been at the Murray Hill Turkish Baths for several days. On a hunch, he went to the massage parlor and obtained the home address of Willie Guldenseppe and made inquiries there. After sketches of the tatoos on the torso of the corpse were published, seven men identified them as Guldenseppe's. Hearst presented a $1,000 bonus to the enterprising reporter.[2] The *World* announced its reporter had a better lead—a ferryman who remembered transporting two covered bundles to Brooklyn. Although this proved to be a red herring, the paper clung to it stubbornly for many days.[3]

So much for identification, but now the *Journal* wanted to find the killer. To that end, it published a huge drawing *in color* to show the pattern on the yellow oilcloth and asked readers if they recognized it. It was probably the first time color printing had been used to add impact to a breaking news story. Too eager to wait for reader responses, the paper sent reporters to interview dry goods dealers, including one in Queens who remembered selling such oilcloth to a woman who lived nearby. Two *Journal* reporters then took the dealer to the police station where she repeated her story. The banner headline across page one on June 30 screamed: **MURDER MYSTERY SOLVED BY THE JOURNAL.**

On July 1 the paper published letters of gratitude from the police chief, the coroner, and two police commissioners. The *World* in an editorial denigrated the *Journal*'s identification and insisted its own pictures really had led to the solution of the crime.[4] The truth was that the *World* had come a cropper with its lead. At least one account suggests that Hearst was personally involved in the cops-and-robbers aspects of the case, and it represented his "greatest success as an amateur detective."[5]

Journal reporters accompanied police when they arrested Mrs. Augusta Nack, a boarder in the same house where Guldenseppe had lived. At different times the beefy forty-year-old unlicensed midwife had been the mistress of both the masseur and Martin Thorn, her accomplice. On July 2 the *Journal* reported that after hours of grilling, Mrs. Nack confessed to helping Thorn rob, kill, and then hack up and dispose of the masseur's body.[6]

Mrs. Nack may not have been faithful but she was pragmatic. She said that while she really liked Guldenseppe better, Thorn, a barber, made more money. She said that on the fatal night the barber shot and stabbed him and cut off his head with his trusty razor. He hacked up the body in the bathtub of a New Jersey farmhouse, and then she wrapped and distributed the oilcloth bundles. Thorn encased the head in plaster of Paris and sank it in the river.[7]

The *Journal* devoted thirty columns to the pursuit and capture of Thorn. A large drawing of Thorn's face on page one pointed out his "cruel mouth and bad eye."[8] (It was a time when many people took seriously such physiological claptrap.) Thorn worked in a shop on Sixth Avenue. Like many in his line of work, Thorn was a blabbermouth. His fellow barbers had often heard him vow to get rid of his rival, and after the killing he had described the bloody deed in great detail for them.

On the day of the capture, the *Journal* devoted most of page four to boasts about its own role. The headline on July 7 read:

NEWS THAT IS NEWS
The *Journal,* as usual, ACTS While the Representatives of
Ancient Journalism Sit Idly By and Wait for
Something to Turn up.

The *Journal* reportedly had to hire guards to keep the eager mobs away from the delivery wagons that day until the copies could be unloaded at the newsstands, but that sounds suspiciously like a Hearst publicity stunt. His son recalled that Hearst often remarked, "Doing something in the paper without promoting it is like winking at a girl in the dark. You know what you're doing but nobody else does."[9]

Thorn and Mrs. Nack were quickly indicted. The *World,* refusing to give up, hired a diver who searched the riverbed without success for the missing head.[10] The murder had been on the front page of the *Journal* for thirteen of the preceding fifteen days, occupying about 140 columns; the *World* had used it on page one nine days, and gave it about 120 columns—wretched excess by almost any measure. Within a few days, the story had disappeared from both papers.

The *World* at the outset had put up a $500 reward for the discovery and identification of the body, so a trade journal chided: "Step up, Mr. Pulitzer and pay Hearst that $500. In doing so, you would make the hit of your life. It would evince an unselfish fulfillment of that so-called 'public service' you have so often advocated in your columns which would actually be refreshing." Of course, the *World* never paid off.[11]

Thorn was convicted of first-degree murder and executed, but Augusta

Nack got off with nine years for manslaughter. During her years in prison would occur the greatest newspaper confrontation in American history.

CUBAN ADVENTURE

Without question the general public, if it thinks at all about newspaper sensationalism, thinks first of the Spanish-American War. The press's exploitation of the conflict was even more evident during the prelude than during the fighting itself. The causes of that war were much more complex, but still it is an unsavory chapter in journalism history, best understood as the culmination in the bitter circulation battle between Hearst and Pulitzer. For the *Journal* and the *World,* Cuba was just one more running story. It was not a new one, either, since in the 1850s James Gordon Bennett, among others, had pressed for American seizure or purchase of the island.[12] Both printed accounts of Spanish atrocities, some real and most faked, and called for America to defend its sullied honor, but their shrill imperialist cries certainly did not "cause" the war. Many other papers and wire services were equally reckless in their cries and coverage.

It is a mistake to assume that either Hearst or Pulitzer lacked genuine concern for the Cubans. As early as 1884, the *World* expressed sympathy for the suffering natives and suggested Americans might eventually have to liberate the island.[13] During the next several years, the paper occasionally voiced similar sentiments, as did Hearst out in San Francisco, but neither publisher became really interested until the festering rebel resentment erupted into open revolt in early 1895.

Spain, although nearly bankrupt, had committed much of its army to Cuba, prompting demands in Madrid for either a quick victory or a negotiated withdrawal. By 1896 the rebels demanded total independence. There was much cruelty on both sides, but because Spain had banned reporters, the American reporters in Florida and New York had to rely almost entirely on the claims of rebel propagandists.[14] American politicians, businessmen, and educators demanded intervention. The chaplain of the House of Representatives was praised for his jingoistic prayers.[15]

James Creelman of the *World* was one of the most bellicose reporters in Cuba. Incensed by his stories, the Spaniards chased him from Cuba in August 1896. After that he sent the same kind of stories from Florida, based on accounts provided by rebel propagandists.[16] Hearst, not the Spaniards, eventually "captured" Creelman, adding him to his staff.

Most of the headline news of 1896 was gathered and often invented on the hotel verandas in Havana, Key West, or Tampa. The correspondents spun tales of beautiful Amazons wielding machetes while riding their fiery steeds into the fray, and rapes of nuns and nurses.[17] As one recent writer suggested, many editors may have expected readers to take such tales with a grain of salt. "The world was a much larger and mysterious place in the 1890s than today, and the popular press, not just in New York but across the country tended to view news from exotic locales as a form of entertainment, a good source of fantasy and horror stories."[18] Other stories, such as this from the *World,* emphasized Spanish barbarism toward rebel soldiers:

> **The skulls of all [the Cuban dead] were split to pieces down to the eyes. Some of these were gouged out. All the bodies had been stabbed by sword bayonets and hacked by sabers until I could not count the cuts; they were indistinguishable. The bodies had almost lost semblance of human form. . . . The tongue of one had been cut out, split open at the base and placed on the mangled forehead. . . . The Spanish soldiers habitually cut off the ears of the Cuban dead and retain them as souvenirs.[19]**

Both papers sought more direct involvement in the rebellion. The *World* even volunteered its intrepid reporter, Nellie Bly, to recruit and lead a regiment of female volunteers to fight for Cuban independence, but nothing came of that proposal.[20] Hearst purchased a jeweled sword at a charity auction and commissioned one of his men to find the rebel general and to present it to him. After the start of hostilities, Hearst maneuvered his own yacht close enough to watch the bombardment of Havana.[21]

THE INFAMOUS CABLE

In December 1896 Hearst lured Richard Harding Davis, the incarnation of the glamorous foreign correspondent, to team with Frederic Remington for a one-month sojourn with the Cuban rebels. He paid each of them $4,000 and provided an unlimited expense account. Remington, already well-known for his cowboy paintings and for illustrating magazine stories for Owen Wister, never really cottoned to the dapper and flamboyant Davis. Both men sympathized with the rebels and dreamed of battlefield glory. Unable after landing to link up with the rebels, Davis and Remington were forced to cover events from Havana. The artist soon tired of the high living on Hearst's expense account, but the arrangement suited Davis just fine. As the month-long contract neared its end, Remington had plenty of notes and sketches he could complete back in New York. He asked permission to come home. [22]

Creelman's memoir is the only evidence for the infamous anecdote about Hearst's cabling Remington that he would provide the war. [23] Although Creelman was in Florida at that time and gave no indication of where or how he learned this story, historians still repeat it. Neither Remington nor Davis mentioned it, either in frequent letters home nor in later memoirs, and Hearst flatly denied the story. [24]

In any case, Remington headed home in early January, and Davis sailed about three weeks later. Aboard ship, three Cuban girls told Davis of their revolutionary adventures, including a search by Spanish officials. Davis fired off an embellished account of their tale, and the *Journal* hired Remington to prepare an illustration. His drawing showed the naked girls trying to cover themselves from the leering gaze of bearded officers. It ran five columns wide and caused a sensation. When they saw the picture, the Cuban girls were outraged and said they told Davis the search was done in private by women. Davis said it was all Remington's fault for misreading his story. (He had not actually said the soldiers did the stripping, but the story left that impression.) [25] Davis never again worked for Hearst, but for decades other papers sent him wherever there was a whiff of gunpowder. [26]

Hearst stoked the fires. In November 1896, the *Journal* published a large map under a banner headline **WHERE THE FIGHTING IS GOING ON IN CUBA.** [27] Subsequent headlines reminded Cleveland of his "grave public duty" to act on behalf of the Cubans. In succeeding weeks, there were many stories about the preparations for war. The *World* was as excited as the *Journal* and warned that "war's worst fury" soon would break over the stricken island. On November 26, the paper heralded the efforts of some Cubans to purchase their island from Spain. [28] The *Sun* was no less jingoistic, although the *Herald, Times,* and *Evening Post* were much calmer. Like the Associated Press, they all sent reporters south. [29]

In October 1897, just as Spain made some conciliatory moves, the *Journal* created its own heroine, a "Cuban Joan of Arc." Hearst's correspondent freed Evangelina Ciseneros from prison, a feat involving more bribery than bravery, and returned her to New York. One of his editors said Hearst "felt himself in the role of Sir Galahad rescuing a helpless maiden." [30] After proving at welcoming rallies that she was not the innocent victim that audiences wanted, she disappeared from the news. Soon the Spaniards stepped up attacks and the White House dispatched the battleship *Maine* to Havana harbor. Congress quickly increased the military budget. [31]

In early 1898, amid mounting public and congressional pressure for action, McKinley scrambled and prayed for a diplomatic solution. The

Journal published an intercepted letter from a Spanish diplomat calling the President weak and indecisive.[32] Less than two weeks later, the *Maine* blew up and sank. To this day no one knows the cause, but the *Evening Journal* had no doubts. Its wood type proclaimed **SPANISH TREACHERY**. The *World* said **MAINE EXPLOSION CAUSED BY BOMB OR TORPEDO**. Both papers doctored old drawings of the battleship to "show" the explosion. The *Journal* published eight to ten pages a day on the sinking, and the *World* and the *Sun* only slightly less. All three papers offered rewards for clues. Although few at the time thought the blast could have been an accident or that it might have been set by the rebels to assure United States entry, those are equally feasible explanations.

As his circulation climbed, Hearst decided it was the perfect time to double the price of the *Morning Journal*. On April 1, it went to two cents. Pulitzer grimly refused to follow suit, convinced that at last Hearst was showing signs of financial strain. When the move cost the *Journal* few readers or ads, the war of the yellows was really over, and the *World* had lost.

The Journal panted for the start of hostilities. Sample headlines: **FLEET AND ARMY READY FOR ACTION** (April 9); **ON THE VERGE OF WAR** (April 13); **READY BLOW FOR SPAIN!** (April 16); **NOW TO AVENGE THE MAINE!** (April 20). Headline type was often four or five inches high. On April 25, when the headline was **CONGRESS DECLARES WAR**, rockets were fired from the *Journal* building. The paper offered $1,000 for the best ideas on how to conduct the war. Hearst offered to equip, arm, and mount at his own expense a regiment for Cuba, but McKinley declined.[33]

For two days in early May, the *Journal* "ears" on either side of the front-page nameplate asked: "How do you like the *Journal*'s war?" Because it fit the picture of Hearst as an evil genius, it is about the only Hearst boast that historians ever believed. The circulation of the yellow papers did soar during June and July, but the public is seldom led anywhere except in directions it is already determined to go. As one historian concluded:

> To newspapers that thrived on large headlines and lurid report-
> ing, Cuba was a running story, but it is too simple to assign
> primary blame for the conflict on Hearst and Pulitzer. They printed
> colorful, exciting bulletins, some of which were true, and they did
> not cool popular emotions. They served the propagandistic pur-
> poses of the junta well. But they did not create the real differences
> between the United States and Spain. They . . . reflected what
> the public wanted, rather than shaping it.[34]

Hearst's attorney was probably correct when he observed, "If Hearst had never published a word, we would have had the same war."[35] Many

Americans were spoiling for a fight and a chance to enter the worldwide race for colonies, a mood that historians such as Richard Hofstadter blamed more on politicians and social conditions than on the press.[36] These motives were entwined with genuine widespread sympathy for Cubans under Spanish rule.

Hearst sent at least thirty-nine correspondents and illustrators to cover the war, and Pulitzer dispatched a similar corps. Dozens of newspapers, magazines, and wire services joined them. For both the *Journal* and the *World* the staggering expenses far outran the circulation profits. At their wartime peaks, both sold about three-quarters of a million copies on weekdays and more than a million on Sundays.[37] Arthur Brisbane wrote shortly after the end of the fighting that had the war in Cuba gone on for two years, every major newspaper in New York would have been bankrupted. He said war coverage cost the *Journal* $3,000 a day over normal expenses.[38] Historian Frederick Merk cautioned against equating circulation gains with public approval of jingoism. He argues much of the public bought copies *without buying* the editorial positions.[39] The news coverage of the war itself is well documented elsewhere.[40]

During the late nineteenth century the *World* and the *Journal* were two peas in a pod. Both newspapers capitalized on technology and changed conditions to build enterprises of a size never before dreamed of. Screaming headlines, big type, colored inks and illustrations lured readers as did unremitting attention to crime, sexual innuendo, and violence. They justified their policies as giving the public what it wanted and as a way to draw them for the more serious content. Both papers showed enterprise in developing and gathering news. Although it is tempting to caricature the yellow papers as being edited for janitors and clerks, both papers published a fair amount of sober financial, political, and diplomatic information, just as the *Evening News, Tribune,* and *Times* covered some murder trials and prize fights. More than the lower-class scandal sheets in England and France, the *World* and the *Journal* probably were read by people in all social classes.

Although both publishers defended sensationalism as important news that had to be printed, later writers believed Pulitzer but doubted Hearst. To sociologist Robert Park, Pulitzer was muckraking, Hearst jazzing; Pulitzer was teaching, Hearst playing on emotions.[41] Some historians call Pulitzer's style "new journalism" and Hearst's "yellow journalism." Yellow was linked to decadence. It was associated with daring departures in the fine arts, such as Aubrey Beardsley's *Yellow Book* and with poetry and paintings of the *fin de siècle* school.[42]

Contemporary trade journals and popular magazines used the terms "new journalism" and "yellow journalism" interchangeably. E. L. Godkin in an editorial in *The Nation* charged that yellow journalism's real offense was its "pervading spirit of vulgarity, indecency and reckless sensationalism."[43] The *Times* frequently denounced the prurience of both yellow journals. Publisher Frank Munsey blamed Pulitzer more than Hearst for creating "hysterical, sensational, untrue" journalism.

The *World* resorted to sensationalism at least a decade before Hearst arrived in New York. From the day he took over the *World* Pulitzer embraced and emphasized the techniques introduced by the penny press.

Hearst unashamedly copied Pulitzer's techniques, although it is unfair to charge, as one critic did, that "Hearst's real news, like everything else, came from the pages of the *World*."[44] Hearst's papers printed more than their share of exclusives, many paid for at previously unheard-of prices. To cite only a few examples, he commissioned and equipped two expeditions to report on the Klondike Gold Rush, others to report distant wars and sports events in Europe. Hearst testified years later that the circulation battle with the *World* had cost him $8 million, but he did not regret a penny of it.[45]

Hearst was as obsessed as Pulitzer with party politics, but unlike his Hungarian-born competitor, Hearst had a real chance to end up in the White House. Nominated in a safe Democratic district, he served four uneventful years in congress. Later he lost in bids to be elected mayor and governor. During his career, he swung from socialism to hidebound conservatism, in later years using his journalistic empire to reward and punish politicians.

The most difficult part about evaluating Hearst's early career is that we view it through a lens clouded by his cranky years. In all fairness, we should ask how we would rate Hearst had he died in 1911 when Joseph Pulitzer did, instead of in 1951.[46] Although many still concur in *Time*'s appraisal that "Hearst never believed in anything, not even Hearst," Will Irwin, a respected press critic and author, found that Hearst's early intimates insisted that "under his cold exterior he kept a real sympathy for the submerged man or woman, a real feeling of his own mission to plead their case."[47] For a generation of intellectuals, Hearst personified all that was wrong in America, an egomaniacal capitalist. And, of course, there is the ineradicable image left by the 1941 Orson Welles movie, *Citizen Kane*. An ambivalent Swanberg closed Hearst's biography with two "obituaries"—one for the Good Hearst and one for the Bad Hearst. Most of the praise was for his early years.[48]

While the wallflowers clucked, the brazen *World* and *Journal* competed in a journalistic can-can.

If they titilated, the yellow papers also told New Yorkers what was going on, what forces were shaping their lives. Each issue bulged with news accounts and feature stories which were little parables about life in the big city. Because parables always simplify, the papers drew the wrath of the uppercrust, many of whom were not eager for the rabble to understand their stake in the issues anyway.

It is fatuous to quibble about the "real" motives of Pulitzer and Hearst, about whether they were more interested in educating and politicizing the public or in turning profits. Whatever their intentions, they accomplished both. Considering their power, Gunther Barth thought they showed remarkable restraint.[49] Like all men, their motives undoubtedly were mixed.

Their success provoked imitators across the land. By the turn of the century in almost every big city, the yellowest paper was the circulation leader.[50] Soon, however, most of the papers toned down from vivid yellows to pastels. Pulitzer loudly proclaimed an end to the *World*'s flirtation with sensationalism, and even Hearst's *Journal* took itself more seriously. Styles change in journalism as in all things.

During the Progressive Era of the early twentieth century, muckraking monthly magazines such as *McClure's* and *Munsey's* stole the march on daily newspapers.[51] In part that was because most of the newspapers had abandoned the frenetic pace of the can can for the more decorous waltz; in the 1920s they would resonate to a decidedly jazzy beat.

Part Three

THE
1920S

10

Not Everyone Charlestoned

F or most Americans, the twenties no more roared than the nineties had been gay. Not many New Yorkers Charlestoned or drank bootleg hootch in speakeasies until dawn; most of them settled for an occasional movie after a long ride home from work on the subway or bus. On a Sunday, they might head for Coney Island or take in a ball game. Although for most nonfarmers the economic times were good, few people met, much less lived like, Jay Gatsby. The man who really set the image, though, was Frederick Lewis Allen, a *Harper's* magazine editor who in 1931 published an incredibly popular history called *Only Yesterday.*[1] Book of-the-Month Club selected it and two weeks after publication it had become a best-seller.[2] Teachers still assign it, and it still colors our views of the decade. Even people who had lived through the real twenties accepted Allen's giddy portrayal as gospel. As one critic has noted, the book tells us more about Allen than about the twenties.[3] His fundamental premise was that the period bounded by the Armistice and the Crash represented a unique era and that the trauma of World War I explained nearly all the events. Allen denied he emphasized the trivial, insisting instead that he was exploring fundamental trends in national life and thought. Whatever his intent, it was the colorful anecdotes that sold the book.[4]

Fueled by credit buying and backed by advertising, the dominant ethos shifted from self-denial and saving for the rainy day to spending or "investing" as a way of multiplying one's resources. Discarding their traditional fear of indebtedness, Americans by the end of the decade were buying three-fourths of their cars and two-thirds of their appliances on credit.[5] Many American intellectuals who denounced the emphasis on materialism found themselves praising the advertising that promoted it. Annual advertising expenditures totaled $1.25 billion. Of this, newspapers got about half, mostly from local retailers.[6] To Malcolm Cowley, Hart Crane, and George Seldes the capsulized sales pitches were symbols of "modernism."[7] No longer satisfied with meeting consumer needs, ads were designed by agencies to create or expand demands.

Enlightened industrialists acknowledged that in the new mass market economy it was in their own interests to keep wages high and selling prices low. During the war years when inflation doubled, wages had barely kept pace. For example, New York printers earned $30 in 1914 and $56 in 1920. In the early twenties, a typical reporter took home $40 a week, more than most American workers. But during the twenties industrial wages, monthly salaries, profits, and dividends all rose sharply. The factory worker's real income rose 15 to 25 percent, and white-collar salaries did a bit better. Unemployment remained relatively high, and unions made relatively little progress during the decade. Per-man-hour efficiency rose by more than 70 percent and total industrial production by 60 percent. In 1920 the six-day work week was standard, but by 1929 it was five and a half days.[8] Historian Henry F. May found in the decade many signs of social disintegration. "The twenties were a period when the common values and common beliefs were replaced by separate and conflicting loyalties."[9]

Employment trends of the 1890s continued until by 1920 eight million women worked outside the home; of this number nearly one-quarter were married. Women filled 92 percent of secretarial positions and were nearly as dominant in teaching and retail sales.[10] Even on their modest salaries they dressed smartly in the ready-to-wear clothes turned out in the garment district. That was the last manufacturing left in lower Manhattan.

Women showed more economic than political clout. When in their first presidential election in 1920 only 35 percent of New York women voted, and most of them the same way their husbands did, politicians stopped worrying about a "women's vote."[11] By the end of the decade articles denouncing sexual equality appeared in leading magazines, one by the famous muckraker, Ida Tarbell.[12]

As always, New York City's wealth and power rested on its commerce and finance. World War I had made New York's port even more important in the world economy. "The wholesale merchants, the banker potentates, and the corporation attorneys set the pace and dominate all the activities of the metropolis," wrote a visiting professor from Germany.[13]

CLOSING THE GATES

Congress sharply restricted the flow of immigrants and set up quotas that favored the "old stocks" over the new. For example, the 1924 law admitted up to 5000 from Italy, but 65,000 from the British isles. Shrill demands for "Americanization" replaced good-natured talk about a "melting pot."[14] Concerns about immigration were linked to fears of Romanism and urbanism, which in turn were tied to Prohibition. Norman H. Clark takes issue with the traditional interpretation of Prohibition as pinched, parochial, and anti-reformist. He sees it as an attempt to protect the values sheltered in the nuclear family.[15] In a similar vein, Paul Carter saw in the dry crusade a reaffirmation of moral values.[16] Prohibition never had much support in New York. By a margin of nearly seven to one, city voters backed a 1926 referendum to permit the sale of light wines and beer. It rolled up huge margins in every borough.[17] Bootleg liquor was so freely available in the city that *Variety* published the prevailing case prices.[18]

The real nightclubs were replace by speakeasies and cabarets, often run by gangsters. Stanley Walker, a leading newspaper editor of the day, said the new places were brassier, busier, and much more expensive. Patrons willingly paid cover charges of $20 or more to drink watered whiskey and dance to the latest fad. The decade began with the shimmy, but in 1923 the Charleston took over; three years after that it was the suggestive Black Bottom. The Charleston was introduced in "Runnin' Wild," a Broadway hit with an all-black cast, and it was spread by recordings and movies. Such suggestive dances prompted widespread demands to crack down on dance halls. The more decorous fox-trot replaced the waltz, polka, and tango on the social dance floor.[19]

New York Governor Al Smith personified all the fears of the villagers. He was Catholic, wet, and the product of Tammany Hall, the most notorious machine in New York, the most wicked of cities. With a vote for Herbert Hoover in 1928, "110 percent Americans" could vote against all those evils at once.[20] Most of them did. (It would be twenty-four years before they elected another Republican to the White House.)

The swollen black population of about 150,000 was now concentrated north of Central Park in Harlem. Many were refugees from the Deep South who had stayed on after the wartime jobs dried up. Many pleasures of the city were off-limits to blacks, but most of the Harlem speakeasies, rib joints and chicken shacks with their pulsating jazz attracted "sports" of all races. More than one hundred entertainment spots were jammed between 125th and 135th between Lenox and Seventh Avenues. The Cotton Club, Harlem's most luxurious nightclub and the longtime base for Duke Ellington, catered to white patrons only.[21]

Racial tensions still ran high. Of the 102 persons lynched in the nation from September 1920 to September 1922, sixty-nine were black. Not all of the outrages were in the South.[22] There were about 16,000 members in the city's twenty-one Ku Klux Klan kleagles (chapters), but thanks to official and newspaper opposition, the Invisible Order never flourished in Gotham. The *World* in its death throes won a Pulitzer Prize for its exposé of the Klan, but the *Daily News* declined to unmask the Klansmen by publishing their names.[23] Most urban members were low-paid blue-collar workers, but there were also many small businessmen. Most who donned the hoods considered the American way of life threatened by nonwhites and non-Christians.[24] Many of the New Yorkers who joined resented the younger Jews who were challenging housing and college quotas. Half of all the Jews in America lived in the city.[25]

YOU ARE WHERE YOU LIVE

In 1920, the population of New York City was 5.6 million. Of that number only 1 million were native-born whites. Except for the Eastern European Jews, Italians, and Orientals still huddled in the Lower East Side and artists drawn to Greenwich Village, nearly everyone lived above Times Square. Millionaires were now concentrated in the baronial apartment buildings along Park Avenue. Most employees headed after work for the suburbs. Zoning laws combined with covenants to enforce economic and racial segregation.

Like much of the nation, the city had a severe housing shortage—even worse than usual. There were tenement blocks on the Lower East Side that housed 1000 or more.[26] By June 1920, rents were nearly 30 percent higher than before the war, and were still rising at the same time the size of new apartments was shrinking. In 1915, the average had been 4.5 rooms; a decade later it was 3.5.[27] Builders, strapped by lack of capital and forced to comply with tougher codes, slowed residential construction, but jackhammers rattled on, erecting office buildings, banks, and public works. Almost as workers completed the Holland Tunnel under the Hudson, work bean on the George Washington Bridge. At about the same time Robert Moses took on his first great project, Jones Beach on Long Island.[28]

As always, New York was noisy, but now in 1925 Bell laboratories offered scientific proof of the painfully obvious. New York City's new Noise Abatement Commission used the audiometer to set acceptable "decibel levels." Alas, quantifying the problem did not solve it.[29] At the end of the decade a city commission concluded that "a tiger from Siberia or Bengal could roar or snarl indefinitely" on many streets "without attracting the auditory attention of passersby."[30] While it is doubtful they were any noisier than the metal-wheeled omnibuses they replaced, subways and electrified elevated trains got much of the blame for the din. With the increase in automobiles, carbon monoxide replaced the horsey smells. Although there were warnings about the health dangers, most people thought horse manure was less hygenic.[31]

Generations of New Yorkers had longed to escape the indignities and rigid schedules of the crowded mass transit system, and the private auto held out that promise. City dwellers bought cars at the same dizzying pace as those in towns and villages. Certainly they acquired them far faster than cities could adjust to them and congestion worsened.

By the 1920s, New York's trademarks were the twinkling theater marquees and gargantuan lighted signs of the Great White Way. The Wrigley gum sign alone consumed $100,000 a year in current. Compared with earlier eras, most of the city was ablaze with electric light, but there were still plenty of dark and dangerous areas such as Hell's Kitchen. Streetwalkers largely had been displaced by dance-hall and speakeasy "hostesses." Call girls with their own apartments served wealthier clients.[32]

Although both police and fire departments were perennially understaffed and plagued by political interference, protection was much improved.[33] Popular perceptions to the contrary, crime rates did not soar in the 1920s; instead, they continued their slow decade-by-decade increase.[34] New York prisons were much fuller, however, in part because the state enacted in 1925 a measure sending any three-time offender behind bars for life. This affected few murderers or rapists but many a burglar or shoplifter. In New York State there were 122 convictions for homicide in 1900 and 121 in 1927; in the intervening years, the figures were remarkably consistent. Robbery and burglary convictions rose modestly during that period.[35] The city crime statistics are less complete and vary with the improved record keeping.

ARTISTIC BOLDNESS CAUSES CONCERN

In literature, the theater, and movies of the twenties the shopgirl and the clerk were allowed to enjoy the vicarious sensations of illicit sex, murder, and kidnapping—always tempered with pious platitudes. While the postal inspectors still kept an eye out for 500 books, many of them tame by then, the mass media "provided a capsule of immorality, to be taken as often as required but always with a Christian bourgeois antidote."[36] Novels and short stories linked jazz with sex, and so did the movies.

"The postwar world came in," wrote jazzman Hoagy Carmichael, "with a bang of bad booze, flappers with bare legs, jangled morals and wild weekends."[37] His "Stardust" was one of the best songs of Tin Pan Alley's golden age. Jazz and dance bands played and recorded hundreds of hit songs each year. Some records sold more than a million copies. Although jazz music was still identified in the public mind with sin, it was inching toward respectability when in 1924 Paul Whiteman produced a jazz concert in Aeolian Hall, a midtown venue for classical music. The evening marked the premier of George Gershwin's *Rhapsody in Blue.*[38]

In spite of competition from radio and movies, Broadway and vaudeville houses were filled. The 1927–28 season saw first nights for fifty-three musicals.[39] Although New York padlocked a dozen or more plays for immorality, the city was spared the obscenity and blasphemy trials that wracked other parts of the country. The police seldom bothered the revues staged by Florenz Ziegfeld or George White, whose annual *Scandals* featured bare-breasted chorus girls.[40] When the shows toured, the chorus girls often donned more clothes, but no one had to look further than the newspaper comics page to ogle scantily clad cuties like Flapper Fanny and Syncopation Sue. On the other hand, there was a time and a place for everything. Fans were outraged when chorus girls pranced among the players during their fielding practice before the opening game of the 1924 World Series at the Polo Grounds. They bombarded the field with oranges and pop bottles to protest such desecration of the National Game.[41]

Whether more people were sexually active or not is debatable; the rate of pregnant brides and illegitimate births did not increase.[42] That they talked much more openly about sex is certain; Freud's revelations about repression seemed to justify the talk. Historian Paula Fass concluded that among collegians, petting was socially acceptable, but intercourse still was not.[43] The emphasis was on youth, and especially on the flapper, the so-called "demivirgin." Anita Loos drew the definitive portrait of the flapper in her 1926 novel and play, *Gentlemen Prefer Blondes.* Cartoonist John Held also did much to popularize the image of flaming youth. Skirts and bathing suits revealed more flesh, and the automobile gave a young couple a private and padded retreat.

Geoffrey Perrett wrote of the progress of the new sexual freedom:

> All the forces of modern life were behind it—the growing economic and intellectual independence of women, the craving for excitement in a world becoming dull and standardized, the sanction of science, the collapse of the old moral order, the rejection of puritanism."[44]

Divorce was often in the headlines, in part because the only grounds in New York was adultery. To get a decree couples often hired private detectives to "catch" one of them in someone else's hotel room. If the screen's "perfect couple" could flout convention, then perhaps ordinary mortals could, too. Actress Mary Pickford's quickie Nevada divorce and overnight remarriage to Douglas Fairbanks charmed rather than shocked the public. The faint odor of adultery leading to both their divorces wore off quickly, and readers panted for every detail about their life on the fabled "Pickfair" estate.[45] Divorce was written about three times as often in popular magazines as it had been during the previous decade. (Few of the articles were critical.)[46] In the Untied States, as throughout the industrialized world, the divorce rate continued its long climb. Between 1900 and 1930, the American population increased by 62 percent, but the number of divorces quadrupled. By 1928 there were more than 200,000 divorces a year.[47] As usual, scholars blamed the city. But the causes ran deeper. Expectations of marriage and family life had changed. Married life was the butt of jokes in movies, comics, novels, and plays; several newspapers published a syndicated column called "Divorce Lawyer."[48]

No domestic fracas drew more attention than a gold digger's separation suit against a Manhattan real estate mogul in 1927. More than 100 reporters covered the legal tiff between "Peaches" and "Daddy" Browning. Papers from coast to coast reported their accounts of bizarre boudouir behavior. A flood of protests resulted in some restraint in future divorce reporting.[49]

By the end of the twenties, American book publishers were issuing twice as many new titles as they had at the end of the war. Book clubs simplified distribution. For the first time American authors outsold British. It is worth remembering that they bought far more copies of Zane Grey than of Fitzgerald or Hemingway. Both fiction and nonfiction reading material became bolder. One lovemaking text promised in its advertisement:

Sixty-four pages of male-female positional pho-
tographs ... intercourse innovations and sexual

> variants which best satisfy a seeking mate's or-
> gasmic need.... It transforms same-old-thing
> "bedroom encounters" into excitingly different
> *LOVE AFFAIRS*—again, again and again ... pas-
> sionately banishes the sameness of old-hat sex.
> Can any marriage, anchored to this solid bed-
> rock of unsuppressed voluptuous sexual variety
> fail to become stronger?[50]

Many communities warred on allegedly salacious "snappy joke books," confession and "arty" photo magazines. *Captain Billy's Whiz Bang* sold 250,000 copies a month and had many imitators. Its he-she jokes, bowdlerized verses, and a few girlie and outhouse cartoons were less wicked than parents assumed. Dashes masked even the mildest profanity. In an era when postal inspectors were vigilant,[51] no issue was ever banned from the mails. Bernarr Macfadden (to whom we return in chapter 11) established *True Story*, the first and most successful confession, and he blazed what became well-worn trail. Because girls devoured these magazines, moralists worried even more about them than about the boys' joke magazines.[52] Macfadden's physical culture magazines bulged with grainy photos of unclad bodies.

Hollywood features moved beyond shoot-'em-up Westerns and custard-pie comedies to crime and immorality. The movies of the twenties began with *Broken Blossoms* and *Pollyanna* and ended with *The Redeeming Sin* and *Companionate Marriage*. The leap from Mary Pickford and Dorothy Gish to Theda Bara and Clara Bow was too long for many. Social scientists documented the impact of the movies on big-city children. Studies confirming that crime films were the favorites among boys and girls heightened fears of reformers that movies promoted delinquency and law-breaking. A judge was quoted in the New York *Times* in 1920 as saying, "At the movies the young see things they never should be allowed even to hear or think about. Under such conditions the downfall of young girls is not remote."[53] Many agreed with him, especially in the wake of a series of Hollywood scandals in the early twenties.

New York City established a censorship board in 1913, the state a more stringent one in 1921. To stem the spread of such boards and to blunt demands for federal censorship, the Hollywood producers hired as a "czar" Will Hays, Harding's eminently respectable Postmaster General. Producers limited glimpses of shimmering lingerie enough to earn the Hays Office seal, without which distributors and exhibitors would not touch a film. The harder part was making the cuts decreed by all the state and local boards, which were tougher on depictions of crime than of sex. Although critics soon charged that Hays was more interested in cleaning up the image of the movies than the films themselves, in his first three years he helped to defeat all thirty-seven referenda to set up local boards.[54]

Building on the war-induced concern about venereal disease, a few producers survived on the fringe of Hollywood with "educational features" on sex hygiene. In the name of education, crowds flocked to look at genitals, diseased though they were. A crackdown on distributors in 1928 by the Hays Office effectively ended bookings in big cities, but the V.D. films played the boondocks for years.[55]

Purveyors of print or celluloid sex had little hope of winning in court, since the accepted legal definition of obscenity was the hoary Hicklin Rule handed down by a British judge in 1868.[56] Under it, material was obscene if there was any chance it might fall into the hands of someone it might deprave or corrupt—in short, a child or an idiot. American courts interpreted the law to mean that a single word or phrase, even if taken completely out of context, could make an entire work legally obscene. To make matters worse, the Supreme Court had ruled in 1915 that motion pictures were simply spectacles and had no constitutional protection as expression.[57]

THE NEWSPAPER PRESS

Just as Allen mythologized American society, so did Ben Hecht and James MacArthur shape the popular view of newspaper journalism with their 1928 Broadway hit, *The Front Page*. The play, quickly turned into a movie, set forever the image of the amoral, wise-cracking newspaperman who would do anything for a story. Although its gamey language shocked some, the *Times* said it had "all the tang of front-page journalism."[58] The fictional editor and reporter conceal an escaped convict and hardly notice when a girl plunges out the press room window. They lie, cheat, and steal, violating the standards the American Society of Newspaper Editors was at that very moment promoting. Rather than taking offense, contemporary journalists gloried in their portrayal as jovial rogues. Heywood Broun, the *World*'s columnist and perhaps the nation's best known journalist, saw it many times.[59]

In 1920, New York boasted eleven daily newspapers, a decade later seven, two of which were tabloids begun in 1924. As the twenties opened, Hearst's *Evening Journal* led in daily circulation with more than 600,000, about double the figures of the *World*, the *Times* and the *American*. Hovering around 200,000 were the *Herald* and the *Sun*, either of which on occasion still displayed some spark. The *Herald*, for example, won the

Pulitzer Prize in 1921 for its account of the entombment of the Unknown Soldier in Arlington National Cemetery.[60] The *Sun*'s biggest drawing card was columnist Don Marquis, who wrote about a cockroach named archy who typed lowercase letters to a cat named mehitabel. (The cockroach was not strong enough to press down the shift key.) The *Globe, Tribune, Morning Telegraph,* and *Evening Post* all had their faithful. The *Daily News* was barely underway.[61]

Most New York papers subscribed to at least two of the three wire services. The reorganized United Press offered real competition to the Associated Press, Hearst's International News Service less so. All three were covering a wider spectrum of news, no longer content to reprocess stories uncovered by affiliated newspapers. A series of international crises since 1897 had spurred the demand for stories from their foreign correspondents.[62]

In April 1920, the *Evening Journal* raised its daily price to three cents, but not all others followed. All charged more for the fat Sunday editions. In 1925, the New York dailies printed and distributed 3 million copies a day. Although carriers delivered more than ever to homes, most of the daily and virtually all of the Sunday copies were purchased from 12,000 newsstands.[63]

In the fall of 1926, the *Daily News* had a circulation of more than a million, the *Evening Journal* 677,000 and the *Times* 391,000. The *Mirror* was next with 379,000, followed by the *American* and *World*, each with more than 300,000. Close on their heels were the *Herald-Tribune, Evening World* and *Sun*. The *Graphic* claimed 242,000, the *Telegram* barely 200,000. The sedate *Evening Post* trailed far behind with 34,000. The soaring tabloids killed Pulitzer's *World* and *Evening World*, forced others to merge and doomed Hearst's *American*.

Except for Hearst and Adolph Ochs at the *Times*, New York journalism had a new cast. Joseph Pulitzer had died in 1911, and his sons were running his newspapers in New York and St. Louis. The *World* commanded great respect but, according to historian James Boylan "was figuratively a shell, waiting for a new form, even a new soul."[64] The *World*'s fatal decline began with its price increase to three cents in late 1925, although Walter Lippmann, the *World*'s last editorial page editor, blamed the folly of trying to be "as yellow as Hearst, as accurate as the *Times* and as intellectual as the old *Evening Post*."[65]

James Gordon Bennett, Jr. had sold the *Herald*, but readers no longer cared about the publisher. Why should they? Papers were beyond the stage of being extended shadows of single owners. They were properties owned by closed and family corporations and managed by others. They looked more and more alike. Within a few years their shares would be purchased on stock exchanges by total strangers and faceless holding companies.

Editor & Publisher wrote in 1922 that the newspaper industry "is in a more secure position than at any time in its history—better manned, better financed, with more adequate reserves."[66] There was a great sense of hubris at conventions of the American Newspaper Publishers Association, as speaker after speaker relayed success stories.[67] Ads in newspaper trade journals boasted of advertising lineage, which was understandable since circulation now brought in only one-fourth of the revenue.[68] There was little incentive to rock the boat. Across the nation, the number of dailies was at its all-time peak of nearly 2200. Circulation exploded from 32 million in 1920 to more than 40 million in 1929.[69] By the end of the decade half the nation's newspapers, including almost all the big ones, were members of the Audit Bureau of Circulation.

Were the newspapers stodgy? Although *most* probably always have been and perhaps always will be, there were many, large and small, that demonstrated the "zip" so admired in the twenties. They printed more news from abroad.[70] Closer to home, they exposed corruption and helped solve crimes. Most big city papers published several editions daily, a habit they had picked up during World War I and which in an age of radio made less and less economic sense.

Modern was "in," and newspapers looked old-fashioned. They still used few photos and usually stuck with small headlines. There were other reasons for an uneasiness in Paradise. From several directions came the faint sounds of apple munching. Chain ownership was spreading, circulation was barely keeping up with population growth,[71] and editorial influence was slipping.[72] "I cannot think of a single newspaper in America today that is primarily important because of its editorial page," wrote the head of United Press in 1930.[73] For the first time, the newspaper faced serious competition for audiences and advertisers. Each evening millions flocked to movie theaters. Newsstands and mailboxes overflowed with new kinds of "fact" magazines, including news weeklies. *Liberty* magazine even printed the estimated reading time above each story and article. *Colliers* featured "short-short" stories of a single page or less.

More ominous was commercial radio, which began in 1920 in Pittsburgh and Detroit (there is still dispute about which was first). Although from its beginning radio broadcasters concentrated on entertainment, they reported Warren Harding's victory over John W. Davis that first fall. Only a handful of sets received that news, but by 1922 there were 100,000 and by 1926 more than 5 million in American homes. By 1922 there were more than 500 stations on the air. But, as one veteran reporter put it, "You still bought the paper for the news."[74] Although few licensees did much with either news or opinion, newspaper publishers scurried for broadcast licenses to protect their turf. By 1923, sixty-nine newspapers had licenses.[75] Practically all New York dailies carried radio columns; among those publishing radio supplements were the *Sun, Globe, Evening World,* and *Evening Mail.* In all there was an initial emphasis on technical information, which shifted to program matters.[76] Late in the decade when 700 of the 900 stations joined in four networks, they built their audiences on singers and comedians, not newsmen. The ads, with their you-deserve-it emphasis, helped promote the revolution in consumer expectations.[77]

FORMULA WRITING

Most news stories were written in the so-called "inverted pyramid" form. That meant summarizing the most important point first and then inserting facts in descending order of significance. It was a form that had been evolving at least since the Civil War but by the 1920s had eclipsed the older forms such as narrative. An almost perfect example was the detached report in the *Times* on the final chapter in one of the most passionate running stories of the twenties:

> **Niccolo Sacco and Bartolomeo Vanzetti died in the electric chair early this morning, carrying out the sentence imposed on them for the South Braintree murders of April 15, 1920.**
>
> **Sacco marched to the death chair at 12:11 and was pronounced lifeless at 12:19.**
>
> **Vanzetti entered the execution room at 12:20 and was declared dead at 12:26.**
>
> **To the last they protested their innocence, and the efforts of many who believed them guiltless proved futile, although they fought a legal and extra-legal battle unprecedented in the history of American jurisprudence.[78]**

As Mitchell Stephens points out, the inverted pyramid organizes stories around facts rather than around ideas or chronologies. In weighing and shuffling the pieces of information, the single-minded focusing on their news value distorts what we accept as "true."[79] The style, especially in Associated Press dispatches, was deadening. Many thought it was time for a fresh style.

TROUBLESOME NEWS CONTENT

At its first convention in April 1923, the American Society of Newspaper Editors (ASNE) adopted the first nationwide statement of journalistic ideals.[80] The standards, while not enforceable, did represent higher aspirations. In affirming the right of a newspaper to attract and hold readers, its Canons of Journalism also urged decency, honesty, and accuracy. The business manager of the *Times* wrote: "When editors in conference acclaim their adherence to high principles, they strengthen themselves in right thinking, help the cause of journalism and point the way to a better world in which to live."[81]

More than ever, crime news troubled editors. They denounced its excesses in professional meetings, and several tried banning it from their front pages. Inevitably they would give up and explain, as editors always had, that the public demanded its publication.[82] In 1923, New York morning dailies published 58 percent more columns about crime than they had in 1899; however, because the editions were so much larger, it still meant that in the 1920s the papers were devoting about 10 percent of the news hole to crime and courts, about what they reserved for business and finance.[83] A study in 1927 found that Hearst's *Evening Journal* and the three tabloids devoted one-quarter to one-third of their space to what was labeled "antisocial" news, while the standard papers ran 3 to 11 percent.[84]

Newspapers—even those in the smallest cities—printed detailed accounts of crimes, scandals and divorces, much of the material supplied by wire services and feature syndicates. Faced with new competitors, the Associated Press livened up its stories and added feature and photo services. Editors of member papers in competitive situations pleaded with the service for more spice.[85] As usual, publishers said they were just giving the readers, most of whom picked up their copies from newsstands or newsboys, what they wanted.[86] Often they cited the demands of women readers, who increasingly were the keys to newspaper success. *Editor & Publisher* believed women were reading more of the serious news, but Frank P. Glass, the president of ASNE, thought they wanted features. The St. Louis editor said: "Perhaps the great element of newspaper readers that all the newspapers are cultivating nowadays, the lovely ladies, require more and more of these features than mere men do."[87] A scholar concluded that readers of both sexes turned to the New York papers more for diversion than information. "The more unreal the news themes, the better he likes them."[88] Many journalists worried about the deluge of syndicated features. Author Ben Hecht, for example, predicted that within fifty years, newspapers would employ no local reporters at all.[89]

All news organizations felt the need to appeal to women. In 1924, a *World* editor advised his publisher that the paper desperately needed a woman to select features. "No man editor can pass judgment on fashions or topics of feminine appeal."[90] The general manager of the Associated Press assured the publisher of a member newspaper that the service was doing "a good deal more than you realize respecting the news of women." The wire was carrying more on home furnishings and style, "all written by women."[91] The national magazines were doing more, too, although their portrayals of educated or independent females were often condescending.[92]

So long as many more readers wanted to be entertained than educated, sociologist Robert Park conceded that the newspapers were "about as good as they can be." Improvements depended upon educated readers. "The real reason that the ordinary newspaper accounts of the incidents of ordinary life are so sensational is because we know so little of human life that we are not able to interpret the events of life when we read them. It is safe to say that when anything shocks us, we do not understand it."[93] Walter Lippmann, while not defending the excesses, said reporters emphasized the sensational aspects of crime because they wanted to involve their readers.[94] Although speaking of the wire services, Richard Schwarzlose's comment could be extended to journalism generally. He wrote that while news horizons widened during the twenties, "events were increasingly treated as one- or two-day sensations and denied thoughtful, reflective follow-up comment, giving the reader a rising sense that disaster or war could spring up anywhere and die away just as quickly."[95] Nelson Crawford, in the first college textbook on journalism ethics, denounced not only the triviality of press content but also the tendency to pander to the "herd lusts" of readers for money, blood, and sex.[96]

News of sports often appealed to the first two of those same instincts. It was the Golden Age of Sports—or at least of sports promoters. One historian wrote, "The triumph of sports in the Twenties was fundamentally a triumph of the sports media."[97] Record crowds poured through the turnstiles to watch Babe Ruth belt home runs out of Yankee Stadium and to thrill to Carl Hubbell at the Polo Grounds. Brooklynites loved their hapless Dodgers. Black athletes competed for peanuts in segregated leagues. Promoters were wary of interracial prize fights. In those halcyon days, there was pro football at the Polo Grounds (not in New Jersey), hockey, and million-dollar prize fights in Madison Square Garden. On autumn Saturdays Columbia, Fordham, and other area colleges drew good football crowds. More and more people participated in sports, too. Public beaches and pools were jammed, and golf and tennis no longer were limited to country clubs.

Sports stars were folk heroes—big news, even when they were not competing. Press agents apprised reporters of their every move. Those in the press boxes were more like cheer leaders than detatched reporters. As George Mowry wrote, "Scarcely ever has prose been more purple than in the sporting pages of even the more dignified newspapers. Nor were statements rarely more unqualified than those uttered by the nationally known radio sportscasters."[98]

Sports news had increased steadily over the decades, but its explosion in the twenties worried ASNE, which in 1926 established a committee on sports news whose reports sparked lively debates at the next four conventions. The committee found the average paper devoted ten columns daily to sports, and twice that on Sunday. Most papers gave at least 15 percent of their space to sports; almost none gave less than 10 percent. The new tabloid newspapers often led their front pages with sports news and pictures. By 1927, even sober papers such as the *Times* and the *Herald-Tribune* were devoting twenty-five or more columns a day to sports.[99] In presenting the 1928 report to ASNE, W. P. Beazell of the New York *World* called sports "the most important classification of news."[100] Newspapers no longer had a monopoly. Sports also had become a staple on radio.

Sensation at a Glance

"Hey, kid—Ya wanna newspaper?"
"Naw—I don't want to read."
"There's some nice murders!"
          —"Skippy" comic strip, December 1, 1928

In spite of their shouted urgings to "Read *all* about it!" vendors never really meant that. Tabloids were designed for those willing to settle for a glance at big headlines and photos. It was the modern way of "keeping up." Anything modern had to be brief—whether skirts, songs, or media forms. Radio and movies were fast and pleasant. So were new magazines such as *Readers Digest* and *Time*. The new tabloid newspapers were even less demanding.

"Tabloid" means a newspaper page half the standard size. Although there is no inherent reason why a small-format paper has to be sensational (certainly today's *Christian Science Monitor* is not), most have been. Because display and emphasis are the usual targets for critics, tabloidism has

come to mean sensationalism. By the 1980s it was even applied to contro-
versial broadcast programs.

Those who actually *read* the tabloids of the twenties found them less
shocking than those who merely glanced—but the papers were designed
primarily for glancers. "Think in terms of pictures," Patterson told his
editors again and again.[1] Had the technology of their day permitted, there
is no doubt Bennett and Pulitzer would have printed multicolumn headlines
and eye-catching photographs.

In *Jazz Journalism,* his aptly named history of the New York tabloids,
Simon M. Bessie echoed Frederick Lewis Allen:

> The tabloid was part of a pattern which included speakeasies,
> jazz, collegiate whoopee, bathing beauties, movie-star worship,
> big-time sports and many other gigantic exaggerations. And, as
> these characteristics of the Twenties were but manifestations of
> deeper forces that were sweeping through American life, so the
> tabloid was a journalistic mirror of the era.[2]

Although popular small-format dailies already had succeeded in England
and France, American publishers remained skeptical. Alfred Harmsworth
(Lord Northcliff), who crammed his own half-penny London *Daily Mirror*
with pictures, sports, and contests, was the Pied Piper of tabloidism.
William Randolph Hearst seemed the best bet to take the plunge with a
tabloid in New York, but he was beaten out by two wealthy cousins from
Chicago. Joseph Medill Patterson and Robert M. McCormick introduced the
Illustrated Daily News on June 26, 1919. Patterson had wanted to call it the
Daily Mirror but was reluctant to copy Harmsworth's title. He considered
his initial title "rotten" and quickly shortened it to the *Daily News.*[3] The
tabloids were first and foremost picture papers. Big photos stared out from
the front and back pages, seldom relating to the stories in the headlines.
The center two pages were given over entirely to photos, and almost every
page included at least one—all this in an era when standard newspapers
scattered a few tiny photos amid their gray pages of small type. Many news
executives had so little appreciation for photos that after a 1920 demonstration they expressed doubts there were enough worthwhile photos to justify
developing a transmission system.[4] That attitude changed, however, and in
1928 they greeted warmly the Associated Press wire photo service. In the
meantime many had added daily picture pages and Sunday rotogravure
sections.[5]

Philip Payne, who at different times edited both the *Daily News* and the
Mirror, said his goal was to illustrate every story in the paper.[6] He called
photos "the very essence of tabloidism," because they conveyed a story in

a flash and made the reader feel he was a part of the event.[7] That was just the trouble, wrote historian Daniel Boorstin a half-century later, because with photos, readers lower their critical guard.[8] A camera lens may not lie, but it can record staged and misleading scenes. Every photograph quotes rather than translates and in the process simplifies. From among the exposures, an editor chooses to publish the most dramatic and sensational photos.[9]

TWO GENTLEMEN FROM CHICAGO

Patterson and McCormick were members of the family that published the Chicago *Tribune,* where both had worked and McCormick remained. The *Daily News* was really Patterson's baby.[10] Although he operated out of Chicago until 1926, he kept a tight rein and insisted editors clear almost everything with him. He was publisher for more than a quarter-century.

Patterson hired his first managing editor away from Hearst's *Journal.* At thirty-six, Philip Payne was the youngest city editor in the city, and most of his staffers were in their twenties. Patterson grew disenchanted with editors as quickly as Pulitzer had. When Payne took over the top newsroom spot in 1922, he was the third. Patterson was not sorry to see Payne depart to become editor of Hearst's new tabloid, *The Mirror.*[11] Because of a "gentlemen's agreement" between Hearst and Patterson, there were few raids on news or photo staffs.[12] The tabloid's staffers were by standards of the day well-paid. In 1927, the average reporter or photographer earned $65, and four of the fifty made at least $100.[13]

The *Daily News* announced in its first editorial that it was seeking an audience not being served by other New York morning newspapers. In a stream of internal memos Patterson made it clear he meant primarily young women. The *Daily News* caught on quickly. Within five months it sold 60,000 copies a day. The largest group of buyers, according to the circulation manager, were women between 17 and 30.[14] When circulation dipped temporarily in late 1920, Patterson scolded the staff: "We have forgotten the origin of our success, which was the interest of young women and have been reaching out too much to men."[15]

The *Daily News* found a new audience among those who had ignored existing papers and from those who welcomed its freshness. From 1920 to 1925, a period of marked population increase, all the standards either lost circulation or barely held their own. The tabloid's success was not lost on either Hearst or the second generation of Pulitzers. Rising costs forced Hearst's *American* to abandon its experiments with a half-size rotogravure section, which was generally seen as a prototype for his new tabloid.[16]

Then Arthur Brisbane made Patterson an offer he hoped he couldn't refuse: sell or face a Hearst tabloid. Patterson swallowed hard but did not blink. In the spring of 1921 and again in 1923, rumors had Hearst ready, but each time he hesitated.[17] The *Mirror* finally appeared in 1924, by which time the *Daily News* was unassailable.[18] Ironically, while Patterson sweated out the entry of Hearst, the Pulitzer family, whose New York papers were dying, was afraid Patterson might start a tabloid in St. Louis.[19]

Despite its frequent claims in editorials, promotional booklets, and ads that it was read by all classes, the *Daily News* never convinced anybody. From 1923 on, promotional ads stressed that the paper was aimed at "Sweeney," the unpretentious and hard-working New York wage-earner.[20] Mrs. Sweeney liked it, too. A survey of newsstands in 1925 confirmed that women bought nearly one-third of the copies.[21] To attract this audience, Patterson was convinced he had to hold the price at two cents, a penny below other dailies.[22] During the early years, most issues were sixteen pages, with four (later five) columns to the page. In part, it was because the printer with whom the *Daily News* contracted had limited capacity, but there were economic and policy reasons, as well. There were few ads, and the publisher wanted the paper easy to handle in a subway or bus. By the mid-twenties most issues were twenty-four pages.

Although photos filled more than half the nonadvertising space, the "picture newspaper" was launched without a photo editor or even a cameraman. For the first front page, the art editor purchased from a syndicate a portrait of the Prince of Wales on his horse but quickly hired Ed Jackson, a former Signal Corps photographer.[23] By 1927, there were twenty-three staff photographers.[24] Although miniature cameras using fast roll films were available, the *Daily News,* like most newspapers, outfitted its photographers with bulky Speed Graphics that required flash bulbs and sheet film but produced large negatives. Patterson was so enamored of photographs that he considered (but did not try) a Sunday edition without any copy except captions.[25]

He was equally enthusiastic about another form of illustration, the daily comic strip. Newspapers had been running Sunday strips since the days of the Yellow Press, but it was not until after World War I that comics became a fixture in weekday editions. There were four strips in the first issue of Patterson's paper, and the number climbed. Surveys confirmed that many readers bought the paper primarily to keep up with the Gumps, Orphan Annie, Smitty, Harold Teen, and Winnie Winkle. Not only did the *Daily News* originate and run many favorite strips, its syndicate sold them to papers elsewhere.

Until the Associated Press accepted its application for membership in 1927, the *Daily News* bought its wire news from United Press and most of its features from the Chicago *Tribune* syndicate.[26] Like most newspapers of the day, the *Daily News* published serial fiction and short stories. The first issue devoted two pages to a detective story. Recognizing the reader appeal of fiction, Patterson was deeply involved with selecting the serials and short stories. Love stories were most popular, but the paper also reprinted such works as *This Side of Paradise* and *The Beautiful and the Damned.* The editor admitted he "chopped the devil out of" the latter.[27] Fiction remained a *Daily News* staple for decades.

The early issues carried only an abbreviated table of stock, bond, and commodity prices, but in October Patterson ordered a full page daily of financial news.[28] Like Bennett, Patterson saw this as a way to broaden the paper's appeal. Sports, which at first rated only two pages, grew even faster. Patterson frequently called for more sports photos. Columnists geared their advice on health, manners, cooking, and fashions to young readers. Doris Blake's love advice was prim.

REDEFINING NEWS

The *Daily New* rarely missed a major news story. In early 1925 it published more than three-fourths of the news stories receiving significant play in the *Times.*[29] Although the *Daily News* had no foreign correspondents, it received the wire service reports. On stories such as the Russian Revolution, the *Daily News* found its own angle:

**GIRL DAZED BY RED NIGHTMARE ESCAPES BOLSHEVIKIS;
YOUNG WOMAN TELLS OF NIGHTLY ORGIES.**[30]

To explain what was different about the way the *Daily News* handled a news story, Payne cited the marriage of movie star Gloria Swanson in 1925:

> The *Times,* for instance, handled the story in the usual way, giving merely the names, the places and other facts involved. We knew that our readers would be greatly interested in Gloria's age, so we spent considerable money cabling France until we found out for sure her exact age. This fact we played up in the lead of our story.[31]

Although the paper was reluctant to send staffers to cover stories beyond the metropolitan area, it occasionally did so lavishly as when it sent twenty-five reporters and photographers to cover Charles Lindbergh's triumphal reception in Washington, D.C. Before he would disembark from the naval vessel sent to bring him from France, he insisted on a few minutes alone with his mother. The huge parade halted at the Washington Monument, where President Calvin Coolidge presented him the nation's first Distinguished Flying Cross. As in all his acknowledgments, Lindy was modest, insisting his feat was the culmination of two decades of achievement by American aviation and industry. (The fact he had been born about the time of the Wright Brothers' flight showed how new aviation really was.) The *Daily News* staffers captured all this and no doubt delighted their readers; their $2,000 expense account nonetheless horrified the accounting department.[32] Three days later, New Yorkers had their turn, and police estimated three to four million turned out for the biggest ticker tape parade in the city's history. The hysteria was repeated all around the country. For weeks, newspapers—large and small—could not print enough about the Lone Eagle.

From the beginning the *Daily News* paid for tips on stories or photos. Every caller got fifty cents, no matter how many had called before him. Most tipsters received $2 to $5. By 1927 the *Daily News* was dishing out $1,000 a week to callers.[33]

The *Daily News* kept the promise it made in its first issue to cover "the doings of the very fortunate." Illustrated stories about society balls and charity events ran all winter, only to be replaced in the summer by accounts from fashionable seaside spas such as Newport and Southampton. It would seem the Sweeneys had little need to know what to wear to the Epsom Derby or on an ocean voyage, but they were as curious about the upper crust as readers had been in Bennett's or Pulitzer's day. Patterson's pleas to cover more weddings and debutante balls grew less frequent after a woman became society editor in 1922.[34]

Gossip about the rich and famous has always been a sure-fire way to please readers. As one social historian put it:

> Our modern exemplars of the shop girls who devoured the saucy tidbits in Bennett's New York *Herald,* the granddaughters of the housewives from Dullsville who quivered with excitement over the international marriages of the early twentieth century, still seek social gods to worship.[35]

May–December weddings were especially interesting. The marriage of a seventy-three-year-old Italian-American contractor to a thirteen-year-old was page one material for several days in 1926. The stories pointed out that he had served two years in prison for statutory rape of this same girl. "Despite the disparity in their ages and the unfortunate incident that marred their early friendship, Ferraro appears to be madly in love with the child."[36]

With such stories the *Daily News* quickened the pulse of people locked in humdrum lives, at the same time reassuring them that the world remained fairly constant from day to day and year to year. This, in James Murphy's phrase, helped readers "to order the bloomin' buzzin' confusion."[37] Whether life was really more hectic than in the past mattered less than that folks thought it was.

Sometimes the publisher complained the paper was getting too heavy and needed to be "jazzed up"; at other times he warned the staff "too much lowbrow stuff" scared off female readers.[38] By 1928 Patterson was worried that the *Daily News* was not different enough from the standard-size papers. "We have to get more distinction from them," he insisted. He wanted more stories with feminine appeal and fewer wire service stories.[39] Fighting by then for a middle ground, he already saw his paper as distinct from the other tabloids.

The "friend in need" column helped people exchange goods, skills, and services. Many toys and clothes were provided. Others found roommates and jobs. Volunteer tutors, sitters, and drivers were found for old people and needy children. When six stray dogs were offered for adoption, there were 3200 responses.[40] As promotions, Sally Joy Brown took groups of children, selected on the basis of essays, to circuses, ball games, picnics, and Coney Island. The paper sponsored citywide boxing, skating, and swimming and diving meets for youngsters.

Burns Mantle reviewed Broadway plays, and Mark Hellinger reported gossip from the Rialto. Although never as popular as Walter Winchell, Hellinger was the highest paid reporter on the staff. Because Sweeney and his wife went to a lot more movies than plays or nightclubs, Hollywood got much attention, not only in news and reviews but in *Daily News* promotions.

The sports staff grew steadily, and included many photographers.[41] The publisher praised the photos of the 1921 World Series but fired the reporter.[42] The twenties were a great time for New York fans. At least one of the local teams was in the World Series in eight of the years. In 1921, 1922, and 1923 it was a subway series between the Giants and Yankees. Many still consider the 1927 Yankees of Babe Ruth, Lou Gehrig, and company the greatest team in the history of the game.

The *Daily News* and Chicago *Tribune* paid Gertrude Ederle $7,500 in 1926 for the rights to her story of her English Channel swim.[43] Although only nineteen, Ederle had been an Olympic gold medalist and held most of the women's distance records. Only five men and no women had ever swum the English Channel. In spite of heavy rains and seas, she did it in fourteen hours and thirty-one minutes, a new record. She told reporters she hoped it would send a message to women all over the world to persevere. She was hailed by such feminists as Carrie Chapman Catt,[44] and her accomplishment inspired a popular tune entitled "Trudy."[45] She received the following cable from the *Daily News* as she headed home: **RED**

BUICK ROADSTER WITH RUMBLE SEAT AWAITS HERE AT DOCK WITH PRIVATE CHAUFFEUR.[46] New York staged one of its gaudiest ticker tape parades for her, but she turned down the paper's offer to attempt a swim to Catalina Island in California.

The paper was quick to report "scientific breakthroughs," such as monkey gland treatments to restore youth and messages monitored from Mars.[47] A science page was a feature when the *Daily News* began its Sunday edition in 1921. Sample Sunday headlines: **GIRL DREAMS OF BEING POISONED, WAKES AND DIES** and **CHECKED CORSET EVIL IS BLAMED FOR LOST MORALS.** On the other hand, the *Daily News* was slow to recognize the significance of radio. Unlike many of his fellow publishers Patterson was not interested in operating a station and only belatedly added radio listings.[48] He resented giving free publicity to a medium competing for his audience and advertisers.

By August 1919, Patterson considered the paper established.[49] Advertisers were less certain. During its first full month, the *Daily News'* ad income amounted to only $1,530, mostly from "help wanteds." The net loss for the first full month was more than $40,000, and for the rest of the year the paper averaged only four pages of ads a day.[50] The ad department took executives from Gimbels, Wanamakers, and other quality stores to watch the activity at newsstands and conducted postcard polls of readers to show how many shopped at those stores. Such tactics finally paid off in 1921 when the first Fifth Avenue retailers and department stores bought ads.[51] Within a decade the *Daily News* would lead all city papers in ad lineage.

Newsstands welcomed the *Daily News,* but because wholesalers balked at the low margin, Patterson successfully organized his own distribution network. The same tactic that had spelled disaster a half-century earlier for James Gordon Bennett, Jr. was a boon for Patterson. Within three years the *Daily News* was selling a half-million copies daily and was the nation's largest newspaper.[52]

CRIME DOES PAY

The writing style was as brash as the photos and headlines. At times the court reporting harkened back to the days of the Penny Press. Here is an example, in full, of a 1926 report:

> **Miss Frances Rathowitz, being made after Eve's pattern, naturally has knees. Miss Rathowitz, being 28 and modern, rolls her stockings down below her knees.**

> Miss Rathowitz, being very warm, rolled her stockings down under the gaze of the statue of George Washington in Union Square. George remained cold and rigid.
>
> But Patrolman Harry Levin grew warm and quick. He removed Miss Rathowitz for performing such an act in public and, after locking her up overnight, brought her sternly into the presence of Magistrate Oberwager in Tombs court yesterday.
>
> "She rolled her stockings right down," testified the patrolman. Magistrate Oberwager frowned.
>
> "There were a lot of men looking," testified the patrolman. Magistrate Oberwager considered.
>
> "Women shouldn't roll their stockings done in public," he decided. "Three months in the House of the Good Shepherd." And there Miss Rathowitz went instead of to her home at 186 First Avenue."[53]

Another reporter fashioned a feature from two routine police court appearances among the 263 cases heard one day. Robert E. Lee was fined $5 for driving without a license and George Washington paid $2 for running a stoplight. Both men were identified as Negroes and Washington's plea was reported in minstrel-show dialect: "Ah could have used this money on the Fo'th of July, boss, but ah pleaded guilty because Ah jest couldn't tell a lie."[54]

As in all subjects, photos made some of the most dramatic statements about crime. Under the one-word headline **DEAD!** the *Daily News* published the most shocking photo of the decade, showing Ruth Snyder, hooded and strapped in the electric chair. (See chapter 12.) To get the first and only photo of an electrocution, the *Daily News* smuggled an out-of-town photographer past prison officials. Tom Howard had strapped a small camera on his ankle; at the fatal moment he reached in his pocket and pressed the cable release. Howard had time for only one exposure, and that was all he needed.[55]

Similarly, large photos of empty buggies or cradles captured the agony of baby kidnapings far better than words.[56] Such "hard news" photos were the exception. In their constant battle to meet deadlines and without knowing when real news would break, newspapers relied more on photos of routinized or predictable events. A scheduled ball game or prize fight was certain to provide photos. So was the appearance in court of a handcuffed prisoner. Even staged photos "looked real." Coney Island bathers arrested for too-brief attire were photogenic, even if they were there specifically to challenge the rules.[57] Press agents learned to include pretty girls in their stunts.

Competition for photos was so intense that thefts were routine. An hour after Hearst's *American* published the only available photos of a murder victim found in a trunk, the *Daily News* copied and ran them; six weeks later, the *American* copied the *Daily News'* prize fight photos.[58] In reporting his feat to Patterson, the new managing editor of the *Daily News* said he thought he was "getting the feel" for sensationalism. He may have been right, since a month later he credited a series of crime stories for a recent jump in sales.[59] Patterson stressed to his editors the importance of sex and crime stories in selling papers, but he also wanted "romantic happenings" emphasized.[60] He admitted his ambivalence about "private scandal or private love affairs outside the law" before they came to trial; once in court, they were fair game.[61]

Victimized or brave women, especially if they were pretty, were favorite topics. The paper carried a chorus girl's *signed* plea for the extradition from Canada of two men she claimed had striped, beaten, and deserted her on a lonely Westchester County road. The men were returned and convicted.[62] Another chorine described the beatings from her "caveman" boyfriend but said she did not want to leave him.[63] Readers also read often about heroic girls, such as the one injured slightly while fighting off a would-be burglar and another who rescued several children in a school fire.[64]

COMPETITION AND CRITICISM

By 1924, when New York got its second and third tabloids, there were small papers in Baltimore, Detroit, St. Louis, Boston, Chicago, Buffalo, and Philadelphia. As with the Penny Press and the Yellow Press, the tabloids thrived only amid the hustle and bustle of the urban landscape. A few experiments in smaller cities failed quickly. By 1926 there were thirteen tabloids in the United States and more on the drawing boards.[65]

With the appearance of two tabloid competitors, Patterson worried about Hearst's *Mirror* but never about Bernard Macfadden's *Graphic*. He cautioned his executive, "Don't make any mistake. You have competition in the *Mirror*."[66] Although he sued the *Mirror* for stealing one of his paper's copyrighted news stories,[67] he often praised its initiative, writing and makeup to his own staff. His editor dismissed the first issues of the *Graphic* as "a newspaper hash of all current Macfadden publications."[68] After an editorial blast from Macfadden, Patterson first told his editor to "kid the life out of him" (even suggesting running pictures of him in his strong man pose) and then decided to ignore him.[69]

If his reporters pursued a story too zealously, Patterson was ready to back them up. He did not hesitate to pledge full legal aid for two *Daily News* reporters arrested in 1929 for breaking into a public official's locked desk.[70]

The appearance of the new tabloids did not slow the upward circulation spiral of the *Daily News,* which passed the million mark in 1926. It was almost all *local* circulation, promotion ads boasted.[71] Out-state New York publishers denounced the tabloids at their 1926 convention, and other journalists accused them of everything from "outright filth" to monopolizing reading time.[72] In answer to such critics, the New York bureau chief of United Press said in 1927, "It hardly matters what the newspapermen think of the tabloids. The people are showing what they think by the way they buy them."[73] Although democratic theory and *laissez-faire* economics insisted the public got what it deserved, a few scholars insisted that newspapers had loftier obligations than maximizing circulation. Leon Flint, a journalism professor, urged them to "give the public *what it ought to have,* what it wants in its better moments."[74]

The tabloids were "a perversion of journalism" one magazine writer charged, making "eavesdroppers of reporters, sensual meddlers of journalists, and reducing the highest ideas of the newspaper to the process of fastening a camera lens to every boudoir door."[75] Writing in the *American Mercury,* George Jean Nathan said the new pictorial newspapers were more boring and less committed than the yellow journals of the 1890s.[76] Reflecting the contemporary fascination with Freudianism, poet E. E. Cummings suggested in *Vanity Fair* that the slogan for the New York tabloids should be "Every Issue an Oedipus Complex."[77] Silas Bent scoffed at attempts by the mainstream press to disown the tabloids, correctly pointing out that they were the lineal and logical outcome of trends stretching back to Bennett. The attacks, he said, were prompted by jealousy.[78]

MODERATE REFORMER

At the top of the paper's editorial platform for many years was providing enough desks for every child in the public schools. Many poor children still could not attend. "Make schools our leading policy," Patterson ordered in 1922. He wanted seven news stories and seven editorials a month on schools.[79] Although by then local and state governments were spending four times as much on education as they had two decades earlier, a 1927 series of illustrated stories documented the continued overcrowding in New York.[80]

In addition to modification of the liquor laws, the paper's 1926 platform also called for more parks, better service on subways, and improved traffic controls. In an effort to reduce its annual toll of 1000 traffic deaths, New York was one of the first cities in the world to introduce traffic lights.[81] On Pattersons' instructions, many editorials were reprinted or localized from those appearing in the *Tribune*.

On local issues, the paper usually lined up with the moderate reformers; in national politics, it leaned toward the Democrats. Patterson had long since abandoned the radical politics of his youth. On matters of morality, the *Daily News* could be quite starchy. Even after three juries failed to convict Fatty Arbuckle, the paper never forgave the screen comedian for his involvement in the death of an actress, and it applauded the prison sentence for showman Earl Carroll, after a backstage party featuring a nude showgirl in a tub of champagne.[82]

Patterson made it clear to his editors he wanted no sentimentalizing over condemned or executed murderers. On at least one occasion he ordered an editorial prepared on the need for capital punishment.[83]

One law for which the *Daily News* had no sympathy was the Volstead Act. In editorials and stories it belittled the dry laws. Not many published entries in its 1925 essay contest on "My Experience With Prohibition" had anything favorable to say.[84] Nor did the other New York newspapers. The paper charged that in the 1926 elections, the drys had outspent the wets by more than eight-to-one but had not changed popular sentiment. "Money won't convince people that a ridiculous law is a good law."[85] It claimed Prohibition was born in tank towns and certainly was not appropriate in cities.[86] The most frequent themes were that morality could not be legislated and that the law was unenforceable.[87] The front-page headline greeting 1927 was **NEW YEAR WRINGING WET**. [88]

The paper insisted that legal beer and light wines would wean the public from bootleg hootch. "Drinking will no longer be thought smart."[89]

READERS LOVE CONTESTS

The *Daily News* paid readers $1 to $5 for submitting their captions, limericks, jingles, embarrassing moments, and bright sayings. As many as 20,000 a day responded. A tongue-twister contest in 1923 drew 80,000 submissions in one week.[90] More than 100,000 were happy to report on "The Queerest Boss I Ever Worked For." A children's drawing contest drew 300,000 entries. Readers also sent in real love stories, amateur photos,

fish stories, and vacation experiences. As soon as the responses fell off, a
new contest was introduced, but always after consultation with Patterson.
Readers competed for bigger prizes by identifying Presidents from scraps
of pictures, matching serial numbers on dollar bills and designing and
solving crossword puzzles. There was such a howl from readers in 1925
that crosswords were returned.[91] Prizes were adjusted upward or down-
ward to match competition in other papers. The *Daily News* paid $10,000
in 1922 for the best solution to a mystery story. Postal authorities vetoed
several proposed contests as lotteries. To be mailable a contest had to
involve skill, not mere luck.

One annual promotion drew bags of entries but offered no cash prize at
all. This was the vote for favorite movie stars. In 1927, John Gilbert
(13,715 votes) and Vilma Banky (nearly 10,000) reigned as Movie King and
Queen.[92]

Four to six times a year, the *Daily News* ran some sort of beauty
contest, each of which provided an excuse for leg art. Photos entered in its
annual search for "Venus" ran daily for most of the summer. Patterson
fired one managing editor for not following his instructions on how to play
the contest.[93] After telling one of his successors he was disappointed in the
pageant photos, Patterson sent a "clarification":

> Legs are all right and desirable when they are a natural part of
> the story. The stories about bathing beauties should be illustrated
> by pictures of them in bathing costumes. What is objectionable is
> simply to force legs into the picture page to drag in anatomy as
> Macfadden does. Whenever it comes in naturally, by all means use
> it.[94]

The *Daily News* cited a city policemen and firemen for heroism each
month. Over the years the cash awards rose from $100 to $250. No one
could fault this civic-minded promotion, least of all the very civil servants
upon whom reporters relied.

In 1930, Patterson ordered the staff to emphasize *only one* sex or crime
story a day.[95] Its finances secure, the *Daily News* was taking itself more
seriously and, like James Gordon Bennett's *Herald* a century earlier, be-
coming more respectable. Almost in spite of itself.

12

Challengers: The *Mirror* and the *Graphic*

I n spite of the old saying, you apparently *can* underestimate the intelligence of newspaper buyers. That is what one old hand at the game of sensationalism and one eccentric newcomer learned when in 1924 they challenged the *Daily News* for supremacy in the tabloid market. In the 1830s and 1890s the lively, innovative newcomers dislodged the stodgy established leaders, but this time the *Daily News,* still young and vigorous itself, prevailed.

THE *MIRROR:* TOO LITTLE, TOO LATE

The William Randolph Hearst who battled the *Daily News* was not the same energetic, imaginative, free-spending Hearst who had slugged it out with Pulitzer's *World.* Hearst in his sixties was starting to act like his cinematic *roman a clef,* Charles Foster Kane. His opposition to World War I and his blatant flexing of editorial muscle had alienated most liberal and moderate politicians and had earned the emnity of New York Governor Al Smith. His brand of progressivism was out of style. Hearst seemed unable to deliver many votes, least of all for his own frequent candidacies.[1] After two lackluster terms in Congress, elected from a safe Democratic district, he made a serious run for the Democratic presidential nomination in 1904 and lost the New York gubernatorial election two years later to Charles Evans Hughes. In 1908 he organized and financed a third-party White House campaign for an obscure Massachusetts businessman.[2]

By the twenties, Hearst had too many irons in the fire to involve himself with any one of his forty newspapers the way he had with the *Journal* in the 1890s. He also owned dozens of magazines, a wire service, and a feature syndicate. There were personal distractions as well. He was producing movies and managing the career of actress Marion Davies, his mistress. He also roamed the world, spending $1 million a year on art, much of which he never even uncrated.[3]

Hearst was so fascinated with the tabloids that observers expected him to launch New York's first. After trying one in Boston and buying the presses to produce another in New York, he hesitated, calculating that his morning *American* and *Evening Journal,* which were as blood-splattered and sensational as any tabloid, could hold that segment of the market. Hearst urged the editors of both papers to emulate the short stories, big pictures, and sprightly headlines in the *Daily News.* For a while, Hearst even tried to hide his ownership of the *Mirror* through some dummy publishing companies, hoping that the newcomer might not inherit the widespread ill will to the Chief.

Alarmed by the *Daily News* success and rebuffed in his bid to buy out Patterson and McCormick,[4] he launched the *Mirror* on June 24, 1924. From its first issue, the *Mirror* set out to beat the *Daily News* at its own game. As he had done in launching his *Journal* in 1895, Hearst copied his established rival's headlines, pictures, and features and lavished money on promotions. He even raided his opposition for his first managing editor, Philip Payne, who was certain readers preferred "trivialities" to news.[5] The *Mirror* announced that it intended to dispense 90 percent features and entertainment and 10 percent news[6] (Later Hearst even hired Emile Gauvreau, editor of the *Graphic,* the exemplar of trivial news.) This time though, Hearst was up against an alert and vigorous publisher who already had a circulation of nearly 800,000. As a result, the *Mirror* never became more than a pale reflection. The *Daily News* predicted in 1926 that the Hearst tabloid would fail because "people always prefer the genuine article."[7]

Soft News Content

The first issue of the *Mirror* contained thirty-two pages and, like the *Daily News*, sold for two cents. Front page photos showed four boxers, one baseball player, and a screen idol (Rudolph Valentino). Like the *Daily News*, the paper filled its center spread with miscellaneous photos. Three other pages were devoted to sports news. "Flaming Youth," the first fiction serial, reeked of sexual innuendo. The headline on the back page read: **WOMAN'S DIARY/LOVE, HATE, MARRIAGE, DIVORCE**. There was no routine news of local government and only a smattering of business, national, and international items. The paper carried nine comic strips plus jokes, cute sayings, and the usual assortment of advice columns and puzzles. One cynic suggested that the *Mirror* was edited for "those who found the *Journal* too scholarly."[8]

The *Mirror* printed larger headlines, more photos, and more crime news than the *Daily News*. An analysis of the *Mirror* for one week in 1925 found that pictures filled *two-thirds of the nonadvertising space*. Probably no daily newspaper in the world ever had published that high a percentage of artwork. In features, which occupied more space than news stories, the *Mirror* emphasized the narrative writing style. Managing editor Walter Howey disliked summary leads and told his writers to "forget journalism as the term is usually used."[9]

Whether, as one writer suggested, the *Mirror* routinely "manufactured" stories of murder and mayhem,[10] it certainly hyped some. During its first summer, the *Mirror* went all out to cover a grisly trial in New Jersey. (See chapter 12 for its role two years later in reopening the Hall-Mills case in the same state.) A mother on trial for the murder of her baby fainted when the state brought in a mummified corpse:

> **Jersey's gruesome show, its Judicial Grand Guignol, continued yesterday to the morbid edification of a packed courtroom at May's Landing.**
>
> **The dead little star of the show, the mummified infant's corpse which the State maintains is the murdered child ... continues to repose on the table where the woman in black sat ...**[11]

Of course, the *Mirror* published every detail in its news accounts of the case. Here are the headlines on some other crime stories from the *Mirror*'s first month: **SHE'LL TELL OF POISON, KILLS WIFE HE HATED, DIES JOKING, ANOTHER FOLLIES GIRL BEATEN, SCORNED, MOTHER OF 5 SHOOTS LOVER**, and **MIR-**

ROR FINDS SLAYER'S SHIRT. In the last, a reporter had turned up a bloody garment near the site of a youth's murder. The story suggested that a psychopath was to blame, a psychopath still on the loose.

Arthur Brisbane, however, refused to allow the reporter covering the Loeb-Leopold trial in the fall of 1924 to use the word "pervert." He changed it to "dreadful failure."[12] Historian Cathy Covert wrote of the journalistic mind of the day. "While 'normal' sex proved a favorite newspaper topic, adherence to social taboos prevented clear and open reporting on such Freudian topics as perversion or the emotional aspects of excretion and other subjects not discussed in public."[13]

The *Mirror* could not print enough about flappers and flaming youth. They were favorites in both the fiction serials ("Shebo: She Rode the Rods on Life's Fast Freight") and the news stories. The paper even reached 3000 miles for the tale of a "dance-crazed beauty" who killed her mother in San Francisco. There were four pictures on the first day and several follow-up accounts.[14] Then there were

MUSIC DRUGGED SOUL, SAYS GIRL SLAYER
Syncopation Madness[15]

and

FLAPPER, 14, AFLAME, KILLS BROTHER
Steak Knife in Heart[16]

The paper even headlined the hardly remarkable position taken by Catholic bishops:

BISHOPS INDICT GAY LIVING
Denounce Divorce, Birth Control and Orgies.[17]

In an editorial, the *Mirror* defended the right of girls to bob their hair and to wear scanty clothes as "outward manifestations of their determination to do as the boys do—and be free."[18]

Marital splits involving the rich or famous were a staple. It was an era with many suits for alienation of affections, usually headlined as "heart balm." In its second issue the *Mirror* had a major story on a policeman who divorced his society wife, and two days later a story on a wife who filed suit to leave a famous vaudevillian (**FAILS TO STAR IN ROLE AS HUSBAND**).[19] A princess seeking to shake her American husband rated front-page treatment as did a divorce suit against one of the Goulds.[20] Even if a person with a problem was not really famous, sometimes a writer could make him *sound* that way. Readers had to go well beyond the headline "Rockefeller in Tears Begs Wife Forgive" to learn it was about the owner of a Brooklyn salt company and not one of the "real" Rockefellers.[21]

Like all Hearst papers, the *Mirror* doted on pseudoscience and freaks. It was delighted when a zoologist "settled" the age-old riddle by declaring the egg came before the hen.[22] The *Mirror* was more impressed than others with reports of a diver's battle on the ocean bottom with a giant lobster and with such stories as "Siamese Twins by Choice" and the 165-pound man who took a 486-pound wife.[23] An interview with an artist about "feminine perfection" was little more than an excuse to run pictures of Helen Wills, Gertrude Ederle, and other underdressed athletes below the headline **"FULSOMELY ROUND" GIRLS.**[24]

In an interview published in 1926 in a trade publication, Hearst spelled out his view that the average reader "wants everything presented to him briefly as well as brightly. . . . It is the editor's business to do the winnowing for him."[25] His papers were true to his vision.

Contests, Confessions, and Counselors

At the end of its first month, the *Mirror* announced a contest to find the "prettiest woman." Each day it printed several photos that had been submitted. In separate contests, readers voted for the best lips and legs in town, and even for their favorite barber. Rarely was the paper without at least one contest. In a tasteless promotion in 1925, the *Mirror* asked readers to elect the city's homeliest girl. Dozens of women sent snapshots, and the most votes went to an Italian seamstress who aspired to be an opera diva. Her prize was free plastic surgery and an audition.[26] Her operatic "career" ended there. The *Daily News* had run a similar promotion in 1920, but it had involved no "election."[27]

The *Mirror* published many photos of the sixteen-year-old who won the Charleston contest at the Polo Grounds. In a by-lined article Mary Suchier wrote: "I attribute the shapliness of my legs to the exercise they get when dancing." She said her mother was learning the dance, too.[28] For a while it seemed almost everyone was fascinated with the dance, which soon gave way to others.

One 1926 contest run by the *Mirror* bordered on self-caricature. Readers were rewarded for sending in nine-word "tabloid stories." One example, not much shorter than some actual *Mirror* stories:

One Piece Suit
Cop Nabs Beast
Crowd Yells Brute.

In a contest to identify pictures of "movie lovers," 845 readers won movie tickets and had their names published. Every day, the paper awarded $1 to $5 to readers willing to share embarrassing moments, baby talk, and jokes.[29] Several times the paper invited readers to submit parodies of songs. In January 1925 it offered $1,000 for solutions to crossword puzzles. One comic strip on the sports page included a tip on a horse race being run that day.

"True stories" submitted by readers ran under such titles as "A Fat Woman's Diary," "I Married a Thief for Revenge" and "The Man Who Fooled Me." An ever-changing corps of columnists advised on graphology, astrology, and numerology. The romantic counsel offered by Eleanor Glyn, one of the most daring novelists of the decade, was prim, as when she advised a letter writer not to be swayed by the behavior of others at a "petting party."[30] Columnist John Blake warned girls to beware of jazz because "like every drug, it is habit-forming."[31] The women's section offered glimpses of sophistication among the dress patterns and household hints. The recipes seldom ventured beyond chicken à la king.

Like most other New York City papers, the *Mirror* consistently denounced Prohibition and called for its repeal. In 1929, Hearst put up $25,000 for the best plan for a "practical alternative." He purchased ads in papers across the country to encourage entries. The prize was claimed by a New York juvenile court judge, who backed the legalization of light wines and beers.[32]

A Blunted Lance

In spite of such efforts, the *Mirror* could not gain on the *Daily News*. In the six months ending March 30, 1925, the *Mirror* had increased its circulation by nearly 40 percent to 218,431, but its rival had gained even more and claimed four times as many readers. Nor could the *Mirror* attract advertisers. In a 1926 promotion ad, the publicity director of Bloomingdale's department store praised the *Mirror*'s "peppy" and growing audience and liked the way ads stood out in the small page format.[33] He might have added that the ads stood out precisely because there were so few of them.

A box in the *Mirror* in 1925 boasted:

DAILY MIRROR has proved that a clean, live pictured newspaper has a strong appeal to a better class of readers in all income groups.[34]

But that was really wishful thinking. Editors came and went with bewildering speed at all three Hearst papers, but none could reverse the circulation losses. In desperation the *Mirror* lured the city's top gossip columnist and city editor, but it was too late. Walter Winchell's column added a few thousand former *Graphic* readers, but *Herald-Tribune* loyalists did not follow Stanley Walker. Finding his principal duty was to reduce the staff,

Walker did not stay long.[35] Hungry for exclusives, the *Mirror* brought two women lumberjacks from Idaho to Central Park, where *Mirror* photographers and writers captured their prowess which captivated neither onlookers nor readers.[36]

Things were even gloomier at the other Hearst properties. As Swanberg noted, "To work for a publication in which Hearst was dissatisfied was to enter a world of madness and pressure that had about equal parts of humor and futility."[37] As he watched the circulation of the *American* dwindle, Hearst ordered the managing editor to condense every story, especially political stories, and to print more about divorces, romances, and human tragedies.[38] The *American* was so desperate that it purchased ads in the *Graphic* to claim it was the paper for the "up-to-date" woman.[39] When the *American* announced a lottery with a top prize of $1,000, the *Daily News* the next day offered $2,500. When Hearst upped the ante to $5,000, Patterson countered with a prize of $10,000. Hearst passed. He no longer had the taste for such high-stakes poker. With the deepening of the Great Depression, he folded the *American* in 1931. It was a wrenching decision since the morning paper was the direct descendant of his *Journal* of the 1890s. He found it easier at about the same time to sell the *Mirror*. Neither Hearst nor New York readers ever developed much affection for the half-pint.

THE GRAPHIC: TOO MUCH FOR *ANY* TIME

New York got its third—and strangest—tabloid on September 15, 1924, a date one writer called the "blackest day in the history of American journalism."[40] The *Evening Graphic* was publisher Bernarr Macfadden's attempt to apply to a daily newspaper the techniques he had developed with his confession and physical culture magazines. Those techniques amounted to sexual titillation. While the other tabloids occasionally smirked, the *Graphic* leered in every story, headline, and picture.

Macfadden readily admitted the *Graphic* did not represent journalism in any ordinary sense of the term, "but fashions change, even in orthodoxy. . . . We expect to become an institution, a human institution."[41] There seldom was anything about mayors or legislatures. The only congress that drew much attention was the sexual sort. Space was found, however, for song lyrics and ukulele chords.

During its eight years, it was denounced, derided, damned, and sued, not only for libel but also for obscenity.[42] Many newsstands refused to sell the paper, and respectable citizens did not want to be seen carrying a copy.

What Upset the Public?

The first twenty-four-page issue of the *Graphic* did *not* look like the *Daily News,* the *Mirror* or any other paper, before or since, although it sold for the same price, two cents. The opening editorial promised: "We intend to interest you mightily. We intend to dramatize and sensationalize the news and some stories that are not new. But we do not want a single dull line to appear in this newspaper." No paper ever came closer to living up to its promises. It did less well in reflecting its front-page slogan: **NOTHING BUT THE TRUTH.**

Editor & Publisher shook its head at the *Graphic*'s "remarkable" news treatment and its "interesting, but not perfectly organized" typography.[43] To Macfadden features and editorials were the heart of the paper, news little more than binder to hold together the photos, features, and columns. He never bothered to subscribe to any news service and employed far fewer local reporters than the other two tabloids.

Macfadden really created a daily magazine, and the layouts and many of the stories came right out of *Physical Culture* and *True Story.* Following the confession magazine practice, the *Graphic* for the first few issues ran most local stories under the by-lines of participants (reporters really wrote most of them). Headlines included **FOR 36 HOURS I LIVED ANOTHER WOMAN'S LOVE LIFE, MY FRIENDS DRAGGED ME INTO THE GUTTER.** and **HE BEAT ME—I LOVE HIM.** In one story an artist's housekeeper speculated about whether her employer would continue painting after marrying an English baronet. Such stories seldom ran longer than six inches—but then neither did much else in the paper.

Gangsters and street murders were staples, but contrary to popular opinion, the *Graphic* ran no more crime news than the other tabloids, but it is easy to explain the basis for that misconception. For example, the front page of the second issue had six pictures of murder cases, and the banner story was **POOR BOY, 19, FACING NOOSE, CRIES MUST I DIE WHEN RICH KILLERS GET LIFE?** Despite its lurid accounts of beastly crimes, the paper consistently opposed capital punishment, even for "thrill killers" Loeb and Leopold, on trial in Chicago at the time.[44] Crime reporters received no by-lines in the paper's early months. (By-lines were still rare in all newspapers.) The paper would reach afar for a good murder story. It devoted a banner headline and five pictures to the conviction in Ohio of a "society flapper" who murdered her husband with a hammer. She was sent to prison for life.[45]

The *Graphic* continually denounced and ridiculed attempts to enforce the dry laws. A headline in 1929 tied this to a favorite topic: **PROBITION HAS MADE AMERICA SEX MAD.**[46]

Even more than crime, though, the *Graphic* front pages emphasized bedroom scandals, sexual deviance, torture, suicide, and divorce. Within the first month, the front page offered titillation like

SHACKLED GIRL FLEES
Chained, She Creeps
Miles to Police.[47]

Others included **DIDN'T MAKE LOVE TO PRINCESS. ELOPING HEIRESS HAPPY** and **MURDERER FIEND STILL AT LARGE.**

Those who called the paper the *Porno-Graphic* often singled out the fiction pieces, usually illustrated with posed studio photos. The *Graphic's* fiction was the same kind of sentimental and suggestive tripe that filled Macfadden's confession magazines. The paper's first serial, "The Romance of an Artist's Model," involved remorse over a premarital affair.

Macfadden wanted every item in his paper to present a point of view. The *Graphic's* hardly revolutionary editorial platform opposed government censorship, intolerance, and business and political graft and supported better subway service, a bridge across the Hudson River to New Jersey, voting by mail, fines for those who did not vote, registration of aliens, and automatic annulment of inactive laws.[48] The eccentric millionaire's battles with the medical establishment prompted quips that the *Graphic* was against vaccination and for fornication.

After a few weeks of experimenting with layouts, the *Graphic* began running a single large front-page photo, which seldom related to the headline story. The favorite headline word was love—frequently in such corrupted forms as love nest and love child.

Every issue of the *Graphic* also included Macfadden's column in which he preached the virtues of exercise and diet. To attract those bored by carbuncles and carrots, he gave sexual advice, illustrating the articles with photos of scantily-clad models.

Beginning in 1925, Macfadden purchased time on WOR in Newark to lead calisthenics. From 6:45 to 8 A.M. he urged sleepy listeners to join him in exercises. A small studio orchestra played, and chorus girls often came along to the studio to join him and to be interviewed. They also had their pictures published in the *Graphic,* which Macfadden promoted throughout the broadcasts.[49]

Mindful of affairs of the heart and not just the libido, the *Graphic* provided a lonely hearts column for those looking for love and "Are You Unhappily Wed?" for those looking for a way out. Those who wrote to the former were invited to the annual Lonely Hearts Ball, which in 1928 attracted 15,000.[50] Numerologists and astrologers also advised on affairs of the heart. A column published under movie actress Norma Talmadge's name advised a girl torn between trying a screen career and marriage, "Silly child. Marry the boy you love and who loves you and settle down in your little house and have the babies. That is my advice, absolutely."[51] The manners columnist once advised emptying one's mouth before kissing in public places.[52] Supporting the publisher's interest in eugenics, the paper offered $10,000 for "ideal marriages" between Dianas and Apollos. Naturally, pictures of the entrants were published for weeks on end.

The paper's most popular writer was Walter Winchell. In his breezy Broadway gossip column he coined words and adopted a breathless tone that made even the most mundane fact seem like a state secret. In addition to writing his column, he also reviewed plays. He wrote for the *Graphic* from September 1924 until the *Mirror* hired him away in 1930. (He had made overtures to the *Daily News,* as well, but the publisher thought he wanted too much money.)[53] Macfadden conceded that Winchell's column sold 75,000 to 100,000 copies of the *Graphic* a day.[54] Winchell's greatest fame came in the 1940s as a network radio commentator. ("Mr. and Mrs. North America and all the ships at sea . . . Let's go to press!" was his staccato opening.)

Stanley Walker thought Winchell deserved more credit than he ever received for making newspapers relevant and interesting to a mass readership. He did it by focusing on personalities. Walker said Winchell was "the perfect flower of Broadway, the product of his period as surely as the tommy gun."[55]

Bearing in mind Bessie's warning that "undertaking a sober analysis of the *Graphic* is about as easy as making a statistical study of the character of the modern burlesque show,"[56] here is an attempt at quantified analysis of the editorial content of the three New York tabloids for two weeks in October 1926:

At one point, when the *Graphic* was gaining circulation, the following notice was posted in the city room by editor Emile Guavreau:

> **The circulation of the *Graphic* has reached the point where it is tearing the guts out of the presses. This has resulted from my policy of sensationalism. Any man who cannot be yellow has no place on the staff.**[58]

Macfadden shrugged off criticisms that his newspaper was too sensational. "Sensationalism is nothing more than a clear, definitive, attractive presentation of the news and is perfectly proper as long as one adheres to the truth."[59]

	Number of Column Inches		
	Graphic	Mirror	Daily News
Crime	879	865	858
Sex crime	10	22	43
Divorce/annulment	874	252	284
General news	679	540	1016
Local news	232	217	295
Foreign news	78	74	102
Editorials	421	229	282
Entertainment, fiction, puzzles	1187	1818	1757
Departments including advice, how-to, sayings[57]	7734	4479	4548

Such assertions of veracity were directly contradicted by the *Graphic*'s use of phony photographs. There was nothing new about faked pictures, but the *Graphic* made a fetish of "composographs." After models posed in the studio, the photo editor would paste on the faces of people in the news. Tiny type identified the pictures as composites.[60] Startling examples showed Enrico Caruso greeting Rudolph Valentino at the Pearly Gates, Vanzetti walking his last mile, and Lindbergh on his way to Paris.

The composograph that got the *Graphic* in the most trouble was published during the infamous separation hearing between Edward "Daddy" Browning, a wealthy Manhattan real estate owner, and his teenage bride Peaches. In 1925 all the newspapers printed reams of testimony about their bedroom antics, but it was the *Graphic* that shocked the city with a photo that seemed to show Peaches standing naked before the jury box.[61] A chorus girl had posed for the infamous shot and for others published during the hearing. *Editor & Publisher* pronounced it "the most shocking news picture ever produced by New York journalism."[62] Although several suburbs banned that issue from their newsstands, it sold an extra quarter-million copies. When the New York Society for the Suppression of Vice charged Macfadden with publishing pictures of "bloodshed, lust and crime," the Browning photo was the star exhibit. The judge called the paper "disgusting" but eventually dismissed the charges.[63]

Promotions Galore

In its first issue the *Graphic* announced that it was sending "Our Subway Girl" to ride the trains and award cash to men who gave up their seats to women riders. Beneath a large picture of her in a bathing suit, the caption asked, "Will you know her in street clothes?"[64] In the fall of 1924 readers voted for the city's prettiest stenographers and later for bookkeepers, clerks, and teachers. The contest editor recalled how one girl plopped on his desk, crossed her legs and said, "The best in Canarsie!"[65]

Born in the midst of the crossword puzzle craze, the *Graphic* offered prizes for solvers and creators. Simon & Schuster's first crossword puzzle book was atop the best-seller list, and newspaper readers were clamoring for puzzles. Of the New York dailies, only the *Times* held out against the puzzle craze. Before long some papers were offering prizes of $25,000.[66] When the New York papers got caught up in a "Lucky Buck" contest frenzy in late 1925, the *Graphic* avoided putting up any cash of its own by printing the winning serial numbers from all the other papers.[67] Perhaps the ultimate in self-serving promotions was the *Graphic*'s essay contest, which carried a $25,000 prize. The topic: "Why the *Graphic* Is the Best New York Newspaper."[68] Like the other tabloids, the *Graphic* regularly offered small cash rewards for cute baby sayings, *faux pas* and the like.

Not Enough Readers or Advertisers

On its peak days the *Graphic* sold about 750,000 copies, but its audited average was much lower. Nearly all copies were sold on city newsstands.[69] The edition with a front-page picture of an executed man under the two-inch high headline **ROASTED ALIVE** sold 30,000 extra copies.[70]

The *Graphic* did not change much with the installation of a new editor in 1929. It still featured such headlines as **HALF-MAD BLUEBEARD TAUGHT RITES OF SEX TO 115 LOVE-CRAZED WOMEN** and **GIGOLO CONFESSES TORSO MURDER; PAID BY SWEETIE.**[71] Except for two months in 1925, there was no Sunday edition. The Audit Bureau of Circulation reported these figures:

1926	95,000
1927	141,000
1928	335,000
1929	295,000
1930	325,000
1931	280,0000
1932	263,000[72]

The paper was labeled the Gum Chewers' Gazette, and no matter how often the executives insisted it drew a quality audience, advertisers remained skeptical. The *Graphic* circulation manager claimed that in the closing hours of a crossword contest, he watched bankers, merchants, ministers, housewives, and newsboys elbowing one another to submit their solutions. He added, "Every grade of society contains honest and sincere people who are lovers of truth."[73] Used-furniture dealers were among the *Graphic*'s few regular advertisers. Bloomingdale's advertised—but only its bargain basement merchandise. It was 1931 before Macy's bought an ad.

The failure of his paper to catch on with either advertisers or readers squelched Macfadden's dream for a nationwide chain of tabloids. Macfadden said the *Graphic* lost $8 million during its eight years, but his comptroller said it was $11 million.[74] He made more than enough on his magazine empire to cover such losses. By 1926 *True Story* alone had a circulation of 2 million and attracted $3 million a year in advertising. There were several European editions and even a radio version.[75] At various times Macfadden owned such magazines as *True Romance, True Experiences* and *True Detective*.[76]

After his employees voted not to buy the *Graphic*, Macfadden filed for bankruptcy on July 1, 1932. There were few mourners.[77] Macfadden lived for another twenty-three years. He was a robust eighty-seven when he died in 1955, outliving Hearst by four years.[78] Like Hearst, Macfadden thought he would make an excellent President of the United States. Perhaps because they both were villified for their flamboyant personal lives and for their sensational journalism, the two men were friends.[79]

Bessie dismissed the *Graphic* as a "madcap venture." One of its editors dubbed it "the World's Zaniest Newspaper."[80] A *Saturday Evening Post* writer, determined to find something positive, credited the *Graphic* with teaching readers not to believe everything they read.[81] In its determination to be different, the *Graphic* forgot to be a newspaper. A daily newspaper must provide some coverage of happenings, no matter how brief. The *Daily News* and the *Mirror* did that in the 1920s, and the *Daily News* and the *Post* continue to do so today. The *Graphic* showed as much disdain for the news as today's supermarket tabloids. But they are weeklies, and readers look to them only for entertainment. Macfadden no doubt would have been delighted when in 1989 the publishing company bearing his name acquired the *National Enquirer*.

13

Murders in Tabloid Land

American mass media were obsessed with homicide in the twenties. Newspapers, magazines, novels, and movies gloried in murder trials, although the actual murder rate was almost unchanged. The fiction writers introduced the "hard-boiled detective" genre with morally ambiguous heroes, more sex, more mayhem and more gunplay.[1] Journalists jazzed up their crime stories and molded the principals into preconceived roles to match.

By any definition, some homicides are inherently more newsworthy than others, but that did not seem to make much difference in how they were featured. Here we will compare the coverage of two murders—one with all the classic elements of interest and the other fairly mundane. Neither involved famous people. One gets the impression in reading the files of the New York newspapers, and especially of the tabloids, there was a "quota" of one *cause célèbre* at a time. The moment it faded, whether after a day or months, another "crime of the century" immediately dominated the headlines. The media were not interested in typical real murders, most of which habitual criminals committed during robberies. They much preferred domestic murders with a sex angle. If the characters were not interesting, the media made them so.

THE PASTOR AND THE CHOIR SINGER
Act One

The Hall-Mills murder case got more ink than any other in the decade. The Reverend Edward Hall was pastor of the largest Episcopal church in New Brunswick, New Jersey, a town where his wife's family was among the most prominent. Mrs. Hall, seven years her husband's senior, looked drab beside Eleanor Mills, the sexton's pretty wife who sang in the church choir. Although both spouses insisted they had heard no romantic rumors, everyone else in town had. The two bodies were discovered in DeRussey's Lane, a popular trysting spot, on the morning of September 16, 1922. Both had been shot in the head; her throat had been slit from ear to ear, and her nearly severed head lay on his arm. Their shredded love notes were sprinkled over them.[2]

Across the Hudson and across the nation, newspapers panted for details of the story that combined a grisly double murder, illicit sex involving a clergyman and a witness so bizarre that other newsmen accused a *Daily News* reporter of inventing her.[3] Jane Gibson, who raised pigs on a farm near the murder site, claimed that on the fatal night she had saddled up her mule Jenny to chase what she thought were people stealing her corn. Instead she witnessed the murders in the lovers' lane. Although it was a moonless night, Mrs. Gibson said she saw four figures silhouetted against the sky, heard a shot and saw one person slump to the ground. (Her story grew more detailed with each retelling.) Then a woman screamed, "Don't! Don't! Don't!" and after more gunfire, a second figure fell. Moments later, one of the two people standing there (and Mrs. Gibson was sure it was a woman) clasped her companion's shoulders and spoke the name Henry.

This time the journalists inherited good *dramatis personae*. The minister and the choir girl, as the ill-starred lovers, needed little hyping. The journalists stressed that he was handsome, dashing, and love-starved, while she was beautiful and infatuated with a father figure. The wronged wife was matronly, cold, and stolid, the husband of the choir singer weak and pathetic. Eleanor Mills' daughter Charlotte personified the brassy flapper that at the time intrigued the nation.[4] One of Mrs. Hall's brothers, Willie with his bug eyes and walrus mustache, provided comic relief. A bit retarded, he lived with the Halls and sometimes chased fire engines. And there was the Pig Woman, as the press quickly dubbed Mrs. Gibson. Over the next few years, many supporting and bit players (at least 140 by William Kunstler's count) appeared to help provide seemingly endless plot twists.[5]

Retracted confessions, police blunders, new leads and reports of bribed witnesses and jurors kept surfacing.

The murder at first attracted full but unremarkable coverage. In its initial headline, the *Daily News* emphasized the adultery: **PASTOR AND MARRIED CHOIR SINGER MURDER PLOT VICTIMS**.[6] The next day's stories focused on the new evidence against the "gray-haired" widow.[7] In its initial story, the *Journal* underlined the Halls' wealth and social status; the next day it spoke of his widow as the "woman of mystery."[8] For three straight days the *Journal* devoted a full page to pictures and cartoons of the case.[9] Charlotte Mills, a perky fifteen-year-old who was always willing to pose for cameramen, took center stage by accusing the Hall family of complicity in the murders. Desperate for some new angle, the *Daily News* even found the mother of a girl who many years before had been engaged to the minister and quoted her about Hall's sex appeal.[10] The *Journal* devoted a full page to the speculations of a detective novelist, which proved to be dead wrong.[11]

Under intense public pressure for an arrest, the prosecutor jailed a teenager placed at the murder scene by the testimony of a romantic rival. The *Daily News*' banner: **SPOONING PAIR HOLD KEY TO HALL MURDER**.[12] Hardly anyone thought there was a solid case against the lad and he was freed two days later. **HALL CASE ACCUSER ADMITS LIE**, was the *Journal*'s headline.[13]

For the next week or so, the murder got more newspaper attention than the Greco-Turkish War and revelations about Oom the Omnipotent, leader of a cult in Nyack, New York.[14] After that, most New York papers, with the notable exceptions of the three Hearst papers, moved their Hall-Mills accounts to inside pages. The Pig Woman's testimony in late October returned the story to the front pages, where it remained until the grand jury dismissed all charges on November 28.

Newspapers competed to reprint the love notes that the widower, James Mills and his daughter, Charlotte, said they found in their house. The Hearst papers outbid the *Daily News* and paid the Millses an undisclosed sum. Far from being erotic, the notes read like the bleating of lovesick high school freshmen. "Call me Babykins," she pleaded in one. The *Journal* published facsimiles of several passages from the minister's diary it accused the *World* and other papers of cribbing.[15]

Convinced that one of the cast of characters knew more than he was telling, Philip Payne of the *Daily News* cooked up an elaborate plot. Learning that the man believed in spiritualism, the editor told a female reporter to bone up on the subject and outfit her apartment for a seance. She sent word to the man that she had a message for him from the spirit world. He showed up, and she went through with the seance, while Payne, two detectives, the prosecuting attorney and two stenographers listened in but learned nothing useful.[16]

Reporters swarmed outside the room where the grand jury deliberated, badgering witnesses as they came and went. The newshounds discovered a transom through which they could peek into the hearing room. Some papers reportedly hired lip readers to "eavesdrop" on the deliberations.[17] The Pig Woman's testimony did not convince the grand jury, which handed down no indictments.

In calling the coverage "a shameless exhibition of the eagerness to exploit crime for profit," educator Leon Flint was on target. Innocent people had suffered merely to entertain the public with a mystery story.[18] Even some reporters admitted their coverage made Mrs. Hall look bad.[19] Amid the flurry of incriminations, the curtain fell on what proved to be only the first act of the mystery. But as Al Jolson told audiences of the day, "You ain't seen nothin' yet!"

Entr'Acte

The newspapers found other sensations to cover, and despite occasional stories about new leads and false confessions, the public lost interest in the Hall-Mills case. A few intrepid reporters and policemen continued to nose around. Jane Gibson saw spies everywhere. James Mills continued as sexton of the same church and Charlotte turned to spiritualism. Mrs. Hall took an extended vacation in Europe, and her brother Willie seldom left the house.[20]

Both the new tabloids hoped to revive the case. The *Graphic* assigned one of its first reporters to interview the Pig Woman. According to another staffer, that reporter "all but courted her," paying her bills and talking with her for weeks; however, in the end, the paper decided not to go with the story.[21] Phil Payne, by then managing editor at the *Mirror,* was still fascinated with the case. He sent his reporters in pursuit of every rumor and was convinced its revival was the best hope for reducing the huge circulation lead of the *Daily News.* On July 14, 1926, the *Mirror* startled readers with headlines about new evidence. The husband of a former maid in the Hall household wanted an annulment because she had concealed from him until after they were married a story, that if proven true, definitely implicated Mrs. Hall and her brother in the murders. She told her husband she had been bribed to keep quiet about how on the night of the murders Mrs. Hall and Willie tailed the pastor to the lovers' lane for a showdown. Payne sent a telegram, daring the Hall attorney to seek a criminal libel action against him personally if the charges were not true.[22]

On July 17, the Hearst papers ran the story with photos of the principals. The next day the *Daily News* published the maid's testimony plus what it claimed was an exclusive interview.[23] The other papers, more wary of libel suits, bided their time. All-out coverage began with the arrest of Mrs. Hall two weeks later. With unseemly relish, the newspapers reconstructed their *dramatis personae* from four years earlier. Editors reprinted photos from 1922, and the *Mirror* even recounted the case in comic strip form.

During the next month, when Willie and Henry Stevens, Mrs. Hall's brothers, and Henry Carpender, her cousin, were arrested and indicted, Hearst's *American* played the case as a banner headline on nineteen days, and few editions of any papers lacked a mention of the case. Only Gertrude Ederle's conquest of the English Channel and Gene Tunney's knockout of Jack Dempsey edged Hall-Mills from the front pages.

As the trial date neared, the papers published grisly details of the exhumation of the bodies, vows by the prosecutors to get the real truth this time, photos of James Mills praying beside his wife's grave and "explanations" of the crime by ministers, doctors, and psychiatrists. Meanwhile, thousands of *Graphic* readers sent in their solutions—in fifty words or less.

Act Two

As the trial got underway, the *Mirror* crowed in an editorial about reviving the case: "It was not until the independent, fearless, intelligent, unpurchasable press began to function according to original principles that the masks were torn away and the majesty of the law tardily rose from the dust in New Jersey."[24] Many journalists were more cynical. A California editor thought the trial a total waste but conceded "Americans must have their favorite sport, which is not baseball but murder trials."[25]

Nearly 400 reporters scrambled for the 130 seats set aside for the press in the Somerset courtroom. The trial judge allowed ten photographers at a time to prowl the courtroom, while another forty took pictures outside. The *Daily News* assigned sixteen photographers and reporters, including the diminutive Grace Robinson, who covered most of the era's big crimes and trials.[26] The *Mirror* sent thirteen. The staid *Times* sent sixteen, an indication of the widespread interest in the trial. Damon Runyon was there for his syndicate,[27] and so were "specials," such as evangelist Billy Sunday. The presence in the press section of mystery writer Mary Roberts Rinehart and novelist Theodore Drieser further blurred the line between fiction and nonfiction. Sinclair Lewis and Eugene O'Neill had been approached to write about the trial but wanted too much money.[28]

The reporters beat the drums. The *Graphic*'s account on the first day began: "A suspense almost terrifying at times hung over the Somerset County Courthouse today when the Hall-Mills trial opened. Is Willie Stevens going to plead guilty to second-degree murder? Will Mrs. Jane Gibson, the Pig Woman, die before her testimony can be written into the record?"

Over a front-page sidebar story by a clergyman was the headline **HALL TRAGEDY SHOWS JUDGEMENT AWAITS ALL WHO SIN.**[29]

The holiday-like behavior of spectators who waited for hours for seats "nauseated" Charlotte Mills, retained as a correspondent by Famous Features Syndicate. With "assistance" from ghost writers, she provided daily accounts to twenty papers, including the _Mirror._ Her accounts included conversations with her mother's spirit.[30] The same syndicate distributed the memoirs of her father. In the third installment, he admitted he had no delusions about himself. "I'm just a plain, drab, ordinary man with simple tastes. Eleanor was different, and that was the thing that turned our married life into a tragedy."[31]

The story was front-page news in every newspaper in New York and throughout much of the nation. On the first day, the New York standards ran 12,000 to 20,000 words each. The _Times_ used a two-column, three-line headline with six decks on the front page, plus thirteen columns, five pictures, a map, and an editorial on the inside.[32] The _Mirror_ published 14,000 words, four times as many as the _Daily News._ The account in the _Mirror_ occupied the first thirteen pages that day.[33] During the rest of the four-week trial, the _Mirror_ gave it about one-third of its total news space. It published two long analyses by a psychiatrist, who traced both lovers' frustrations over producing no male heirs.[34] The _Times,_ the _World,_ the _Sun,_ the _Herald-Tribune,_ and the _Evening Post_ published several columns daily of transcript testimony, The _American_ and the _Journal_ usually illustrated their long accounts with three or four pictures. In the background of a photo of Mrs. Hall on the stand, _Journal_ artists sketched in the spirit of her dead husband. In a _Mirror_ composite, Willie was shown placing a calling card at the feet of the slain rector.[35]

The first two weeks were not very exciting as a parade of fingerprint, ballistic, and medical experts testified. One day on page one the _Mirror_ featured Charlotte Mills' tale of feeling the presence of her mother's ghost in the courtroom. "My mother's wounds cry out for justice!"[36]

The prosecutor was nonplussed when his key witness destroyed the murder motive he suggested for Mrs. Hall. The maid (whose husband had since dropped his request for an annulment) told the 1926 grand jury that Mrs. Hall had picked up the extension phone when the pair were planning their rendezvous, a few hours before their deaths. On the witness stand, the former maid said that Mrs. Hall hung up too quickly to hear their discussion. When the prosecutor asked why she had not told that part to the grand jury, the shapely brunette shrugged and said they never asked about it.[37]

The real drama came in the daily medical reports on the condition of the Pig Woman. One day she was at death's door and the next recovering nicely. The prosecution would not even reveal which private hospital she was in. As it should with any good mystery, the suspense built until on November 18 four state troopers carried in the Pig Woman on a stretcher. Amid exploding flash bulbs, Mrs. Gibson was transferred to a hospital bed that faced the jury. A physician checked her pulse, gravely nodded his approval and she was sworn in. The story she told in a quavering voice was much the same as the one she had told to two grand juries and countless law enforcement officials and newspaper reporters. Avid newspaper readers could have recited it almost as well as she.

Recognizing that the case rested on whether the jury believed her, the defense attorneys in cross-examination impugned both her veracity and her character. Her own mother called her a liar, and Mrs. Gibson seemed hazy on how many times she had been married and divorced.[38] As she finished her testimony, Jane Gibson rose on one elbow, glared at the defendants and screeched, "I have told the truth, so help me God, and you know I've told the truth!"

Runyon likened the scene to "attending a wake and having the dead suddenly begin talking in an out-of-the-grave sort of voice."[39]

The *Journal* devoted all of its first four pages to her testimony. The *Mirror*'s headline read: **DEFENSE MERCILESS TO JANE, DYING.** (She actually lived three more years.) The *Times* described her as "weak but defiant."[40] The *World* was not exaggerating when it wrote, "Never had a more theatrical day in court been staged."[41] Newspapers from coast to coast published her picture.

The Jersey City hospital to which she returned reported Mrs. Gibson was doing "remarkably well." She delighted in the floral bouquets (including one from Charlotte Mills) and fruit baskets that filled her room. Congratulatory letters and cards poured in. "It was a wonderful thing," the Pig Woman told visitors, "to go down there when I was needed."[42]

The rest of the trial was anticlimax. All the defendants, including the slightly addled Willie, retained their composure under intense questioning. He insisted he had retired early the night of the murders and that Reverend Hall was a dear friend. Runyon said that even if, as the prosecution charged, Willie had been carefully coached before he took the stand, he made a strong witness for the defense.[43]

Day after day, Mrs. Hall sat in the courtroom, her expression seldom changing. What novelist Fannie Hurst, a Universal Press special writer, praised as dignified bearing,[44] others interpreted as cold indifference. Her testimony was exactly as it had been for four years, prompting columnist Dorothy Dix to suggest she lied like a lady. "If there is ever a lie on which the recording angel drops a tear that blots it out, it is the one a wife tells to cover up her husband's deficiencies."[45]

As the lawyers made their summary arguments, Runyon estimated the odds on acquittal at one hundred to one.[46] Even the prosecutor told reporters he expected a speedy acquittal but that he would file for a mistrial.[47] (Among other grounds, he said three jurors had slept through some of the testimony. Although they had heard testimony that filled 500 pages, the jury returned after only five hours. As soon as the foreman sounded his third "Not Guilty" the reporters raced for the doors.[48] Jurymen later said the vote on the first ballot had been ten to two for acquittal, the second unanimous. The jurors simply did not believe the Pig Woman. One said, "I would rather remain here for thirty years than vote a verdict of guilty on such evidence."[49]

Despite her well-known aversion to cameras, Mrs. Hall posed willingly on her front steps when she returned to New Brunswick. "I cannot tell you how happy I am," she said.[50] Informed of the verdict, Mrs. Gibson expressed dismay. Charlotte Mills was furious, but she soon found a way to capitalize on her fame by accepting an offer to play herself in a drama based on the case.

After the Curtain

At the curtain, there was little applause for either the case or its coverage. The *Mirror* and the *Daily News* denounced the verdict, but editorials in the other New York dailies generally approved. The *Times* conceded that even if "Jersey Justice" could not always find the guilty, at least it could acquit the innocent.[51] No mistrial was granted, and the state showed no interest in reopening the investigation.

To the surprise of many observers, studies showed that the standard papers had printed more words about the case than the tabloids; of course, the standards had bigger news holes. One count showed the *Times* published 338,000 words, more than twice the total in the *Daily News*.[52]

Bruce Blivin wrote in the *New Republic*: "Not only did a single paper, half size at that, reach into New Jersey from across the river, like an instant Hercules reopen Pandora's Box so that Anteus might rise again (good tabloid mythology); not only has the case been tried in the newspapers even more casually and irresponsibly than in Somerset, no mean achievement," but that reporters had filed millions of words to say, in effect, nothing much has happened."[53] (Estimates ran from five to fifteen million words.) It drew twice as many reporters as had the Scopes "Monkey Trial" the summer before.

The *Graphic* flayed the *Mirror* "which, for the purposes of circulation, caused an innocent woman and three of her menfolk to be arrested."[54] The *Mirror* apologized in an editorial for excesses of "partisan reporting" arising out of its zeal to see justice done. The *Daily News* thought its extensive coverage justified. Compared with the Browning divorce, it had been a "nice, clean case."[55] Not, of course, from the viewpoint of the Halls, who sued the *Mirror* for $500,000 each under civil libel, later adding suits against the *Journal* and Hearst personally. They accepted an undisclosed out-of-court settlement (rumored to be $20,000 each) in December 1928. By then editor Phillip Payne of the *Mirror* was dead, the victim of an airplane crash. Hearst sold the tabloid during the Depression, but under various owners it survived until 1965. By then all the featured players from the Hall-Mills drama were long dead.

Who really killed the pastor and the choir singer that night in 1922? There have been speculations. William Kunstler, a noted criminal attorney, sifted the evidence forty years later and put the blame on the Ku Klux Klan. He concluded the Halls had solid alibis and were not the sort of people who murdered to solve their problems. He found no one else with enough motivation. As he said, it was a ritual killing and thieves would not have arranged the murder scene so carefully. Because the Invisible Empire was quite active in that part of New Jersey and disciplined other wayward clergymen,[56] Kunstler's Klan theory makes sense, but not to Mary Hartman, a historian of crime who happens now to live in the Hall residence. She is persuaded by the confession of a dying man in 1970 that on the day after the murders he delivered $6,000 from Mrs. Hall to two local hoodlums. While the man claimed he knew nothing about the arrangements, he said Willie Stevens had tried earlier to recruit him in a plan to get rid of the minister. The old man passed two polygraph tests before he died.[57] Dr. Hartman also believes that because the sleazy Pig Woman offended the middle-class jurors, they refused to take her testimony seriously.

Whatever the reality behind the deed, the case fueled old concerns about excessive crime news, not only from outside critics but among journalists themselves. Stanley Walker, a leading journalist of the era, wrote:

> In any event, the conduct of the *Mirror* and Payne, which might have been defended as "vigorous, crusading journalism," if the evidence had stood up, brought general public condemnation upon the tabloids. It gave tabloids a bad name from which they still suffer. It gave the "reporter-detective" a black eye. It disgusted the press with the sensational press generally, and even affected the esteem in which all the press was held.[58]

Although nearly forgotten today, Hall-Mills was one of the greatest murder cases of the twentieth century. It had a great opening scene, a minister found murdered beside his paramour. It had a flamboyant cast of characters. Above all, it had suspense and remained a mystery even after the curtain. Hooked on such vicarious excitement, newspaper readers clamored for more. As a writer in *Harpers* predicted, the press quickly found for them a new "crime of the century."[59] The sordid little murder that occurred in March 1927 in a Long Island bungalow had a less interesting cast than Hall-Mills and no suspense, but sequels usually are inferior.

THE SEQUEL: SNYDER-GRAY

On March 20, 1927, Ruth Synder and her lover, Judd Gray, bashed in the skull of her husband, an artist in an advertising agency, with a window sash weight. Arrested almost immediately, their clumsy cover stories collapsed under questioning, and they both confessed. A month later they were on trial for first-degree murder.

As an *Evening Post* columnist complained, the Snyder murder was "not really first-rate."[60] Reporters tried to build interest by dubbing it The Dumbbell Murder, but the name never caught on. They were happy that at least it had adultery.

Gray was as dull as his name, but the press did its best to glamorize his accomplice. Writers called her beautiful and mysterious, but photos showed an unremarkable bleached blond who would not turn a head on the street. (Damon Runyon called her "a chilly looking blonde with frosty eyes and one of those marble, you-bet-you-will chins.") She was depicted as the one who planned the killing, which considering its ineptitude, was no great compliment. The real subtext was that she was likely to be the first woman ever to die in the electric chair. Gray was her dupe, described by Runyon as "an inert, scare-drunk fellow that you couldn't miss among any hundred men as a dead setup for a blonde, or the shell game, or maybe a gold brick." Here there was no disguising the love triangle and lust factors. Humdrum defendants could be an advantage, since far more readers knew folks like Ruth Snyder and Judd Gray than the snooty Halls.

During the three weeks from arrest to trial, the *Journal* devoted 4070 inches to the case, which represented 5.5 percent of its newshole, a higher percentage than the *Mirror* (5 percent), the *Graphic* (4.2 percent) or the *Daily News* (4 percent). The *Daily News* reprised the case in comic-strip form for its readers.[61] Many of the stories were generated by reporters who goaded one defendant by relaying what the other allegedly had said. Because Mrs. Snyder and Gray were denied all direct communication, the tactic worked well. The *Daily News* turned down first-person series written from Sing-Sing by both Mrs. Snyder and Gray.[62]

On the opening day, fifteen Western Union operators transmitted 62,711 words from the two press rooms.[63] There was no other story in the first fourteen pages of the *Daily News* on May 6. There were fewer sob sisters in the press section. Although the judge barred photographers from the courtroom, the dozen waited on the steps. Even more than with Hall-Mills, photos were the mainstay of the coverage. The tabloids and the Hearst standards ran eight to ten a day, including many of Mrs. Snyder behind bars. Perhaps the low point was a front-page photo in the *Daily News* of nine-year-old Lorraine Gray sending a Mother's Day card.[64] Although photographers dogged the little girl's every move, Judd Gray's photo seldom appeared.

The quick trial went according to script, and the jury needed only seventy-one minutes to find both defendants guilty.[65] On January 13 (Friday the thirteenth), they both died in the electric chair. The *Daily News'* smuggled photo of the death of Mrs. Snyder is a classic.[66] As with the Hall-Mills case, there was a play; however, *Illicit Love* died during its preview run in the Bronx.[67]

Spurred by demands from bar and civic groups for legal curbs on press coverage of crime, newspapers promised to do better. In an attempt to distance themselves from the flashier papers, the twenty-five newspapers in the Scripps-Howard chain bragged in ad in *Saturday Evening Post* that they employed no sob sisters and printed no brutal pictures "to wring the last circulation penny from the salacious and emotional aspects of the case."[68]

Although the crime rate remained unchanged, crime news soon tapered off, the front pages of the tabloids paling from crimson to pink. Editors sensed readers were tired of crime and scandal and pointed to the hysteria that greeted Charles Lindbergh's solo flight across the Atlantic in the spring of 1927. As one social historian put it, the flight "gave the American people a glimpse of what they liked to think themselves to be at a time when they feared they had deserted their own vision of themselves."[69] In a record no murder ever matched, Lindbergh's flight was on the front pages of New York dailies for thirty straight days.[70] It also inspired more than twenty popular songs, the most successful of which was "Lucky Lindy."[71] The public loved the modest, wholesome farm boy who, by turning down stage and movie offers, refused to cash in on his fame.[72] As the Crash of 1929 further sobered the nation (**WALL STREET LAYS AN EGG** was the *Variety* headline), newspaper sensationalism was reduced even further. But with a rhythm as eternal as the moon and the tides, it would return.

14

In the Tradition:
Supermarket Tabloids

Today, as always, the public thinks its newspapers are sensational. Pressed for examples, people will cite some sex crime that the newspapers "blew out of proportion." As we have seen, modern critics equate sensationalism with display and emphasis. In truth, today's daily newspapers are pretty tame, which is precisely why each week the supermarket tabloids sell millions of copies. Freed of any obligation to cover the news, the tabs ladle up what ordinary dailies sprinkle on as a garnish.

They are Bennett's heirs. Like his *Herald,* they print what respectable competitors turn up their noses at. They have redefined the boundary between what is public and what is private. Like the yellow press, they exploit the sensational angle in any story. As jingoistic as Pulitzer and Hearst ever were, their editorial slant is almost reactionary. Like the tabloids of the 1920s, they tell their stories primarily through headlines and photos (lots of cheesecake but no nudity.) Their "dumbed down" writing style certainly is colloquial. Thus they meet George Juergens' criteria (outlined in the first chapter) for sensationalism. [1]

The crucial distinction is that these tabs are not really newspapers at all; they are weekly or biweekly magazines that appear in newspaper format. In this they are like *Rolling Stone* or the *Village Voice*. Unlike the *Daily News, Post,* and *Newsday,* they make no pretense of covering the news. Even Macfadden's *Graphic* had *some* news. Another difference is that these papers have no sense of place. The papers discussed in earlier periods were all products of New York City, and much of their content reflected that milieu. The supermarket tabs are published in Florida and mostly by veterans of British tabloidism. Not one reader in 10,000 could name the editor of *National Enquirer.*

Few stories run longer than 12 inches and can be read in a couple of minutes. The prose is third-grade level and peppered with slang. Their advertisers include psychics, diet plans, and get-rich-quick schemes.

Their audience buys them for what is not in the other papers. Much of the content of the six garish tabloids at the checkout lines—the *National Enquirer, National Examiner, Sun, Star, Globe,* and *Weekly World News*—is pseudoscience, miraculous and monstrous births, the occult, and scandals. They also pander to the obsession of today's public with celebrities and miracle diets.

If they shock readers less than their predecessors, it is not for lack of trying. Their publishers want to provoke, to titillate, to get noticed. Perhaps in the late twentieth century, we are too blasé or too satiated to pay much attention. The rare obscenity actions are almost all against movies, not print media. The tabs fight off libel suits, but those do not arise out of *societal* outrage but merely the wrath of individuals who believe they have been victimized.

Although at one time the *National Enquirer* featured gore **(I RIPPED OUT HER HEART AND STOMPED ON IT)**, it toned down when it went for the female food shopper. So did *Midnight,* which evolved into the present *Globe.* Gruesome photos of death crashes and murder victims gave way to diets, horoscopes, and gossip about soap opera stars.

The *Enquirer* later spun off *Weekly World News* (WWN) as Globe Communications did the *Sun.* These two are the most bizarre. They reportedly have the greatest popularity among male readers, which may also explain why they run more photos of muscular wrestlers and actors like Arnold Schwarzenegger. Typical WWN headlines: **MAN BURIED AT SEA IN 1926 FOUND ALIVE** and **ADAM AND EVE FOUND IN ASIA.** The *Sun* has published such gems as **WOMAN WHO DIED SIX TIMES COMES TO LIFE IN MORGUE** and **COUNT DRACULA'S GRAVE FOUND GUARDED BY BATS.** These papers specialize, as did Pulitzer on his first day in New York, in finding small wire stories and embellishing them. Pulitzer used a bomb in Haiti; WWN and the *Sun* prefer attacks by killer bees, alligators, pit bulls or sharks. Today's tabs often add (unverifiable) details and stock photos. Most events seem to occur in remote regions of the world. Jungles and mountains of South America are favorite sites.

A 1988 story in WWN echoed the Guldenseppe murder of a century before. Police charged a Las Vegas man with chopping off the head of a victim and tossing it onto his victim's front lawn. Unlike Pulitzer or Hearst, the tabloid editors published a photo of the grisly find.

Given their emphasis, the tabloids might revive the standing headline some early American papers ran above improbable stories: Interesting, If True. The tabs dote on monsters and the supernatural. Bigfoot is the favorite. WWN even published a photo of Bigfoot's baby, allegedly captured in 1989 in a remote corner of China. There are many tales of weird aquatic beasts, such as a story about the recovery of an enormous dorsal fin off Indonesia. WWN illustrated the story with an artist's conception of a 300-foot prehistoric monster. The story quoted a Singapore expert, "It is truly the single greatest discovery in scientific history." Quite a claim. Haunted houses, messages from beyond the grave, and exorcisms are standard fare. Families often flee houses where things go bang in the night or when they are harrassed by ghostly visitors. One lucky fellow was haunted by a nude Marilyn Monroe. A dead husband communicated with his wife through the set of false teeth he left behind. He only did this when she was alone, never when others were present. Two children killed in an accident assured their mother that they were happy in Heaven.

Although most of the papers devote much space to celebrities, none comes close to matching Rupert Murdoch's *Star*. So much of its space is given over to television and show business personalities; that for all practical purposes, it is another fan magazine. Rumors of romances or divorces are treated with the same rapt attention the London tabloids reserve for the Royal Family. Jackie Kennedy is, of course, always front-page news. The *National Enquirer*'s largest sale came the week it published a photo of Elvis Presley in his casket.

One category of news was not found in earlier eras. That is visits by space aliens. In 1987, WWN reported **UFO RAISED FROM DEVIL'S TRIANGLE,** uniting two favorite tabloid themes, which while new are in the best pseudoscience tradition of the Sunday supplements of Pulitzer and Hearst. In 1988 the *Sun* (ironically the same name as Benjamin Day's penny paper) reported Noah's Ark really had been a UFO. According to a WWN "exclusive," Soviet doctors delivered the alien baby of an extraterrestrial rescued from the wreckage of a starship in July 1989. When the same tabloid missed with its prediction that flying saucers would land during a televised Monday night football game, the paper said the UFOs had been scared off by the Goodyear blimp; it did not explain what was so scary about the blimp.

Perhaps no story better epitomizes the affinity between pseudoscience and the media than one in the *Weekly World News* in February 1989: **SPACE ALIEN NEWSPAPER FOUND AT UFO SITE!** A Bolivian scientist had translated the violent and depressing stories in a "newspaper" found by a farmer after a close encounter with a UFO.

> **"This proves beyond doubt that extraterrestrials are visiting Earth and have much the same interest in news events that we do," Dr. Canelas told newsmen. "The newspaper itself is circular and printed on a thin white metal that has been tested by experts who say it is unlike anything on Earth and obviously came from another planet.**
>
> **"I simply cannot overstate the significance of this newspaper," the scientist continued. "The stories concern events that have happened on 22 different planets. This is a clear indication that extraterrestrial life is thriving all over the universe."**

Stories told of a drought on one planet, a death-battle between two creatures on another, and a UFO collision. (Apparently interest in sensationalism really *is* universal.) The doctor said the stories were written in a simple mathematical code that "is almost surely a universal language." The stories were etched within grooves like those on a record album. Although the story reported experts from around the world were planning to fly to Bolivia to inspect the newspaper firsthand, nothing more was heard of the story.

Six months later, the same paper reported a woman in Switzerland had videotaped seven minutes of a program from outer space. The tape allegedly showed bug-eyed humanoids clicking and squealing noises like dolphins. A scientist was quoted as saying sunspots may have diverted the signal. A French astrophysicist said the tape "if genuine" could offer the strongest proof to date of life in outer space.

Like story-tellers of every era, the supermarket tabloids dote on freak births. The *Sun* in 1988 claimed a woman had artificially inseminated herself, using three men (two of them priests). WWN reported in 1989 that "adorable little Tiffany Yorks" had survived a year with her legs joined but that doctors finally had saved the "mermaid baby." In addition to tales of Siamese twins and children born with tails or weighing only a few ounces, there are often accounts of children or grannies giving birth. A typical headline from the *Sun*: **"GRANNY, 87, EXPECTING 62ND BABY BY TEEN LOVER.** Longevity is another favorite topic, as it was in the almanacs of old. In 1989 the *National Examiner* described a woman, 114, who had no wrinkles, thanks to daily rubs with olive oil. A woman claimed in 1989 to be the widow of Jack the Ripper, who terrorized London a century earlier. An ex-poultryman, 106, was "still eyeing the chicks."

Tab columnists tend to be staunchly conservative and nationalistic, none more so than WWN's Ed Anger, who urges castration of "sand-sucking terrorists" and slow slicing up in public of flag burners. Anyone favoring gun control is an "anti-American wimp." He got 35,000 readers to sign petitions urging President Bush to pardon Oliver North after his conviction in the Iran-Contra affair.

TABS AND URBAN LEGENDS

Many stories in the supermarket tabloids are no more than variations on familiar urban legends, contemporary folk tales such as the alligators in the New York sewers, or the car thief who did not know there was a dead grandmother in the trunk. Urban legends are always reported as fact; often they happened to a friend of a friend (FOAF, to folklorists). Many professional folklorists have come to recognize that myths, tales, and legends are circulated by the mass media, often in their attempts to debunk rumors. With remarkable speed, the same stories pop up all over the nation and sometimes the world, sped along in conversations, news accounts, and even by office copiers and computer bulletin boards.

The foremost American authority is Jan Harold Brunvand of the University of Utah, who has published four collections[2] and writes a syndicated newspaper column. He reported that in 1988 one of the wire services was gulled into reporting as fact the old exploding toilet legend. In a typical version a fellow enters the bathroom just after painting the room, his wife has dropped the leftover thinner in the toilet. He sits down, strikes a match to light a cigaret and is blasted several feet. The story has been told and printed all over the world for at least a quarter-century, but there is no evidence it ever really happened. After printing the wire service story, several reputable newspapers ran corrections, but a supermarket tabloid not only defended the veracity of the story but promised to print the proof. Of course, it never did.[3]

It is a rare issue that does not include at least one bizarre story about food, a standard theme in urban legends. There is a hoary legend about injesting snake eggs while drinking in a stream and having the reptiles mature in the host's stomach. Brunvand writes that although this is one of the most ancient of legends, it never happened. It is a similar motif to the

Sun story in 1988 that told of a Mexican's awful experience after swallowing melon seeds.

> **Stunned doctors have confirmed that a man who swallowed a mouthful of melon seeds during the course of a few days last summer now has a melon growing in his stomach.**

Like most stories in the supermarket tabloids, no exact location was given.

With striking regularity, the tabloids report on people who burst into flame and within seconds are reduced to ashes. "We don't know what to make of it," a researcher told WWN about a report that a kissing couple had self-detonated in an Austrian shopping mall. No wonder, since scientists have yet to document such a case.

WHAT THE TABS TRY TO DO

Mike Nevard, editorial director of the *Globe,* wrote that although the covers are aimed at women, who buy the tabloids, stories are selected for every member of the family. His comment that "we aim to catch those who watch the most popular TV shows,"[4] is but a slight paraphrase from the observation by Juergens:

> Bennett and Day before, as surely as Hearst and Patterson after, understood that the goal of sensational journalism is to catch the interest, even to titillate, the vast body of men and women who for one reason or another are unconcerned with happenings in government, business and the arts.[5]

Like his predecessors, the *Globe* editor argues his paper communicates with, rather than panders to, readers: "The tabloids—all of them—are popular because their editors know what the public is interested in and gives it to them." Publishers of broadsides also said they were giving the public what it demanded.

"We hope that our readers feel better when they get to the end of a tabloid than when they opened it," says Nevard. All six tabs print more upbeat stories than scares. For example WWN readers were told that a land of eternal youth has been discovered, deep in the jungle of Brazil. (On the other hand, the Amazon explorer quoted in the *Sun* found a race of monkeymen.) Space invaders generally are depicted as friendly. The psychics seem always to foresee good things. Countess Sophia reassures letter writers to WWN that their loved ones are in Heaven. As she assured

"Late" in Roanoke, "Everything happens for the best." The *Examiner* psychic reportedly receives several thousand letters a week.

Miracle diets are published frequently. One need only eat nothing for a few days except hot dogs, or popcorn, or Twinkies. None of them ever involve exercise or will power.

One would think readers eventually would wonder why the stories never appeared in standard media. But then, 3000 people pay $20 a year to support the Flat Earth Research Society in its efforts to expose the widespread conspiracy to treat the world as round. Tabloid readers know all about such conspiracies.

"I found this parallel universe—its like ours but with more gusto—while waiting in a supermarket checkout line," wrote a feature writer in *Smithsonian* magazine. He learned Tabloidworld had no problems with national debt, ecological blight, or nuclear tension but was overrun with invaders from outer space, vampires, and above all, exclamation points. Like many another who happened in, he found Tabloidworld an amusing diversion.[6] He took them no more seriously than have many—perhaps most—Americans of many eras who lay down their coins for the escapism provided by sensational papers.

Notes

1. "The More Things Change..."

1. Colin Wilson and Donald Seaman, *An Encyclopedia of Scandal,* p. 9.
2. Emile Durkheim, *The Rules of Sociological Method.*
3. Shelley Ross, *Fall From Grace,* p. xviii.
4. Mitchell Stephens, *A History of News,* p. 114.
5. Frank Luther Mott, *American Journalism,* p. 442; Edwin and Michael Emery, *The Press and America,* p. 119.
6. Joyce Milton, *The Yellow Kids,* p. 14.
7. Jack Korty, "What Makes Crime News?" A classic analysis of the appeal of crime news is Helen M. Hughes, *News and the Human Interest Story.*
8. George Juergens, *Joseph Pulitzer and the New York World,* pp. viii–ix.
9. Warren Francke, "An Argument in Defense of Sensationalism."
10. Joseph R. Dominick, "Crime and Law Enforcement in the Mass Media," in Charles Winick, ed., *Deviance and Mass Media,* pp. 105–07; Stanford Sherizen, "Social Creation of Crime News: All the News Fitted to Print," in Winick, pp. 223–34; James Garofalo, "Crime and the Mass Media: a Selective Review of Research," *Journal of Research in Crime and Delinquency* (1981), pp. 319–50; B. Roshier,

"The Selection of Crime News by the Press," in Stanley Cohen and Jock Young, eds., *The Manufacture of News*, pp. 28–39; W. Clinton Terry III, "Crime and the News," in Ray Surette, ed., *Justice and the Media*, pp. 31–50.

11. P. M. Pickard, *I Could a Tale Untold*, pp. 160–61.

12. Joseph Frank, *The Beginnings of the English Newspaper*.

13. Bernard Capp, *English Almanacs 1500–1800*.

14. Lise Andries, "Almanacs: Revolutionizing a Traditional Genre," in Robert Darnton and Daniel Roche, eds., *Revolution in Print*, p. 213.

15. Simon Schama, *Citizens*, pp. 174–75, 225–26.

16. *The Tattler*, May 21, 1709.

17. Marjorie Plant, *The English Book Trade*, pp. 114–15.

18. Lincoln B. Faller, *Turned to Account*.

19. Ted Peterson, "British Crime Pamphleteers: Forgotten Journalists"; Peterson, "James Catnach: Master of Street Literature."

20. Thomas Boyle, *Black Swine in the Sewers of Hampstead*, pp. 42–45.

21. Deborah Cameron and Elizabeth Frazier, *The Lust to Kill*, p. 38.

22. Gershon Legman, quoted in Garth S. Jowett, Penny Reath and Monica Schouten, "The Control of Mass Entertainment Media in Canada, the United States and Great Britain: Historical Surveys," in *Violence in Print and Media* (Toronto: Royal Commission on Violence, 1976), p. 4.

23. David P. Nord, "Teleology and News."

24. Cited in W. S. Lilly, "The Ethics of Journalism."

25. Ronald A. Bosco, "Lectures in the Pillory."

2. New York, Crime, and the Newspapers

1. Robert G. Albion, *The Rise of the New York Port*, pp. 235–36.

2. M. Wayne Thomas, "Walt Whitman and Mannahatta-New York."

3. Kenneth T. Jackson and Stanley K. Schultz, eds., *Cities in American History*, pp. 114–15.

4. *The Writings of Thomas Jefferson* 15 (Washington: Thomas Jefferson Memorial Association, 1907), p. 469.

5. The new social sciences of the late nineteenth and early twentieth centuries, and especially the sociology championed by the "Chicago School," reinforced hoary anticity views. Robert E. Park and his followers found that traditional social controls broke down in big cities. In the transition from community to metropolis, police and courts were inadequate substitutes for families as teachers of values. They concluded that urban growth meant more crime, vice, suicides, diseases, and insanity. Statistical comparisons of rural and urban areas undergirded all these conclusions. In sociology, in history and in the public's mind, cities were necessary evils. When in the 1970s scholars reexamined these premises, they found little to support Park in his insistence that city size and impersonality explained violent disorder. For decades researchers had relied on official figures without recognizing that law enforcement agencies categorize events for their own reasons. Some information was inaccurate; all of it was based on ever-changing definitions. See Roger Lane, "Urbanization and Criminal Violence in the 19th Century: Massachusetts as a Test

Case," In Hugh D. Graham and Ted R. Gurr, eds., *The History of Violence in America*, pp. 468–84.

6. James F. Richardson, "To Control the City," in Jackson and Schultz, pp. 272–73; Paul A. Gilje, *The Road to Mobocracy*, pp. 278–82.

7. James F. Richardson, *The New York Police*, pp. 17–22.

8. Richardson, p. 26; unpublished report by Kenneth Conboy for Prof. Kenneth Jackson; *Herald*, February 15, 1840.

9. Morton and Lucia White, *The Intellectual Versus the City;* Adrienne Siegel, *The Image of the American City in Popular Literature, 1820–1870;* Charles N. Glaab, "The Historian and the Urban Tradition."

10. Recent historical scholarship on literacy is summarized in a special issue of *Communication* (1988), 11(1).

11. Charles Tilley, "Collective Violence in European Perspective," in Graham and Gurr, p. 484; Michael Feldberg, *The Turbulent Era;* pp. 1–120.

12. Gilje, p. 205.

13. Edward Pessen, *Jacksonian America*, pp. 77–101.

14. Thomas C. Cochran, *200 Years of American Business*, p. 29.

15. The birth rate (55 per 1000) was double that of the 1960s "Baby Boom" and rivaled those in less developed nations in the 1980s. Harry N. Scheiber, Harold G. Vatter, and Harold U. Faulkner, *American Economic History*, p. 170.

16. William V. Shannon, *The American Irish*, pp. 1–41.

17. Daniel E. Sutherland, *Americans and Their Servants*, pp. 30–40.

18. Allan Nevins, ed., *The Diary of Phillip Hone*, p. 190.

19. Gilje, pp. 139–42.

20. For an account of the most publicized disclosures, those of Maria Monk, see chapter 3.

21. Gilje, pp. 162–70.

22. Allan R. Pred, *Urban Growth and the Circulation of Information*, p. 59.

23. Alexis de Tocqueville, *Democracy in America*, p. 52.

24. Cash books for the New York *Evening Star* indicate that from 1833 through 1835, only rarely did daily individual sales exceed 100 copies; the average was nearer fifty. Manuscript collection of the New-York Historical Society. There are no known records for other New York papers of the period.

25. Schudson suggested the penny papers "invented" news, which was in sharp contrast to the opinion matter in the six-cent papers. *Discovering the News*, pp. 3–4. In contrast, Stephens emphasized the continuity through the centuries from oral to printed reports in *A History of News*.

26. Thomas C. Leonard, *Power of the Press*, pp. 142–43; *Niles' Weekly Register*, March 27, 1824.

27. Total story: "The trial of John Williams, the oculist, before the Circuit Court in Washington has resulted in his acquital." *American*, January 11, 1837.

28. Albion, pp. 256–57.

29. *Journal of Commerce*, April 29, 1831.

3. A Press for the Masses (Sort of)

1. Merle Curti, *The Growth of American Thought*, p. 347.

2. Lee Soltow and Edward Stevens, *The Rise of Literacy and the Common School in the United States;* The term "preordained" is used in Russell Nye, *Society and Culture in America*, p. 367.

3. A less gracious but more accurate term, since many of the new breed of papers sold for more than one cent. There were a few workingmen's papers earlier. These were distributed free or at very low cost by early unions and seldom survived for long.

4. Anthony Smith, *The Newspaper: An International History;* Marshall MacLuhan, *Understanding Media.* Of course, technological determinists do not see it as a coincidence.

5. Day shared these characteristics with most of the publishers who began cheap papers in New York and other cities before 1837; however, James Gordon Bennett was an exception. Alexander Saxton, "Problems of Class and Rank in the Origins of the Mass Circulation Press."

6. John Nerone, "The Mythology of the Penny Press."

7. "A dozen a year" were established during the 1830s in New York, according to Frank M. O'Brien, *The Story of the Sun,* pp. 84–85. There were "scores" of them, according to Saxton, p. 216.

8. *Working Man's Advocate,* November 17, 1832. Unfortunately, the article did not list the papers or the cities. Major research libraries have no copies.

9. The many biographies of Greeley are so uncritical one may as well rely on his autobiography, *Recollections of a Busy Life.*

10. Dan Schiller, *Objectivity and the News;* Saxton, pp. 220–30.

11. Willard G. Bleyer, *Main Currents in the History of American Journalism,* pp. 155–156; Mitchell Stephens, *A History of News,* pp. 204–07; Soltow and Stevens, pp. 147–90.

12. Quoted in Silas Bent, *Ballyhoo,* p. 50.

13. Even in 1840, less than 9 percent of the workforce was in manufacturing. Statistics for clerks are less exact, but they certainly were increasing rapidly. Walter Hugins, *Jacksonian Democracy and the Working Class,* pp. 51–52.

14. Robert Ernst, *Immigrant Life in New York City,* p. 96.

15. The *Working Man's Advocate* claimed a huge weekly circulation by the late 1820s, as did some of the Irish nationalist weeklies; however, most copies were distributed free or through labor and church organizations.

16. Thomas C. Cochran and William Miller, *The Age of Enterprise,* pp. 28–29. Even in the 1840s, clerk salaries seldom exceeded $300 a year, according to Ernst, p. 96.

17. *New Era,* October 3, 1836; *Herald,* July 14, 1836.

18. Robert E. Park, *The Immigrant Press and Its Control,* p. 14; Paul J. Folk, *Pioneer Catholic Journalism,* pp. 12–43; Ernst, pp. 150–55.

19. O'Brien, p. 49.

20. A Journalist [Isaac C. Pray], *Memoirs of James Gordon Bennett and His Times,* pp. 181–82. Literary examples include *Jemmy Daily; or the Little News*

Vendor (1843) and *The Newsboy* (1854). Horatio Alger featured news vendors in *Ragged Dick* (1868) and *Ben, the Luggage Boy* (1870).

21. Howard B. Rock, *Artisans of the New Republic*, p. 158.
22. Michael Schudson, *Discovering the News*, pp. 18–20.
23. James S. Bradshaw, "George W. Wisner and the New York Sun."
24. *Sun*, May 19, October 23, 1833.
25. *Sun*, October 9, 1834.
26. The city's most notorious slum and center of vice.
27. *Sun*, May 16, 1835.
28. For example, the *Transcript* used dialect to report a dispute between rival French chefs, August 28, 1835, and recounted the outcome of nineteen cases in one forty-seven-line story, October 31, 1835. The *Man* devoted more space than the other small papers to both partisan politics and labor meetings.
29. *Herald*, March 17, 1836.
30. Pray, p. 183.
31. Seymour M. Lipset (ed.), *Harriet Martineau's Society in America*, p. 104.
32. Thomas C. Hamilton, *Men and Manners in America*.
33. *Sun*, June 8, 1834.
34. Allen R. Steinberg, "The Criminal Courts and the Transformation of Criminal Justice in Philadelphia, 1814–1874," pp. 73–78; Schiller also makes this argument.
35. *Sun*, August 6, 1834.
36. *Sun*, May 6, 1835; June 28, 1838.
37. *Sun*, August 25–29, 1835.
38. Bleyer, p. 162.
39. *Evening Post*, August 28, September 1, 1835.
40. *Herald*, August 29, September 3, 1835.
41. In 1844, the *Sun* created far less stir with its faked stories about an Atlantic crossing by a balloonist. *Sun*, April 13, 1844.
42. *Sun*, July 21, 1834.
43. *American*, January 27, 1838; *Sun*, January 26, 1835.
44. Phillip Hone Diary, October 5, 1835. See also Allan Nevins, ed., *The Diary of Phillip Hone*, p. 179.
45. Edwin and Michael Emery, *The Press and America*, p. 119.
46. Jean Folkerts and Dwight L. Teeter, *Voices of a Nation*, p. 138.
47. Saxton, p. 220.
48. Donald L. Shaw, "At the Crossroads: Change and Continuity in American Press News, 1820–1860."
49. Nerone, p. 377.

4. Bennett and His Damned *Herald*

1. Oliver Carlson, *The Man Who Made News: James Gordon Bennett*, pp. 74–117; Wallace Eberhard, "Mr. Bennett Covers a Murder Trial."
2. *Life and Adventures of Editor Bombast*.
3. Quoted in Gary Giddins, *Satchmo* (New York: Doubleday, 1988), p. 102.

4. James L. Crouthamel, *Bennett's New York Herald and the Rise of the Popular Press,* pp. x–xi.

5. A Journalist [Isaac C. Pray], *Memoirs of James Gordon Bennett and His Times.*

6. Pray, p. 134.

7. Robert K. Stewart, "Jacksonians Discipline a Party Editor: Economic Leverage and Political Exile."

8. *Herald,* October 26, 1836.

9. Crouthamel, pp. 69–111.

10. Douglas Fermer, *James Gordon Bennett and the New York Herald,* pp. 83–125.

11. *Herald,* March 26, 1856.

12. Fermer, pp. 44–82; Crouthamel, pp. 56–68.

13. *Herald,* August 30, 1836.

14. Philip S. Foner, *History of the Labor Movement in the United States,* pp. 118–20.

15. Crouthamel, pp. 96–97.

16. Fermer, pp. 106–227; Crouthamel, pp. 69–73.

17. *Herald,* July 19, 1836.

18. Russell Nye, *Society and Culture in America,* p. 53; Richard O'Connor, *The Scandalous Mr. Bennett,* pp. 25–26; Fermer, pp. 67–68.

19. *Herald,* April 4, December 19, 1836.

20. *Herald,* August 19, 1836.

21. Carlson, p. 168.

22. *Herald,* February 15, 1836.

23. *Life and Writings of James Gordon Bennett.*

24. *Herald,* July 5, 1836.

25. *Herald,* December 17–26, 1835.

26. R. Smith Schuneman, "Art or Photography: A Question for Newspaper Editors of the 1890s."

27. *Herald,* February 3, 1836.

28. Richard A. Schwarzlose, *The Nation's Newsbrokers,* vol. 1, chapter 3; Carlson, pp. 191–231.

29. Quoted in O'Connor, p. 21.

30. Allan Nevins, ed., *The Diary of Phillip Hone,* p. 195.

31. Ray A. Billington, *The Protestant Crusade, 1830–1860,* p. 67; John Cogley, *Catholic America,* pp. 42–43.

32. Billington, pp. 85–89.

33. Frederick Marryatt, *A Diary in America.*

34. Billington, pp. 101–02.

35. *Herald,* March 1, 1836. Note that this is several weeks *before* the interview with the madam, discussed in chapter 5.

36. *Herald,* March 27, July 19, 27, August 6, 20, 31, 1836.

37. William V. Shannon, *The American Irish,* p. 43.

38. Henry Steele Commager, *The American Mind,* p. 412.

39. Fermer, pp. 27–28.

40. Robert Park, "The Natural History of the Newspaper."

41. For a long attack aimed at both Protestant and Catholic churchmen and for one directed specifically against Presbyterian leaders, see *Herald*, July 9, 20, 1836.

42. *Herald*, August 8, 1849. Although particularly pointed, this attack typified years of such charges. Bennett had been raised a Catholic.

43. *Herald*, July 9, 14, 1836.

44. Crouthamel, pp. 52–53.

45. *Herald*, July 14, August 12, 1836. Fermer is one of the few historians to point out the apparent significance of women readers to the *Herald*, p. 21.

46. For an early booster editorial, see *Herlad*, July 22, 1835.

47. Crouthamel, pp. 92–111.

48. *Herald*, September 5, 1836. Bennett wrote that the *Sun printed* 15,000 but sold far fewer. He gave no figure for the *Transcript* but said almost all its circulation was "out of town." He said the *Courier and Enquirer* sold 6300, far more than the other six-centers.

49. *Herald*, December 9, 1836.

50. *Herald*, October 17, 1836. The essays began appearing in December.

51. Melvin L. Adelman, *A Sporting Time,* pp. 41–58.

52. Only scattered copies survive, but Bennett quoted from the *New Era* several times. *Herald*, October 3, 4, 7, 17, 1836.

53. *Herald*, October 6, 7, 1836.

54. *Herald*, December 8, 1836.

55. *New Era*, January 5, 1837; *Sun*, January 6, 1837; *Herald*, January 7, 13, 1837. A few months later, Bennett called the *New Era* the "most wretched of the lot." *Herald*, May 4, 1837.

56. *Herald*, December 4, 1836.

57. *Herald*, March 27, June 21, 1839; June 3, 1840; Clifford Browder, *The Wickedest Woman in New York;* Marvin Olasky, "Advertising Abortion During the 1830s and 1840s: Madame Restell Builds a Business."

58. Schudson, pp. 55–57.

59. *Herald*, June 1, 1840; Michael Schudson, *Discovering the News,* pp. 95–97.

60. O'Connor, pp. 30–35.

61. Even the *Man,* which itself was often at odds with Bennett, called Webb "impudent, blustering, impertinent, self-important." December 16, 1835.

62. James L. Crouthamel, *James Watson Webb: A Biography,* pp. 20–83; *Herald,* January 18, 21, 1836.

63. *Herald*, May 10, 1836.

64. *Herald*, July 5, 19, 1836.

65. *Sun*, January 22, May 19, July 19, 1836.

66. *Herald*, October 5, 1836.

67. *Courier*, April 10, 1833. See also *Evening Post* of the same date.

68. *Herald*, November 18, 1836.

69. Fermer, pp. 34–35.

5. The Robinson–Jewett Case

1. Brothel owners, like other entrepreneurs, were not reluctant to call on the watchmen and courts to protect their interests. Timothy J. Gilfoyle, "Strumpets and Misogynists: Brothel 'Riots' and the Transformation of Prostitution in Antebellum New York City"; Paul A. Gilje, *The Road to Mobocracy,* pp. 236–41.

2. Allan Nevins and Milton H. Thomas (eds.), *The Diary of George Templeton Strong,* vol. 2, p. 15.

3. Patricia C. Cohen, "The Ellen Jewett Murder: Violence, Gender and Sexual Licentiousness in Antebellum America."

4. *Documents of the Board of Aldermen of the City of New York,* 7:585–86; J. W. Gerard, *London and New York: Their Crime and Police,* p. 16.

5. Thomas Boyle, *Black Swine in the Sewers of Hampstead,* pp. 47–54.

6. In 1988, *New York* Magazine included the case in its article on the most famous crimes in the city's history. Jewett's alleged likeness even graced the cover. "The Annals of Manhattan Crime," (November 14, 1988), 21(45):40–55.

7. David B. Davis, *Homicide in American Fiction,* pp. 156–70. For a discussion of similar themes in magazines of the day, see Barbara Welter, "The Cult of True Womanhood: 1820–1860."

8. Sociologist Dan Schiller makes too much of this point in explaining the great interest in the Robinson-Jewett case. *Objectivity and the News,* pp. 57–65.

9. Sidney Ditzion, *Marriage, Morals and Sex in America,* pp. 108–09.

10. *Evening Post,* July 9, 1831; *Courier and Enquirer,* July 6, 1831; *Working Man's Advocate,* July 23, 1831; *Courier and Enquirer,* August 22, 1831; *Journal of Commerce,* August 16, 1831.

11. *Herald,* October 29, 1836.

12. Larry H. Whiteaker, "Moral Reform and Prostitution in New York City, 1830–1860," p. 7.

13. Timothy J. Gilfoyle, "The Urban Geography of Commercial Sex: Prostitution in New York City, 1790–1860." During periodic bursts of civic reform, the police would raid a few houses, but almost always the ones in the worst slums. See also *Courier and Enquirer,* January 23, 1832; *Commercial Advertiser,* March 29, 1830.

14. *The Sun* called it "a terrible affair of the most horrible and melancholy" type; the *Transcript* lead referred to "one of the most cold-blooded, atrocious, and as far as is known, unprovoked murders that has ever been recorded in the annals of crime." Justice moved swiftly in those days. Jack Finney described an inquest in an 1857 murder in New York. Within hours, that coroner had impaneled a full jury of twelve men, who began hearing testimony within a few hours and in the very blood-splattered room where the stabbing death had occurred. The corpse lay in the next room. Newspaper reporters were present throughout. Jack Finney, *Forgotten News,* pp. 55–80.

15. *Herald,* April 12, 1836. Fiction writers of the day were obsessed with detailed descriptions of corpses, according to Davis, p. 163.

16. *Times,* April 11, 1836; *Herald,* April 15, 18, 19, 20, 1836.

17. *Herald,* April 21, 1836.

18. Many other versions of her biography were published, most of them varying only in details. See Cohen paper.

19. *Life and Writings of James Gordon Bennett.*

20. Herald, April 11, 1836.

21. *Herald,* April 14, 1836.

22. *Herald,* April 12, 1836.

23. "Odds and Ends," *The Knickerbocker* (April 1836), 7(2):365–67.

24. *Transcript,* April 16, 1836; *Sun,* April 14, 16, 1836; *Herald,* April 16, 1836. Twenty years after the trial, Bennett sued an editor for repeating the bribery rumor.

25. In fairness, there was much news published during these weeks concerning the Seminole war in Florida and the battles for Texas independence, stories for which even Bennett had to find space.

26. *Herald,* April 27, 28, May 16, 17, 1836.

27. Robinson earned only $60 a year, plus lodging, according to the *Sun,* April 13, 1836.

28. *Sun,* April 20, 1836.

29. *Herald,* April 13, 1836.

30. Thomas C. Leonard, *Power of the Press,* pp. 147–49.

31. Nils G. Nilsson, "The Origin of the Interview"; Mitchell Stephens, *A History of News,* p. 247.

32. *Herald,* April 17, 1836.

33. Frederic Hudson, *Journalism in the United States,* p. 453; "Odds and Ends," *The Knickerbocker;* 7(2): *Herald,* July 9, 23, 1836; Judith M. Buddenbaum, " 'Judge . . . What Their Acts Will Justify': The Religion Journalism of James Gordon Bennett."

34. Philip S. Foner, *History of the Labor Movement in the United States,* p. 155.

35. *Appleton's Encyclopedia of American Biography,* vol. 2, p. 313; *Dictionary of American Biography,* p. 298.

36. Unintimidated by a hostile crowd, Edwards not only imposed heavy fines on the tailors but chastized the agitators. Although widely denounced, the decision squared with several others that had used common law to brand unions as conspiracies because strikes and higher wages forced up prices and interfered with the liberty of employees and employers to contract. The Chief Justice of New York upheld this logic in 1835, but in less than a decade the courts abandoned it.

37. Hone Diary, June 5, 1836. Strong passed up a chance to attend, "not caring particularly about being squeezed to death." Strong Diary, June 4, 1836.

38. Quoted in Robert G. Albion, *The Rise of the New York Port,* p. 252.

39. *Herald,* April 30, 1836.

40. Robinson never stopped maintaining his innocence of the murder but admitted his sinful ways. *Letter From Richard P. Robinson* (New York: 1837).

41. *Sun,* June 21, 23, 1836.

42. *Herald,* June 9, 1836.

43. George C. Wolling, *Recollections of a New York Chief of Police,* pp. 25–26; *Transcript,* June 13, 1836; *Sun,* June 9, 1836; Hone Diary, June 7, 1836; Strong Diary, June 5, 1836.

44. *Evening Post,* June 9, 1836.

45. Strong considered it a fabrication, "No more his diary than mine." In his June 11 entry he added, "By the by, I wonder if ever I shall be placed in a predicament of the same sort—and shall have this scrawl brought up to be argued on by lawyers and explained by that glorious trio, the *Sun, Transcript* and *Herald?*" Strong Diary, p. 24.

46. *Herald,* July 1, 1836.

47. *Sun,* July 9–15, 1836. The stories referred to Robinson as "the murderer" and "consummate libertine."

48. *Times,* July 11, 1836.

49. Boston *Daily Times,* June 6, 1836.

50. Copies of both novels and six pamphlets, published between 1836 and 1841, at the New-York Historical Society.

51. Gilfoyle, *City of Eros.,* chapter 5. Cohen sounded a similar theme.

52. *Advocate of Moral Reform,* July 1, 1836, p. 92.

53. English newspapers increased their sensational news even more sharply in the 1840s and 1850s, according to Boyle, pp. 39–45.

54. *Sun,* August 2, 1836.

6. Gilded-Age New York and Its Newspapers

1. Greater New York was incorporated in 1897. Ira Rosenwaike, *Population History of New York City,* pp. 55–56.

2. Sean D. Cashman, *America in the Gilded Age,* pp. 12–13; Edward C. Kirkland, *Industry Comes of Age,* pp. 237–61.

3. Arthur M. Schlesinger, *The Rise of the City,* pp. 79–80.

4. James Ford, et al., *Slums and Housing,* vol. 1, p. 187.

5. Gunther Barth, *City People,* pp. 46–47.

6. Harold U. Faulkner, *Politics, Reform and Expansion,* pp. 91–93, 141–43; Charles Hoffman, *The Depression of the Nineties,* pp. 3–17; Carl N. Degler, ed., *The Age of the Economic Revolution,* pp. 129–30.

7. Richard E. Welch, Jr., *The Presidencies of Grover Cleveland,* pp. 115–16.

8. Barth, p. 23.

9. Ian Whitcomb, *After the Ball,* pp. 4–5; David A. Jasen, *Tin Pan Alley,* pp. 1–13.

10. Bayrd Still, *Mirror for Gotham,* pp. 209–25.

11. Still, p. 252.

12. Compiled from annual editions (1891–1900) of the *Report of the Secretary of State on Statistics of Crime in the State of New York.*

13. The sheet music carried this notation: "The theme of this song is indeed a delicate one to handle, and is offered in sympathy, and not defense, for the unfortunate erring creature, the life of one of whom suggested its construction." Jasen, p. 28.

14. Cashman, pp. 114–15.

15. Robert H. Wiebe, *The Search for Order,* p. 27.

16. Margery Davis, "Woman's Place is at the Typewriter"; Susan E. Lyman,

The Story of New York, p. 189; Susan P. Benson, *Counter Cultures,* pp. 22–25; Robert E. Mackay, "Managing the Clerks: Office Management from the 1870s Through the Great Depression."

17. Barth, pp. 110–47; Michael Schudson, *Advertising, the Uneasy Persuasion,* pp. 150–52.

18. Theodore Dreiser, *Sister Carrie,* p. 17.

19. Annie M. MacLean, "Two Weeks in a Department Store"; Daniel Boorstin, *The Americans: The Democratic Experience,* pp. 107–09. For a more thorough history of the department store, see Michael B. Miller, *The Bon Marche.*

20. Robert H. Bremner, *From the Depths,* p. 12.

21. Faulkner, pp. 87–88; Cashman, pp. 143–63.

22. John F. Kasson, *Civilizing the Machine,* p. 183; Neil Harris, ed., *The Land of Contrasts,* pp. 6–7.

23. Richard A. Schwarzlose, *The Nation's Newsbrokers,* vol. 2, pp. 63–108. The New York AP members were the *Times, Tribune, Herald, World, Sun, Journal of Commerce,* and *Evening Express.*

24. James D. Hart, *The Popular Book,* pp. 188–194. The same romantic themes dominated popular music and melodramas of the period.

25. Richard Shenkman, *Legends, Lies and Cherished Myths of American History,* p. 70.

26. Quoted in Joseph Durso, *Baseball and the American Dream,* p. 31.

27. David Q. Voigt, *American Baseball: From Gentlemen's Sport to the Commissioner System,* pp. 212–13.

28. Julius Ward, "The Future of Sunday Journalism."

29. S. N. D. North, "History and Present Condition of the Newspaper and Periodical Press of the United States," vol. 7:51.

30. Not only did Bennett chafe under what he considered excessive wire rates, but he never forgave Gould for distributing a scathing 10,000-word personal attack. Schwarzlose, vol. 2, pp. 90–91.

31. George Juergens, *Joseph Pulilzer and the New York World,* p. 8; Douglas Fermer, *James Gordon Bennett and the New York Herald,* p. 312.

32. *The Journalist* (May 20, 1893), 17(10):5.

33. Charles T. Rosebault, *When Dana Was the Sun,* p. 159.

34. Barth, p. 87.

35. Cashman, pp. 47–49.

36. *The Journalist* (January 1, 1893), 17(1):9.

37. David Potter, *People of Plenty,* p. 169.

38. Edwin Emery, *History of the American Newspaper Publishers Association;* Jean Folkerts and Dwight L. Teeter, *Voices of a Nation,* pp. 283–84.

39. Mitchell Stephens, *A History of News,* pp. 258–59; Michael Schudson, *Discovering the News,* pp. 106–20.

40. *The Autobiography of Lincoln Steffens* (New York: Harcourt, Brace, 1931), pp. 285–91.

41. Ted C. Smythe, "The Reporter, 1880–1900: Conditions and Their Influence on the News." Nationwide, reporter salaries doubled between 1870 and 1890, according to Richard A. Hofstadter, *The Age of Reform,* p. 191.

7. Pulitzer Shows the Way

1. W. A. Swanberg, *Pulitzer,* pp. 145–70; *World,* December 10, 11, 1890.
2. Julian S. Rammelkamp's *Pulitzer's Post Dispatch* details this period of his career.
3. Gay Talese, *The Kingdom and the Power,* p. 53; Michael Schudson, *Discovering the News,* pp. 106–09.
4. George Juergens, *Joseph Pulitzer and the New York World,* introduction.
5. Ballots could be cast only for editors and publishers active in the preceding fifty years. Runners-up were Adolph Ochs, New York *Times;* Robert McCormick, Chicago *Tribune;* E. W. Scripps and William Randolph Hearst. *Editor & Publisher* (July 21, 1934), 67(10):266.
6. Hazel Dicken-Garcia, *Journalistic Standards in Nineteenth-Century America,* pp. 202–5.
7. Swanberg, *Pulitzer,* pp. 67–70; Kenneth Stewart and John Tebbel, *Makers of Modern Journalism,* pp. 91–92; W. A. Hurlbert to Joseph Pulitzer, January 10, 1883, Joseph Pulitzer Papers, Columbia University (hereafter JPC), box 1. He expressed confidence that goal could be met.
8. John M. Holmes to Joseph Pulitzer, December (?), 1883, JPC, box 4.
9. Allen Churchill, *Park Row,* p. 6.
10. *World,* May 11–15, 1883.
11. *World,* May 16, 17, 1883.
12. *Herald,* May 23–25, 1883.
13. *World,* May 22, 25, 1883.
14. Don C. Seitz, *Joseph Pulitzer: His Life and Letters,* pp. 142–43.
15. David G. McCullough, *The Great Bridge,* pp. 544–45.
16. *World, Herald, Sun, Times, Tribune,* May 31, 1883.
17. *World,* May 13, 14 and 29 and June 2, 1883.
18. *World,* Aug. 11, 1883.
19. Juergens, p. 316.
20. Frank Luther Mott, *American Journalism,* pp. 437–39.
21. Homer W. King, *Pulitzer's Prize Editor,* pp. 194–206.
22. Several long letters a month from his editor and from his business manager outlined the most minute details of *Post-Dispatch* business. Many of these, although not his responses, are found in JPC.
23. Ted C. Smythe, "The Reporter, 1880–1900," p. 3; Jean Folkerts and Dwight Teeter, *Voices of a Nation,* pp. 281–82.
24. Seitz, p. 148; Swanberg, *Pulitzer,* pp. 83–85.
25. Juergens, pp. 350–59; Swanberg, *Pulitzer,* pp. 136–47.
26. Charles T. Rosebault, *When Dana Was the Sun,* pp. 177–79.
27. Juergens, pp. 359–61.
28. "Story of the N.Y. Herald Fight With the Newsdealers," undated and unsigned memo in Joseph Pulitzer Papers, Library of Congress (hereafter JPL), box 11; Seitz, pp. 145–48.
29. "Daily Circulation of New York Newspapers, August, 1898" in The World Papers, Columbia University. Daily circulations were: *Journal,* 319,000;

World, 283,000; *Herald,* 167,000; *Sun,* 125,000; *Tribune,* 58,000; *Times,* 44,000.

30. *The Journalist* (December 16, 1893), 18(14):62.

31. Undated 1898 memo of circulation figures, The World Papers.

32. Printed price list, JPC, box 4. (A pencilled note indicates these are "about the same as the *Herald*"); "Ten Years of Advertising Revenue," undated 1897 memo, The World Papers.

33. Swanberg, *Pulitzer,* p. 75.

34. Swanberg, *Pulitzer,* pp. 133–34.

35. Juergens, pp. 288–97.

36. John Heaton, *The Story of a Page,* p. 49.

37. Swanberg, *Pulitzer,* pp. 173–74.

38. *World,* February 13, March 2, 3, 1884.

39. *World,* July 20, 1884.

40. *World,* March 8, 1891.

41. Seitz, p. 100.

42. *World,* May 17, 1883.

43. Juergens, pp. 175–330.

44. Pulitzer to O. H. Merrill, March 26, 1899, JPL, box 2.

45. Juergens, p. 329.

46. A Hungarian scholar has established Pulitzer was born in 1840 to a well-to-do merchant in Mako. Both his parents were Jewish. Andra's Csillag, "Joseph Pulitzer's Roots in Europe: A Genealogical History."

47. *World,* March 15–16, August 11, 1885; Seitz, pp. 156–59.

48. Bernard Weisberger, *The American Newspaperman,* p. 138.

49. Swanberg, *Pulitzer,* p. 73.

50. She departed on November 14, 1889. Verne's telegram was published in the *World,* January 26, 1890. The other papers virtually ignored her trip.

51. *World,* August 7, 1890. In an editorial the same day, the *World* called for an end to electrocutions; the *Times* thought the experiment deserved more of a chance.

52. *World,* December 26, 1884.

53. *World,* January 25, 1884; Juergens, pp. 34–35.

54. *World,* June 5, 1886.

55. *World,* August 6, 1884.

56. Sean D. Cashman, *America in the Gilded Age,* p. 50.

57. Schudson, pp. 94–95.

58. *World,* February 21, 1884.

59. Juergens, p. 57.

60. James W. Barrett, *Joseph Pulitzer and His World,* pp. 81–82; Juergens, pp. 115–17.

61. Stephen Hess, "The Ungentlemanly Art." The Associated Press dispatch which quoted one speaker at a Blaine rally as being against "rum, Romanism and rebellion" may have been even more decisive. The AP was heavily criticized for its attention to the phrase. Richard A. Schwarzlose, *The Nation's Newsbrokers,* vol. 2, pp. 124–25.

62. *The Journalist* (June 3, 1893), 17(12):6.

63. "Indecent Journalism," *The Journalist* (August 5, 1893), 17(21):8.

64. James Melvin Lee, *History of American Journalism*, p. 448; *World*, May 6, 1884.

65. *World*, November 4, 1883.

66. *World*, December 27, 1884.

67. Juergens, pp. 140–45.

68. Juergens, pp. 69–70.

69. *World* editorial, April 13, 1884.

70. *World*, September 15, 1883; September 14, 1884.

71. *World*, January 10, 1892.

72. Juergens, p. 149.

73. *World*, January 15, 1892.

74. *World*, January 14, 15, 1892.

75. Gunther Barth, *City People*, pp. 81–83.

76. An editorial expressed preference for women "rocking the cradle to running the caucus." *World*, April 4, 1895.

77. Michael T. Isenberg, *John L. Sullivan and His America*, pp. 378–81; Juergens, p. 125, counted eighteen front-page stories on Sullivan during the *World's* first year and a half.

78. Don Seitz to Joseph Pulitzer, October 20, 1898, JPL, box 2.

79. Barth, pp. 149–53.

80. David Q. Voigt, *America Through Baseball*, pp. 79–91.

8. With Skirts Higher and Higher

1. Mrs. Fremont Older, *William Randolph Hearst: American*, p. 128. Mrs. Older was a family friend and the only biographer who had access to many Hearst manuscripts.

2. James Feister, "The Other Pulitzer—Albert." The purchase was reported in the *Times*, October 5, 1895 and in the *Tribune* the next day. The *World* took no notice.

3. Oliver Carlson and Ernest S. Bates, *Hearst: Lord of San Simeon*, p. 74. This is one of the most negative biographies of Hearst.

4. Carlson and Bates, p. 80.

5. W. A. Swanberg, *Citizen Hearst*, p. 97; Don C. Seitz, *Joseph Pulitzer: His Life and Letters*, pp. 210–13.

6. *Journal, World*, November 7, 1895.

7. Hazel Dicken-Garcia, *Journalistic Standards in Nineteenth Century America*, pp. 92–95.

8. *Journal, World*, November 10, 11, 12, 13, 1895; *Journal*, November 19, 1895.

9. *Journal, World*, November 9, 1895.

10. *Journal, World*, November 10, 1895.

11. "A Most Unfeeling Man: Doesn't Make the Slightest Objection When You

Thrust Daggers and Brads in His Arms" and "Deadly Poisons Cannot Harm Him," were features on November 17, 1895.

12. John K. Winkler, *William Randolph Hearst: A New Appraisal*, pp. 106–07.

13. With the inclusion of ads, the supplement was sold to non-Hearst papers and eventually reached a circulation of ten million. In 1944 it became a tabloid insert and lasted until 1961.

14. Willis J. Abbot, *Watching the World Go By*, pp. 34–35.

15. Richard A. Schwarzlose, *Newsbrokers to the Nation*, vol. 2, pp. 175–77.

16. *Journal*, December 6–10, 1895. The *World* devoted as much space to the story but did not go to court on her behalf or claim credit for her release. *World*, December 6–10, 1895.

17. *Journal*, December 1, 1896. Hearst was an outspoken animal lover.

18. *Journal*, December 3, 1897.

19. Edward C. Kirkland, *Industry Comes of Age: Business, Labor and Public Policy, 1860–1897*, p. 250.

20. *Journal, World*, December 29, 1895; September 3, 1896.

21. *Journal*, November 24, 1895; September 6, 1896.

22. *The Journalist* (July 17, 1897), 21(13):99.

23. Older, p. 145.

24. John Francis Neylan to W. A. Swanberg, December 8, 1959; James Swinnerton to W. A. Swanberg, November 2, 1959, Swanberg Papers, Columbia University (hereafter SP), Citizen Hearst file. For an argument that Hearst was "intellectually lazy," see Joyce Milton, *The Yellow Kids*, pp. 195–96.

25. The first half of the Weber and Fields shows were the usual singers and comedy acts, but the last acts were parodies of current hit productions. David A. Jasen, *Tin Pan Alley*, pp. 19–20.

26. *The Journalist* (April 16, 1898), 22(26):232, 248.

27. *The Journalist* (April 16, 1898), 22(26):251.

28. Don Seitz to Joseph Pulitzer, November 18, 1898, in The New York World Papers.

29. Michael Schudson, *Discovering the News*, pp. 102–04.

30. *Journal*, September 5, 1896; Paul W. Glad, *McKinley, Bryan and the People*, pp. 170–72.

31. *The Journalist* (February 12, 1898), 22(17):176; Schudson, p. 99.

32. Daniel Boorstin, *The Americans: The Democratic Experience*, p. 371.

33. R. Smith Schuneman, "Art or Photography: A Question for Newspaper Editors of the 1890s"; Older, p. 203. The *Graphic* died in 1889 and was no relation to the *Evening Graphic* described in chapter 11.

34. Older, p. 28.

35. W. A. Gleeson interview, October 10, 1959, SP, Citizen Hearst file. Gleeson worked for many years at San Simeon.

36. William Randolph Hearst, Jr., to W. A. Swanberg, May 30, 1959, SP, Citizen Hearst file.

37. Harry Hershfield interview, September 10, 1959, SP, Citizen Hearst file. Hershfield, one of the pioneers in cartoon art, joined Hearst in 1899.

38. Swanberg, *Citizen Hearst*, p. 398.

39. Oliver Carlson, *Brisbane: A Candid Biography*, p. 112; Arthur Brisbane Papers.

40. Older, p. 203.

41. Correspondents for both papers in the Spanish-American War were often referred to as Yellow Kid reporters, according to Milton, p. 141.

42. Seitz to Pulitzer, October 4, 1898, JPL Papers, box 2; Seitz to Pulitzer, undated 1898, in The World Papers. A copy of a similar agreement among the Chicago papers, dated 1898 is found in The World Papers, 1898.

43. Seitz to Pulitzer, December 19, 1898, JPL Papers.

44. Moses Koenigsberg, *King News: An Autobiography* (Philadelphia: Stokes, 1941), pp. 367–71; *The Journalist* (October 20, 1894), 19(32):8.

9. Yellow, Yellow, Everywhere

1. *Journal, World,* June 28, 1897. Some citations are from the morning and others from the evening editions of the *Journal.*

2. *Journal,* June 29–July 1, 1897. The paper devoted seventeen, nineteen and twenty-seven columns, respectively, to the murder.

3. *World,* June 29–July 1, 1897. The paper printed about nine columns a day about the murder.

4. *World,* July 2, 1897.

5. Oliver Carlson and Ernest H. Bates, *Hearst: Lord of San Simeon,* p. 88.

6. *Journal,* July 2, 1897.

7. Edmund Pearson, *Masterpieces of Murder,* pp. 230–32.

8. *Journal,* June 29–July 7, 1897.

9. William Randolph Hearst, Jr., to W. A. Swanberg, December 8, 1959, SP, Citizen Hearst file.

10. *World,* July 9, 1897.

11. *The Journalist* (July 10, 1897), 21(12):94.

12. James L. Crouthamel, *Bennett's New York Herald and the Rise of the Popular Press,* pp. 62–66.

13. W. A. Swanberg, *Pulitzer,* pp. 224–25; Swanberg, *Citizen Hearst,* p. 128; *World,* April 17, 1884.

14. Swanberg, *Citizen Hearst,* pp. 141–43.

15. *Times,* January 18, 1896.

16. *World,* January 12, 14, 1896.

17. Charles H. Brown, *The Correspondents' War,* p. 41.

18. Joyce Milton, *The Yellow Kids,* p. 92.

19. Quoted in Swanberg, *Pulitzer,* pp. 227–28.

20. *World,* March 8, 1896.

21. Swanberg, *Citizen Hearst,* pp. 177–201.

22. Peggy and Harold Samuels, *Frederic Remington,* pp. 244–49.

23. James Creelman, *On the Great Highway,* p. 178.

24. William Jr. told a researcher that his father always denounced the story as pure fabrication. Everett Littlefield III, *William Randolph Hearst: His Role in*

American Progressivism, p. 43. Milton repeated the story, but admitted there was no evidence to support it, pp. 140–42.

25. Samuels, pp. 249–50.

26. Phillip Knightley, *The First Casualty,* pp. 66, 115–16.

27. *Journal,* November 15, 1896.

28. *World,* November 9, 26, 1896.

29. Swanberg, *Citizen Hearst,* p. 138.

30. Milton, pp. 194–202; *Journal,* October 10, 1897; Willis S. Abbot, *Watching the World Go By,* p. 216.

31. Lewis J. Gould, *The Presidency of William McKinley,* pp. 65–90; Swanberg, *Citizen Hearst,* pp. 137–53.

32. *Journal,* February 9, 1898.

33. *Journal,* June 10, 1898.

34. Gould, pp. 62–63.

35. John Francis Neylan to W. A. Swanberg, December 8, 1959, SP, Citizen Hearst file.

36. Richard A. Hofstadter, *The Paranoid Style in American Politics,* p. 158.

37. Jean Folkerts and Dwight L. Teeter, *Voices of a Nation,* p. 275.

38. Arthur Brisbane, "The Modern Newspaper in War Time."

39. Frederick Merk, *Manifest Destiny and Mission in American History: A Reinterpretation* (New York: Knopf, 1963), p. 193.

40. In addition to works cited in this chapter, see Frank Freidel, *A Splendid Little War* (Boston: Little, Brown, 1958); Robert E. Beisner, *Twelve Against Empire: The Anti-Imperialists, 1898–1900* (New York: McGraw-Hill, 1968); Walter Millis, *The Martial Spirit: A Study of our War With Spain* (Boston: Houghton Mifflin, 1931); Richard Harding Davis, *The Notes of a War Correspondent* (New York: Scribner's Sons, 1910); Marcus Wilkerson, *Public Opinion and the Spanish-American War* (Baton Rouge: Louisiana State University Press, 1932); Joseph E. Winan, *The Cuban Crisis as Reflected in the New York Press* (New York: Columbia University Press, 1934).

41. Robert E. Park, "The Natural History of the Newspaper," in Park, *The City,* pp. 80–98. Silas Bent suggested that Hearst might have produced a great paper if he had not been so absorbed in besting Pulitzer. *Ballyhoo* (New York: Horace Livermore, 1927), p. 150.

42. Holbrook Jackson, *The Eighteen-Nineties,* p. 23.

43. E. L. Godkin, editorial, *The Nation* (September 26, 1901), 73(1891): 239.

44. Ferdinand Lundberg, *Imperial Hearst,* p. 54.

45. Seitz, p. 215.

46. Edwin Emery, "William Randolph Hearst: A Tentative Appraisal."

47. *Time,* March 13, 1939, p. 49; Will Irwin, "The American Newspaper: A Study of Journalism in Its Relation to the Public. Part 3."

48. Swanberg, *Citizen Hearst,* pp. 622–26. During his research, Swanberg interviewed a psychiatrist, who pronounced Hearst a "classic megalomaniac" who never got over his childish insistence on immediate satisfactions, SP, Citizen Hearst file.

49. Gunther Barth, *City People,* pp. 66, 229.

50. Delos F. Wilcox, "The American Newspaper: A Study in Social Psychology."

51. For an introduction, see Arthur and Lila Weinberg, eds., *The Muckrakers* (New York: Simon & Schuster, 1961). For individual magazines, see Theodore Peterson, *Magazines in the United States* (Urbana: University of Illinois Press, 1956), and the five volumes of Frank Luther Mott, *A History of American Magazines* (Cambridge: Harvard University Press).

10. Not Everyone Charlestoned

1. Frederick Lewis Allen, *Only Yesterday.*

2. Darwin Payne, *The Man of Only Yesterday,* p. 99. Payne was told by the publisher that by 1971 the 1931 edition had sold 67,300 copies; a one-dollar text edition in 1932, 4760; Blue Ribbon Edition, 1933, 40,290; Bantam paperback, 1946, 283,100; Bantam paperback reissue, 1963–64, 76,000; 1957 regular edition reissue, 36,500; Harpercrest edition, 1961, 14,100, and Perennial paper edition, 1964, 589,211. It continues to sell steadily.

3. Kenneth Lynn, "Only Yesterday."

4. Payne, pp. 100–101. Many historians now dispute the assertion about the decade's uniqueness, placing developments in longer time frames.

5. Michael Schudson, *Advertising, the Uneasy Persuasion;* Daniel Bell, *The Cultural Contradictions of American Capitalism;* George E. Mowry, *The Urban Nation, 1920–1960,* pp. 6–7.

6. A survey in 1927 found twenty successful non-chain newspapers ran 42 to 58 percent advertising. In almost all papers classifieds were the leading category, accounting for nearly one-third of the ad space. See *Editor & Publisher* (April 9, 1927), 60(46):26.

7. David E. Shi, "Advertising and the Literary Imagination During the Jazz Age."

8. Roy Lubove, *Community Planning in the 1920s,* p. 26; *Editor & Publisher* (November 6, 1920), 53(23):7; (August 27, 1921), 55(13):11; George E. Mowry, *The Urban Nation,* pp. 15–16; Irving Bernstein, *The Lean Years,* pp. 47–82.

9. Henry F. May, "Shifting Perspectives on the 1920s," p. 425.

10. Alba M. Edwards, *Comparative Occupational Statistics for the United States, 1870–1940,* tables 9 and 10; Mary C. Anderson, "Gender, Class and Culture: Women Secretarial and Clerical Workers in the United States, 1925–1955."

11. William H. Chafe, *The American Woman,* pp. 30–31. Some feminists insist historians and journalists misinterpreted these developments because of their inability to think of women in other than their sexual roles. See Estelle B. Freedman, "The New Woman: Changing Views of Women in the 1920s."

12. Ida Tarbell, "Ten Years of Women's Suffrage."

13. Bayrd Still, *Mirror for Gotham,* pp. 262–63.

14. Milton W. Gordon, "Assimilation in America: Theory and Reality"; Marion Marzolf, "Americanizing the Melting Pot," in Catherine L. Covert and John D.

Stevens, *Mass Media Between the Wars,* pp. 107–27; Max Lerner, *America as a Civilization,* pp. 92–94.

15. Norman H. Clark, *Deliver Us From Evil.* Representative of the more traditional interpretation are Richard A. Hofstadter, *The Age of Reform;* Andrew Sinclair, *Prohibition: Era of Excess* (New York: Little, Brown, 1962); and Joseph H. Gusfeld, *Symbolic Crusade* (Urbana: University of Illinois Press, 1963).

16. Paul A. Carter, *Another Part of the Twenties,* pp. 85–86.

17. *Times,* November 3, 1926; Thomas M. Coffey, *The Long Thirst,* pp. 189–91.

18. *Variety,* September 30, 1925; February 3, October 27, December 22, 1926; October 29, 1927; September 19, 1928; May 8, 1929, and many others. The same paper reported street prices for opium, morphine and cocaine, February 17, 1926.

19. Stanley Walker, *The Night Club Era,* pp. 77–102; David A. Jasen, *Tin Pan Alley,* pp. 155–56; Elisabeth Perry, "Cleaning Up the Dance Halls."

20. Edmund A. Mooney, *A Catholic Runs for President,* pp. 41–108.

21. Arnold Shaw, *The Jazz Age,* pp. 57–63.

22. American Civil Liberties Union, "Mob Violence in the United States," (New York: ACLU, 1923) in ACLU Papers.

23. Patterson to Philip Payne, December 8, 1922, in Joseph Medill Patterson Papers, box 19.

24. Kenneth T. Jackson, *The Ku Klux Klan in the City, 1915–1930,* pp. 175–78, 237–41.

25. John Higham, *Send These to Me,* pp. 157–95.

26. James A. Richardson, *The New York Police,* p. 166.

27. R. D. McKenzie, *The Metropolitan Community,* pp. 219–20.

28. Robert A. Caro, *The Power Broker.*

29. Raymond W. Smilor, "Cacophony at 34th and Sixth: The Noise Problem in America, 1900–1930."

30. Quoted in Kenneth T. Jackson and Stanley K. Schultz (eds.), *Cities in American History,* p. 256.

31. Michael L. Berger, "The Automobile and the City."

32. *Variety,* June 17, 1925, p. 11; Timothy Gilfoyle, *City of Eros;* Geoffrey Perrett, *America in the Twenties,* p. 154.

33. Richardson, pp. 168–71.

34. President's Research Committee on Social Trends, *Recent Social Trends in the United States,* vol. 2, p. 1128. See also, Perrett, pp. 307–99; J. C. Burnham, "New Perspectives on the Prohibition Experiment of the 1920s," p. 61.

35. *Report of the Crime Commission* (Albany: State of New York, 1927), p. 31. Although there are limits to the usefulness of conviction rates, most legal writers consider them more reliable indicators than arrest or imprisonment figures.

36. Frederick Hoffman, "Philistine and Puritan in the 1920s," in Hennig Cohen, ed., *The American Experience,* p. 124.

37. Hoagy Carmichael and Stephen Greenstreet, *Sometimes I Wonder,* p. 43.

38. Shaw, pp. 46–53.

39. Jasen, p. 192.

40. Shaw, pp. 231–33.

41. Richard C. Crepeau, *Baseball: America's Diamond Mind,* pp. 46–47.

42. Daniel S. Smith, "The Dating of the American Sexual Revolution: Evidence and Interpretation," in Michael Gordon, ed., *The American Family in Social-Historical Perspective,* pp. 321–35.

43. Paula Fass, *The Damned and the Beautiful,* pp. 260–70.

44. Perrett, p. 156.

45. Elaine T. May, *Great Expectations,* pp. 75–76.

46. Authors in *Atlantic, Cosmopolitan, Ladies' Home Journal* and *Saturday Evening Post* also wrote more favorably about education for women. Role stereotyping continued in both articles and short stories. See Teresa M. Hynes, "The Portrayal of Women in Selected Magazines From 1911–1930."

47. F. Ivan Nye and Felix M. Bernardo, *The Family: Its Structure and Interaction,* pp. 466–67.

48. The *World* publisher dropped the feature in 1926, calling it "too raw and too unimportant." Joseph Pulitzer, Jr., to Arthur Krock, January 26, 1926, JPL, reel 22.

49. John D. Stevens, "Social Utility of Sensational News: Murder and Divorce in the 1920s."

50. Ad for *Sexual Lovemaking,* quoted in May, p. 92.

51. For example, a Brooklyn housewife was convicted for mailing a much-praised short compiliation of sex facts for adolescents. *U.S. v. Dennett,* 39 F.2d 564 (2d Cir., 1930).

52. John D. Stevens, "Media and Morality in the 20s."

53. *Times,* January 18, 1925.

54. Robert Fisher, "Film Censorship and Progressive Reform: The National Board of Censorship of Motion Pictures"; Howard T. Lewis, *The Motion Picture Industry,* p. 370; Will H. Hays, *The Memoirs of Will H. Hays,* p. 333.

55. John D. Stevens, "Sex as Entertainment: Social Hygiene Films Before 1930."

56. *Regina v. Hicklin,* L.R.Q.B. 360 (1868). Adapted into American law in *U.S. v. Bennett,* 24 Fed. Cas. 1093 (S.D.N.Y., 1879).

57. *Mutual Film Corp. v. Industrial Commission of Ohio,* 236 U.S. 230 (1915). The Supreme Court finally declared movies protected in *Burstyn v. Wilson,* 343 U.S. 495 (1952).

58. *Times,* August 15, 1928.

59. Mildred Gilman interview, 1969, Oral History Collection, Columbia University. She was a young reporter who attended performances with the columnist.

60. *Herald,* November 11, 1921.

61. Figures for all except the *Daily News* were rounded from those filed with Audit Bureau of Circulation, October 1, 1920, as reported in *Editor & Publisher* (October 2, 1920), 53(18). The *Daily News* was not yet audited but made its claim in a promotion ad in the same magazine (October 16, 1920), 53(20).

62. Schwarzlose, vol. 2, pp. 213–235.

63. *Editor & Publisher* (October 3, 1925), 58(19):11.

64. James Boylan, *The World in the 20's,* p. 4.

65. Walter Lippmann interview, 1950.

66. *Editor & Publisher* (August 5, 1922), 55(10):26.

67. *Editor & Publisher* (November 13, 1926), 59(25):3.

68. *Editor & Publisher* (October 9, 1926), 59(20):27.

69. *N. W. Ayer and Son's American Newspaper Annual and Directory.*

70. See, generally, Robert W. Desmond, *The Press and World Affairs,* and John Hohenberg, *Foreign Correspondence: The Great Reporters and Their Times.*

71. Book sales fell behind population growth, but public library usage gained. Preston W. Slosson, *The Great Crusade and After,* pp. 362, 423–24.

72. Morris L. Ernst, *The First Freedom,* p. 280. In 1923, the mean circulation for all U.S. dailies was about 4000. James N. Rosse, "The Decline of Direct Newspaper Competition."

73. Karl A. Bickel, *News Empires,* p. 39.

74. Gilman interview.

75. Erik Barnouw, *A Tower in Babel,* p. 4.

76. Barnouw, p. 98.

77. Barnouw, pp. 224–34; Mowry, pp. 4–5.

78. *Times,* August 23, 1927.

79. Mitchell Stephens, *A History of News,* pp. 254–55.

80. In the early years membership was open only to newspapers of at least 100,000 circulation; of those 80 percent joined within the first year. See *Problems of Journalism, 1927* (Washington: American Society of Newspaper Editors, 1927).

81. *Problems in Journalism, 1923* (Washington: American Society of Newspaper Editors, 1923); Louis Wiley, "The Making of a Newspaper," p. 118.

82. *Editor & Publisher,* 57:(47), April 18, 1925, 57(47):42.

83. *Editor & Publisher,* March 10, 1923, 55(41):p. 28.

84. Edith E. Switt, "Comparative Analysis of Eight New York City Papers With Especial Reference to Anti-Social News," p. 63.

85. Richard A. Schwarzlose, *The American Wire Services,* p. 396; Sally F. Griffith, *Home Town News,* p. 219; Minutes of Central Division AP Meeting, November 24, 1925, in William T. Evjue Papers, box 7.

86. An undated *Times* promotion flyer of the period claimed that 80 percent of afternoon papers were sold by single copy "below Forty-Second Street." The *Times,* by contrast, had 75 percent home delivery.

87. *Editor & Publisher* 54:(26), November 26, 1921, 54(26):32; *Problems of Journalism 1925* (Washington: American Society of Newspaper Editors, 1925), p. 107.

88. Wiggins DuBois, "Recent Newspaper Tendencies in New York City," p. 79.

89. Quoted in DuBois, pp. 24–25.

90. William Johnston to Joseph Pulitzer, Jr., April 12, 1924, in Joseph Pulitzer Papers, Library of Congress, reel 22 (hereafter JPL).

91. Kent Cooper to Owen Billings, September 4, 1928, in Kent Cooper Papers, box 2.

92. Lyman D. Gordon, "The Gibson Girl Goes to College: Popular Culture and Women's Higher Education in the Progressive Era, 1890–1920."

93. Robert M. Park, "The Natural History of the Newspaper." This seminal article is widely reprinted.

94. Walter Lippmann, *Public Opinion*, pp. 350–55.

95. Schwarzlose, vol. 2, p. 237.

96. Nelson Crawford, "Mental Health and the Newspaper," p. 304.

97. Gilman Ostrander, *American Civilization in the First Machine Age*, p. 231.

98. George Mowry, *The Twenties: Fords, Flappers and Fanatics*, p. 82.

99. *Problems of Journalism 1928* (Washington: American Society of Newspaper Editors, 1928), pp. 13–15.

100. *Problems of Journalism 1929* (Washington: American Society of Newspaper Editors, 1929), pp. 176–79.

11. Sensation at a Glance

1. See for example, Patterson to S. H. Bloomer, September 9, 1922, box 15. Joseph Medill Patterson Papers, hereafter JMP.

2. Simon Bessie, *Jazz Journalism*, p. 24.

3. Patterson to William Field, November 6, 1919, JMP, box 17.

4. *Editor & Publisher* (November 20, 1920), 55(25):23.

5. Mark Monmonier, *Maps With the News*, p. 85; *The Fourth Estate* (October 28, 1922), 29(1496):12.

6. Arthur S. Rudd, "The Development of Illustrated Tabloid Journalism in the United States," p. 55.

7. *Editor & Publisher* (July 26, 1924), 57(9):7.

8. Daniel Boorstin, *The Image*, p. 14.

9. John Berger, "Appearances" in John Berger and Jean Mohr, *Another Way of Telling*, pp. 93–129; Beaumont Newhall, *Photography, 1839–1937*, p. 80.

10. John Chapman, *Tell It to Sweeney*, pp. 27–44; Leo E. McGivena, *The News: The First Fifty Years of New York's Picture Newspaper*, pp. 27–29.

11. Titles varied but the rapid rotation continued. Patterson's policy of promoting from within the staff did not stem the flow.

12. Eddie Doherty to Patterson, April 18, 1931, JMP, box 16. Doherty, long a mainstay of the *Daily News* reporting staff, was an exception. The remark was in his friendly letter telling the publisher of his departure for the *Mirror*.

13. M. C. Feenor to Patterson, July 1, 1927, JMP, box 18.

14. Max Annenberg to Patterson, November 20, 1919, JMP, box 15.

15. He specifically complained of too much boxing and horse racing and too little about divorces. Patterson to William Field, October 18, 1920, JMP, box 17.

16. William Field to Patterson, July 16, 1919, JMP, box 17.

17. Max Annenberg to Patterson, March 23, 1921; Philip Payne to Patterson, January 15, 1923, JMP, boxes 15, 19.

18. Chapman, pp. 125–28.

19. There is no evidence Patterson ever contemplated such a paper. Swope to Joseph Pulitzer, Jr., November 27, 1923, JPL, reel 22.

20. Chapman, pp. 145–46.

21. Rudd, pp. 112–13.

22. Patterson to William Field, May 28, 1920, JMP, box 17.

23. Chapman, pp. 98–111.

24. M. C. Feenor to Patterson, July 1, 1927, JMP, box 18.

25. He thought it was a great way to use up the "by-product" of daily journalism, the unpublished shots. Patterson to William Field, November 5, 1919, JMP, box 17.

26. Kent Cooper to Patterson, January 29, 1927, Kent Cooper Papers, box 2.

27. Philip Payne to Patterson, February 12, 1929, JMP, box 19.

28. Patterson to William Field, October 20, 1919, JMP, box 17. Field, the general manager, added the page but thought it a poor use of space. "The success of the newspaper will be based upon two things—first, pictures, and second, condensed news." Field to Patterson, November 4, 1919, JMP, box 17.

29. Rudd, pp. 77–83.

30. *Daily News,* October 9, 1919.

31. Quoted in Rudd, p. 56.

32. M. C. Feenor to Patterson, July 1, 1927, JMP, box 18.

33. M. C. Feenor to Patterson, July 1, 1927, JMP, box 18.

34. Patterson to William Field, October 18, 1920; Patterson to Merton E. Burke, December 26, 1921, JMP, boxes 16, 17.

35. Gerald Gordon, *The Polite Americans* (New York: William Morrow, 1966), p. 222.

36. *Daily News,* July 19, 1926.

37. James Murphy, "Tabloids as an Urban Response," in Catherine L. Covert and John D. Stevens, eds., *Mass Media Between the Wars,* pp. 62–67.

38. Patterson to Frank Hause, September 29, 1925; Hause memo to staff, May 29, 1930; Patterson to Merton E. Burke, May 3, 1922; Patterson to Arthur Clayton, December 1, 1922; Patterson to Harvey Duell, August 10, 1925; Patterson to Frank Hause, October 10, 1928, JMP, boxes 16, 17.

39. Patterson to Frank Hause, October 10, 1928, JMP, box 17.

40. Philip Payne to Patterson, December 26, 1922, JMP, box 17.

41. The managing editor was proud of arrangements to photograph baseball games in New York stadiums, including the use of a camera with a twenty-four-inch lens. Merton E. Burke to Patterson, September 14, 1920, JMP, box 16.

42. Patterson to Merton E. Burke, October 14, 1921, JMP, box 16.

43. *Editor & Publisher* (August 4, 1926), 59(12):18.

44. Paul A. Carter, *Another Part of the Twenties,* pp. 116–19.

45. Arnold Shaw, *The Jazz Age,* p. 175.

46. *Daily News* to Ederle, August 11, 1926, JMP, box 16.

47. *Daily News,* February 3, October 11, 1919; October 2, 1921.

48. Patterson to Frank Hause, July 15, 1928, JMP, box 17.

49. Patterson to William Field, August 19, 1919, JMP, box 17.

50. Chapman, p. 62.

51. Roy C. Hollins to Patterson, May 7, May 16, 1921, JMP, box 17.

52. *Daily News,* June 25, 1922. It passed the million mark in the middle of 1925 and kept growing. It topped two million in 1933 and three million in 1938.

53. *Daily News,* August 5, 1926.

54. *Daily News,* July 3, 1926.

55. Chapman, pp. 99–100.

56. *Daily News,* August 16, 1919; August 19, 1921.

57. *Daily News,* June 29, 1926.

58. Merton E. Burke to Patterson, August 2, September 8, 1920, JMP, box 16.

59. Merton E. Burke to Patterson, July 29, 1920, JMP, box 16.

60. Patterson to Merton E. Burke, August 29, 1920; Patterson to William Field, July 8, 1919, JMP, boxes 16, 17.

61. Patterson to William Field, March 11, 1921, JMP, box 17. In ordering Field to "jazz up" the paper, he cautioned against getting "smutty." Patterson to William Field, September 22, 1924, JMP, box 17.

62. *Daily News,* June 30, July 4, 1926.

63. *Daily News,* June 7, 1924.

64. *Daily News,* August 1, December 20, 1919.

65. Richard G. deRochemont, "The Tabloids." *Editor & Publisher* (July 26, 1924), 57(9):7.

66. Patterson to William Field, October 30, 1925, JMP, box 17.

67. Patterson to Philip Payne, August 26, 1924, JMP, box 20.

68. Philip Payne to Patterson, September 15, 1924, JMP, box 20.

69. Patterson to William Field, December 6, December 10, 1924, JMP, box 17.

70. Patterson to Frank Hause, May 15, 1929, JMP, box 17.

71. *Editor & Publisher* (June 26, 1926), 59(5):1.

72. *Editor & Publisher* (February 12, 1927), 59(38):12; (June 12, 1926), 59(3):6.

73. Quoted in Rudd, p. 54.

74. Leon N. Flint, *The Conscience of a Newspaper,* pp. 125–27. Italics added.

75. Aben Kandel, "A Tabloid a Day."

76. George Jean Nathan, "Clinical Notes: the Tabloids."

77. e. e. cummings, "The Tabloid Newspaper: An Investigation Involving Big Business, the Pilgrim Fathers, and Psychoanalysis."

78. Silas Bent, *Ballyhoo,* pp. 180–98.

79. Patterson to S. N. Blossom, January 23, 1922; Patterson to Merton E. Burke, June 7, 1922, JMP, box 16.

80. George Soule, *Prosperity Decade;* Harold U. Faulkner, *American Economic History,* p. 622.

81. Perrett, p. 251.

82. *Daily News,* January 7, 17, 1927.

83. Patterson to Merton E. Burke, August 27, 1921; Patterson to Philip Payne, November 5, 1922, JMP, box 16.

84. Patterson to Frank Hause, June 24, 1925, JMP, box 17.

85. *Daily News,* July 2, 1926.

86. *Daily News,* August 9, 1926; May 5, 1927.

87. For example, *Daily News,* July 4, July 7, August 1, 1926; May 5, 1927. On December 24, 1926, the paper began a series on the New York booze business.

88. *Daily News,* January 1, 1927.

89. *Daily News,* July 20, 1926. Contrary to many claims, Prohibition *did* reduce alcoholic consumption in the United States by at least one-third. *First Federal Report to the United States Congress on Alcohol and Health;* Perrett, pp. 176–78.

90. Philip Payne to Patterson, January 18, 1923, JMP, box 19.

91. Patterson to Philip Payne, April 20, 1925, JMP, box 20.

92. *Daily News,* April 8, 1927.

93. Extensive correspondence between Patterson and Merton E. Burke is found in JMP, box 16.

94. Patterson to Frank Hause, September 15, 1925, JMP, box 17.

95. Frank Hause memo to staff, May 23, 1930, JMP, box 17.

12. Challengers: The *Mirror* and the *Graphic*

1. Rodney P. Carlisle, "The Political Ideas and Influence of William Randolph Hearst, 1928–1936"; Bruce Blivin, "Hearst."

2. W. A. Swanberg, *Citizen Hearst,* pp. 205–314; Peter Baida, "Hearst's Little Time Bomb."

3. Swanberg, *Citizen Hearst,* pp. 383–430.

4. John Chapman, *Tell It To Sweeney,* pp. 22–26.

5. *Editor & Publisher* (October 31, 1925), 58(23):7.

6. William Q. Parmenter, "The News Control Explanation of News Making: The Case of William Randolph Hearst," pp. 156–89; Swanberg, *Citizen Hearst,* pp. 503–04.

7. *Daily News,* August 4, 1926.

8. Richard G. deRochemont, "The Tabloids," p. 191.

9. Arthur S. Rudd, "The Development of Illustrated Tabloid Journalism in the United States," pp. 61–63.

10. Herman Klurfeld, *Winchell: His Life and Times,* p. 53.

11. *Mirror,* July 19, 1924. An editorial in the same issue likened the display to the Chinese practice of lashing a murder victim's corpse to a killer and making him carry it for several days. The mother was found not guilty and released the next day.

12. Mabel D. Luhan, *Movers and Shakers,* p. 509.

13. Catherine L. Covert, "A View of the Press in the Twenties," p. 96.

14. *Mirror,* January 16, 1925.

15. *Mirror,* January 19, 1925.

16. *Mirror,* July 5, 1924.

17. *Mirror,* October 17, 1925.

18. *Mirror,* July 3, 1926. Reckless, out-of-control youths symbolized for many the unhinging of society. Paula S. Fass, *The Damned and the Beautiful,* pp. 17–20.

19. *Mirror,* June 26, 28, 1924.

20. *Mirror,* October 10, 1924; April 7, 1925.

21. *Mirror,* October 10, 1925.

22. *Mirror,* June 30, 1924.

23. *Mirror,* October 13, 1925; June 28, July 1, 1924.

24. *Mirror,* July 2, 1926.

25. *Editor & Publisher* (October 23, 1926), 59(22):5.

26. *Mirror,* April 2, 3, 7, 1925.

27. Patterson to Merton E. Burke, April 18, 19, 1922, in JMP, box 15.

28. *Mirror,* July 1, 1926.

29. *Mirror,* July 1–September 10, 1926.

30. *Mirror,* August 9, 1926.

31. *Mirror,* July 7, 1926.

32. Announcement ad in Detroit *Free Press,* January 29, 1929. Winner announced in *American,* April 26, 1929.

33. *Mirror,* November 4, 1926.

34. *Mirror,* April 6, 1925.

35. Stanley Walker to W. A. Swanberg, February 8, 1960, Swanberg Papers, Columbia University, Citizen Hearst file.

36. Swanberg, *Citizen Hearst,* p. 507.

37. Swanberg, *Citizen Hearst,* p. 503.

38. Parmenter, 37–38, p. 169.

39. *Graphic,* June 4, 1927.

40. Robert Lewis Taylor, "Physical Culture." This was a three-part profile of Macfadden.

41. *Graphic,* September 24, 1924. He was responding to a remark in *Time* magazine that the newcomer was "hardly a newspaper."

42. In spite of many suits, the *Graphic* paid only $5,200 in settlements and judgments. *Editor & Publisher* (July 9, 1932), 65(8):8.

43. *Editor & Publisher* (September 20, 1924), 57(17):5.

44. *Graphic,* September 16, 1924.

45. *Graphic,* March 6, 1928. An editorial had complained four years earlier (and two years before Ruth Snyder died in the electric chair) about the refusal of jurors to condemn a woman to death, *Graphic,* October 18, 1924.

46. *Graphic,* June 8, 1929.

47. *Graphic,* October 2, 1924.

48. *Graphic,* September 15, 1924.

49. Erik Barnouw, *A Tower in Babel,* pp. 167–68.

50. *Graphic,* September 10, 1928.

51. *Graphic,* September 19, 1924.

52. Quoted in Stanley Walker, *The Night Club Era,* p. 27.

53. Winchell claimed the *Mirror* offered him $1,000 a week and syndication rights. Frank Hause to Patterson, August 21, September 5, 1930, JMP, box 17.

54. Ed Weiner, *Let's Go To Press,* pp. 44–49; Bob Thomas, *Winchell,* pp. 55–58.

55. Walker, *Night Club,* pp. 128–50.

56. Simon Bessie, *Jazz Journalism* p. 192.

57. Edith E. Switt, "Comparative Analysis of Eight New York City Newspapers With Especial Reference to Anti-Social News," p. 61.

58. Quoted in Stanley Walker, *City Editor,* p. 72.

59. *Editor & Publisher* (August 31, 1929), 62(15):5.

60. Douglas Steinbauer, "Faking It With Pictures."

61. John D. Stevens, "Social Utility of Sensational News: Murder and Divorce News in the 1920s." Photo published in *Graphic,* November 25, 1925.

62. Gauvreau said the technique created no real trouble until the Browning case. Emile H. Gauvreau, *My Last Million Readers,* p. 111.

63. *Editor & Publisher* (February 12, 1927), 59(38):5, (July 9, 1927), 60(7):11; *Times,* October 22, 1926.

64. *Graphic,* September 15, 1924.

65. Lester Cohen, *The New York Graphic,* p. 61.

66. Gauvreau, p. 108.

67. Cohen, pp. 93–94.

68. Cohen, pp. 61–65.

69. Rudd, p. 76.

70. Gauvreau, pp. 112–13.

71. *Graphic,* September 1, 1931; June 6, 1931.

72. Data provided by William H. Taft, Columbia, Mo.

73. Rudd, p. 75.

74. Alva Johnston, "The Great Macfadden"; Cohen, p. 219.

75. William H. Taft, "Bernarr Macfadden: One of a Kind," p. 631.

76. He operated dailies in Philadelphia, Detroit, and several smaller cities. His magazines included *Liberty, Photoplay, Radio Mirror,* and *Sports-Life.*

77. *Editor & Publisher* (July 9, 1932), 54(8):8; *Times,* July 8, 1932.

78. William H. Taft, "I Love Life: The Life of Bernarr Macfadden."

79. Like Hearst, Macfadden sought the nomination for mayor and governor, but he never actually ran. Cohen, pp. 209–10.

80. Bessie, p. 184; Cohen title.

81. Johnston, p. 92.

13. Murders in Tabloid Land

1. John R. Brazil, "Murder Trials, Murder and Twenties America."

2. Of the two book-length accounts of the case, the fuller and more reliable is William M. Kunstler, *The Minister and the Choir Girl.* A more popularized account is Charles Boswell and Lewis Thompson, *The Girl in Lover's Lane.*

3. John Chapman, *Tell It To Sweeney,* p. 227.

4. There was no universal definition, but the term generally referred to a girl whose dress and behavior flaunted accepted conventions. G. Stanley Hall, "Flapper Americanus Novissima," *Atlantic* (June 1922), 129(6):771–80. A writer who identified herself as an ex-flapper distinguished the "prep-school type—still a little crude" from her older sister "who has learned to be soulful, virtuous on occasions and, under extreme circumstances, even highbrow." *Times,* July 16, 1922.

5. Kunstler, pp. 335–44.

6. *Daily News,* September 17, 1922.

7. *Daily News,* September 18–19, 1922.

8. *Journal,* September 18–19, 1922.

9. *Journal,* September 19–21, 1922. Neither the *Mirror* nor the *Graphic* appeared until 1924.

10. *Daily News,* September 23–24, 1922.

11. *Journal,* September 22, 1922.

12. *Daily News,* October 8, 1922. The arrest report on October 10 included six

photos, a rundown on the cast of characters, and a boxed list of unanswered questions.

13. *Journal,* October 13, 1922.

14. Oom had wealthy supporters, including some of the Vanderbilts, who put pressure on the newspapers to lay off the veteran con artist, who had spent several years in prison. Philip Payne to Patterson, February 7, 1923, JMP, box 19.

15. *Journal,* October 17–23, 1922.

16. Ishbel Ross, *Ladies of the Press,* p. 270.

17. Boswell and Thompson, p. 33.

18. Leon N. Flint, *The Conscience of the Newspaper,* p. 214.

19. *Editor & Publisher* (April 7, 1923), 55(45):28.

20. Kunstler, pp. 104–12.

21. Lester Cohen, *The New York Graphic,* pp. 9–10.

22. A criminal libel action can be brought only by an officer of the state, and in the twentieth century such actions have been much rarer than civil libel suits. Stanley Walker, *City Editor,* pp. 203.

23. *Daily News,* July 18, 1926. For the next few days the *Daily News* ran little or nothing on the case. Unfortunately, there is no microfilm of the *Graphic* for this period.

24. *Mirror,* November 6, 1926.

25. Napa (Calif.) *Morning Journal,* November 4, 1926.

26. Ross, p. 270.

27. Damon Runyan, like several other writers, had just covered the Peaches and Daddy hearing. Both accounts are reprinted in Damon Runyan, *Trials and Other Tribulations.*

28. *Editor & Publisher* (November 6, 1926), 59(24):3–4. Dreiser was selected because of the murder trial scene in his recent *An American Tragedy,* according to *Variety,* September 22, 1926, p. 1.

29. Quoted in Cohen, p. 107. These issues are missing from the microfilm.

30. An advertisement urged papers, large and small, to sign up for territorial rights. *Editor & Publisher* (September 25, 1926), 59(18):47. She was paid only $75 a week, far less than most of the other special writers. *Editor & Publisher* (November 6, 1926), 59(24):3–4. See *Mirror,* November 13, 1926.

31. Detroit *Free Press,* October 28, 1926.

32. *Times,* November 4, 1926.

33. Martin Weyrauch, "The Why of the Tabloids,"

34. *Mirror,* October 30, November 1, 1926.

35. *Journal,* November 30, 1926; Walker, p. 202.

36. *Mirror,* November 10, 1926.

37. Boswell and Thompson, pp. 83–84.

38. Attorneys frequently used such tactics to badger female witnesses, according to Mary S. Hartman, "The Hall-Mills Murder Case: The Most Fascinating Unsolved Murder Case in America."

39. Runyan, p. 55.

40. *Journal, Mirror, Times,* November 19, 1926.

41. *World,* November 18, 1926.

42. Kunstler, p. 255.

43. Runyan, p. 71.

44. *Journal,* November 29, 1926.

45. New Orleans *Times-Picayune,* November 8, 1926.

46. Runyan, p. 80.

47. *Journal,* December 2, 1926.

48. Boswell and Thompson, p. 168.

49. Kunstler, p. 304.

50. Kunstler, p. 306.

51. *Evening Post,* December 4, 1926; *Sun, Herald-Tribune, Times,* December 6, 1926.

52. Silas Bent, "The Hall Mills Case in the Newspapers."

53. Bruce Blivin, "The Hall-Mills-Press Case."

54. Quoted in Cohen, p. 111.

55. *Mirror,* December 11, 1926; *Daily News,* February 5, 1927.

56. Kenneth T. Jackson, *The Ku Klux Klan in the City,* pp. 178–79.

57. Hartman, pp. 13–14.

58. Walker, p. 204.

59. Merz, pp. 338–43.

60. *Evening Post,* March 31, 1927.

61. The *Times, Herald-Tribune, World,* and *Evening Post* each printed more than 600 inches on the case; however, for none of these standard papers did the coverage occupy as much as 1 percent of the space. Edith E. Switt, "Comparative Analysis of Eight New York City Papers With Especial Reference to Anti-Social News," p. 64.

62. Patterson to Frank Hause, May 24, 1927, JMP, box 17.

63. *Editor & Publisher* (April 23, 1927), 59(48):84.

64. *Daily News,* May 8, 1927.

65. *Mirror,* May 12, 1927.

66. *Daily News,* January 14, 1928. For details on how the picture was taken, see chapter 10.

67. *Variety,* January 11, 1928.

68. *Saturday Evening Post* (July 21, 1928), 201(3):68.

69. John W. Ward, "The Meaning of Lindbergh's Flight," in Joseph J. Kwiat and Mary C. Turpie, eds., *Studies in American Culture,* pp. 27–40.

70. *Variety,* June 22, 1927.

71. David A. Jasen, *Tin Pan Alley,* p. 190.

72. *Variety,* June 15, August 3, 1927. In spite of the public's belief to the contrary, Lindbergh cashed in handsomely on endorsements and personal appearances. Geoffrey Perrett, *America in the Twenties: A History,* p. 283.

14. In the Tradition: Supermarket Tabloids

1. George Juergens, *Joseph Pulitzer and the New York World,* pp. viii–ix.

2. Jan H. Brunvand, *The Vanishing Hitchhiker (New York: Norton, 1981); The*

Choking Doberman (New York: Norton, 1984); *The Mexican Pet* (New York: Norton, 1986); *Curses! Broiled Again! The Hottest Urban Legends Going* (New York: Norton, 1989).

3. Jan H. Brunvand to author, June 23, 1989.

4. Mike Nevard to author, May 9, 1989. Nevard was the only tabloid executive to respond for a request for information. His help is appreciated.

5. Juergens, p. viii.

6. Richard Walkomir, "With Tabloids, 'Zip! You're in Another World.' "

Bibliography

A note on sources: Consult notes for newspaper and trade journal sources as well as for sources of uncited background information.

UNPUBLISHED SOURCES
Manuscript Collections

American Civil Liberties Union Papers. Library of Congress, Washington, D.C.
Arthur Brishbane Papers. Arents Library, Syracuse University, Syracuse, N.Y.
Kent Cooper Papers. Lilly Library, Indiana University, Bloomington.
William T. Evjue Papers. State Historical Society of Wisconsin, Madison.
Phillip Hone Diary. New-York Historical Society, New York City.
New York Evening Star Collection. New-York Historical Society, New York City.
New York World Papers. Butler Library, Columbia University, New York City.
Joseph M. Patterson Papers. Lake Forest College, Lake Forest, Ill.
Joseph Pulitzer Papers. Butler Library, Columbia University, New York City.
Joseph Pulitzer Papers. Library of Congress, Washington, D.C.
George T. Strong Diary. New-York Historical Society, New York City.
William A. Swanberg; Papers. Butler Library, Columbia University, New York.

Letters and Interview

Brunvand, Jan. Letter to author, June 23, 1989.
GIlman, Mildred. Transcribed interview. Oral History Collection, Columbia University, New York.
Lippmann, Walter. Transcribed interview. Oral History Collection, Columbia University, New York.
Nevard, Mike. Letter to author, May 9, 1989.

PUBLISHED SOURCES
Government Documents

Board of Aldermen. *Documents.* New York: City of New York, 1836–37.
Crime Commission, *Annual Report of the Commission.* Albany: State of New York, 1927.
Edwards, Alba M. *Comparative Occupational Statistics for the United States, 1870–1940.* Washington, D.C.: Bureau of the Census, 1943.
First Federal Report of the United States Congress on Alcohol and Health. Washington, D.C.: Department of Health, Education, and Welfare, 1971.
North, S. N. D. "History and Present Condition of the Newspaper and Periodical Press of the United States." Washington, D.C.: Bureau of the Census, 1884.
Royal Commission on Violence. *Violence in Print and Media.* Toronto: Royal Commission on Violence, 1976.
Secretary of State. *Reports on the Statistics of Crime.* Albany: State of New York, 1891–1900.
Burstyn v. Wilson. 343 U.S. 495 (1952).
Mutual Film Corp. v. Industrial Commission of Ohio. 236 U.S. 230 (1915).
Regina v. Hicklin. L.R.Q.B. 360 (1868).
United States v. Dennett. 39 F.2d 564 (1930).
United States v. Bennett. 24 Fed. Cas. 1093, S.D.N.Y. (1879).

Books, Articles, Pamphlets

Abbott, Willis J. *Watching the World Go By.* Boston: Little, Brown, 1934.
Adelman, Melvin L. *A Sporting Time: New York City and the Rise of Modern Athletics, 1820–1870.* Urbana: University of Illinois Press, 1986.
Albion, Robert. *The Rise of the New York Port.* New York: Scribner, 1939.
Allen, Frederick L. *Only Yesterday.* New York: Harper & Row, 1931.
American Society of Newspaper Editors. *Problems in Journalism.* Washington, D.C.: American Society of Newspaper Editors, 1923–30.
Anderson, Mary C. "Gender, Class and Culture: Women Secretarial and Clerical Workers in the United States, 1925–1955." PhD dissertation, Ohio State University, 1986.
Appleton's Encyclopedia of American Biography. New York: D. Appleton, 1881–1901.

Ayer, N. W. and Son. *American Newspaper Annual and Directory.* Philadelphia: N. W. Ayer and Son, 1920, 1929.

Baida, Peter. "Hearst's Little Time Bomb." *American Heritage* (April 1988), 39(3):18–20.

Barnouw, Erik. *A Tower in Babel: A History of Broadcasting in the United States I.* New York: Oxford University Press, 1966.

Barrett, James W. *Joseph Pulitzer and His* World. New York: Vanguard Press, 1941.

Barth, Gunther. *City People: The Rise of Modern City Culture in Nineteenth Century America.* New York: Oxford University Press, 1980.

Bell, Daniel. *The Cultural Contradictions of American Capitalism.* New York: Basic Books, 1976.

Benson, Susan P. *Counter Cultures: Salesmen, Managers and Customers in American Department Stores, 1890–1948.* Urbana: University of Illinois Press, 1986.

Bent, Silas. *Ballyhoo.* New York: Horace Livermore, 1927.

Bent, Silas. "The Hall Mills Case in the Newspapers." *The Nation* (December 8, 1926), 123(3205):580–81.

Berger, John, and Jean Mohr, eds. *Another Way of Telling.* New York: Pantheon, 1982.

Berger, Michael L. "The Automobile and the City." *Michigan Quarterly Review* (Fall 1980), 19(4):459–71.

Bernstein, Irving. *The Lean Years: A History of the American Worker, 1920–1933.* Baltimore: Penguin Books, 1966.

Bessie, Simon. *Jazz Journalism.* New York: Dutton, 1938.

Bickel, Karl A. *News Empires.* Philadelphia: Lippincott, 1930.

Billington, Ray A. *The Protestant Crusade: A Study of the Origins of American Nativism, 1800–1860.* Gloucester, Mass.: Peter Smith, 1963.

Bleyer, Willard G. *Main Currents in the History of American Journalism.* Boston: Houghton Mifflin, 1927.

Blivin, Bruce. "Hearst." *New Republic* (July 4, 1928), 55(709):165–67.

Blivin, Bruce. "The Hall-Mills-Press Case." *New Republic* (December 1, 1926), 49(626):39–40.

Bosco, Ronald A. "Lectures in the Pillory: The Early American Execution Sermon." *American Quarterly* (Summer 1978), 30(2):156–76.

Boorstin, Daniel. *The Americans: The Democratic Experience.* New York: Vantage, 1974.

Boorstin, Daniel. *The Image: A Guide to Pseudo-Events in America.* New York: Atheneum, 1961.

Boswell, Charles, and Lewis Thompson. *The Girl in Lover's Lane.* New York: Fawcett Gold Medal, 1953.

Boylan, James. *The World in the 20's.* New York: Dial Press, 1973.

Boyle, Thomas. *Black Swine in the Sewers of Hempstead.* New York: Viking, 1989.

Bradshaw, James S. "George W. Wisner and the New York *Sun.*" *Journalism History* (Winter 1984), 6(4):112–21.

Brazil, John R. "Murder Trials, Murder and Twenties America." *American Quarterly* (Summer 1981), 33(3):163–84.

Bremner, Robert H. *From the Depths: The Discovery of Poverty in the United States.* New York: New York University Press, 1956.

Brisbane, Arthur. "The Modern Newspaper in War Time." *Cosmopolitan* (September 1898), 25(5):541–56.

Browder, Clifford. *The Wickedest Woman in New York: Madam Restell, the Abortionist.* Hamden, Conn.: Archon, 1988.

Brown, Charles H. *The Correspondents' War: Jouralists in the Spanish-American War.* New York: Scribner, 1967.

Brunvand, Jan H. *The Vanishing Hitchhiker.* New York: Norton, 1981.

Buddenbaum, Judith M. " 'Judge . . . What Their Acts Will Justify': The Religious Journalism of James Gordon Bennett." *Journalism History* (Summer 1987), 14(2):54–67.

Burnham, J. C. "New Perspectives on the Prohibition Experiment of the 1920s." *Journal of Social History* (Fall 1968), 2(1).

Cameron, Deborah and Elizabeth Frazier. *The Lust to Kill: A Feminist Interpretation of Sexual Murder.* London: Polity Press, 1987.

Capp, Bernard. *English Almanacs, 1500–1800.* Ithaca, N.Y.: Cornell University Press, 1979.

Carlisle, Rodney P. "The Political Ideas and Influence of William Randolph Hearst, 1928–1936." PhD dissertation, University of California, 1965.

Carlson, Oliver. *The Man Who Made News: James Gordon Bennett.* New York: Duell, Sloan, and Pearce, 1942.

Carlson, Oliver, and Ernest S. Bates. *Hearst: Lord of San Simeon.* New York: Viking, 1936.

Carlson, Oliver. *Brisbane: A Candid Biography.* New York: Stackpole, 1937.

Carmichael, Hoagy, and Stephen Longstreet. *Sometimes I Wonder: The Story of Hoagy Carmichael.* New York: Farrar, Straus & Giroux, 1965.

Caro, Robert A. *The Power Broker: Robert Moses and the Fall of New York.* New York: Knopf, 1974.

Carson, Gerald. *The Polite Americans: A Wide-Angle View of Our Mores and Less Good Manners Over 300 Years.* New York: William Morrow, 1966.

Carter, Paul A. *Another Part of the Twenties.* New York: Columbia University Press, 1977.

Cashman, Sean D. *America in the Gilded Age.* New York: New York University Press, 1984.

Chafe, William H. *The American Woman: Her Changing Social, Economic and Political Roles, 1920–1970.* New York: Oxford University Press, 1972.

Chapman, John. *Tell It to Sweeney: An Informal History of the New York Daily News.* Garden City, N.Y.: Doubleday, 1961.

Churchill, Allen. *Park Row.* New York: Rinehart, 1958.

Clark, Norman H. *Deliver Us From Evil: An Interpretation of American Prohibition.* New York: Norton, 1976.

Cochran, Thomas C. *200 Years of American Business.* New York: Basic Books, 1977.

Cochran, Thomas C., and William Miller. *The Age of Enterprise: A Social History of Industrial America.* New York: Harper & Row, 1961.

Coffey, Thomas M. *The Long Thirst: Prohibition in America, 1920–1933.* New York: Norton, 1975.

Cogley, John. *Catholic America.* New York: Dial Press, 1973.

Cohen, Hennig, ed. *The American Experience: Approaches to the Study of the United States.* Boston: Houghton Mifflin, 1968.

Cohen, Lester. *The New York* Graphic: *The World's Zaniest Newspaper.* Philadelphia: Chilton, 1964.

Cohen, Patricia C. "The Ellen Jewett Murder Case: Violence, Gender and Sexual Licentiousness in Antebellum America." Paper presented to Organization of American Historians, 1989.

Cohen, Stanley and Jock Young, eds. *The Manufacture of News.* London: Constable, 1973.

Commager, Henry S. *The American Mind.* New Haven: Yale University Press, 1950.

Communication. Special issue on literacy. *Communication* (1988), 11(1).

Conboy, Kenneth. "Murder and Violence in New York Papers." Report for Professor Kenneth Jackson, Columbia University, 1977.

Covert, Catherine L., and John D. Stevens, eds. *Mass Media Between the Wars.* Syracuse: Syracuse University Press, 1984.

Covert, Catherine L., "A View of the Press in the Twenties." *Journalism History* (Autumn 1975), 2(3):66–67, 96.

Crawford, Nelson. "Mental Health and the Newspaper." *Mental Hygine* (April 1922), 6(2):299–304.

Creelman, James. *On the Great Highway.* Boston: Lathrop, 1907.

Crepeau, Richard C. *Baseball: America's Diamond Mind, 1919–1941.* Orlando: University of Central Florida Press, 1980.

Crouthamel, James L. *Bennett's New York* Herald *and the Rise of the Popular Press.* Syracuse: Syracuse University Press, 1989.

Crouthamel, James L. *James Watson Webb: A Biography.* Middleton, Conn.: Wesleyan University Press, 1969.

Csillag, András. "Joseph Pulitzer's Roots in Europe: A Genealogical History." *American Jewish Archives* (April 1987), 39(1):49–68.

cummings, e. e. "The Tabloid Newspaper: An Investigation Involving Big Business, the Pilgrim Fathers, and Psychoanalysis." *Vanity Fair* (December 1926), 27(4):83, 110.

Curti, Merle. *The Growth of American Thought.* 2d ed. New York: Harper & Brothers, 1943.

Darton, Robert and Daniel Roche, eds. *Revolution in Print.* Berkeley: University of California Press, 1989.

Davis, David B. *Homicide in American Fiction.* Ithaca, N.Y.: Cornell University Press, 1957.

Davis, Margery. "Woman's Place Is at the Typewriter." *Radical America* (July/August 1974), 8(4):1–28.

Degler, Carl N., ed. *The Age of the Economic Revolution, 1876–1900.* Glenview, Ill.: Scott, Foresman, 1977.

DeRochemont, Richard G. "The Tabloids." *American Mercury* (October 1926), 9(34):187.

Desmond, Robert W. *The Press and World Affairs.* New York: Appleton-Century-Crofts, 1837.

Dicken-Garcia, Hazel. *Journalistic Standards in Nineteenth Century America.* Madison: University of Wisconsin Press, 1989.

Dictionary of American Biography. Boston: James R. Osgood, 1872.

Ditzion, Sidney. *Marriage, Morals and Sex in America.* New York: Bookman, 1953.

Dreiser, Theodore. *Sister Carrie.* New York: Bantam Books. 1958.

Dubois, Wiggins. "Recent Newspaper Tendencies in New York City." M. A. thesis, Columbia University, 1924.

Durkheim, Emile. *The Rules of Sociological Method.* 5th ed. Glencoe, Ill.: Free Press, 1938.

Durso, Joseph. *Baseball and the American Dream.* St. Louis: the Sporting News, 1966.

Eberhard, Wallace B. "Mr. Bennett Covers a Murder Trial." *Journalism Quarterly* (Winter 1970), 47(4):457–63.

Emery, Edwin. *History of the American Newspaper Publishers Association.* Minneapolis: University of Minnesota Press, 1950.

Emery, Edwin. "William Randolph Hearst: A Tentative Appraisal." *Journalism Quarterly* (Fall 1951), 28(4):428–35.

Emery, Edwin and Michael. *The Press and America.* 6th ed. Englewood Cliffs, N.J.: Prentice-Hall, 1988.

Ernst, Morris L. *The First Freedom.* New York: Macmillan, 1946.

Ernst, Robert. *Immigrant Life in New York City: 1825–1863.* New York: King's Crown Press, 1949.

Faller, Lincoln B. *Turned to Account: The Forms and Functions of Criminal Biography in Late Seventeenth and Early Eighteenth Century England.* New York: Cambridge University Press, 1987.

Fass, Paula. *The Damned and the Beautiful: American Youth in the 1920s.* New York: Oxford University Press, 1977.

Faulkner, Harold U. *Politics, Reform and Expansion, 1890–1900.* New York: Harper, 1959.

Faulkner, Harold U. *American Economic History.* 7th ed. New York: Harper, 1954.

Feister, James. "The Other Pulitzer—Albert." *Media History* (Spring–Summer 1988), 8(1):2–8.

Feldberg, Michael. *Turbulent Era: Riot and Disorder in Jacksonian America.* New York: Oxford University Press, 1980.

Fermer, Douglas. *James Gordon Bennett and the New York* Herald: *A Study of Editorial Opinion in the Civil War Era, 1854–1867.* New York: St. Martin's Press, 1986.

Fisher, Robert. "Film Censorship and Progressive Reform: The National Board of Censorship of Motion Pictures." *Journal of Popular Film* (April 1975), 4(2):143–56.

Flint, Leon N. *The Conscience of a Newspaper.* New York: Appleton-Century, 1925.

Finney, Jack. *Forgotten News.* New York: Simon & Schuster, 1983.

Folk, Paul J. *Pioneer Catholic Journalism.* New York: U.S. Catholic Historical Society, 1930.

Folkerts, Jean, and Dwight L. Teeter. *Voices of a Nation.* New York: Macmillan, 1988.

Foner, Philip S. *History of the Labor Movement in the United States.* New York: International Publishers, 1947.

Ford, James, Katherine Morrow, and George H. Thompson. *Slums and Housing, With Special Reference to New York City.* Cambridge: Harvard University Press, 1936.

Frank, Joseph. *The Beginnings of the English Newspaper: 1620–1660.* Cambridge: Harvard University Press, 1961.

Francke, Warren. "An Argument in Defense of Sensationalism." *Journalism History* (Autumn 1970), 5(3):70–73.

Freedman, Estelle B. "The New Woman: Changing Views of Women in the 1920s." *Journal of American History* (September 1974), 61(2):372–93.

Gauvreau, Emile H. *My Last Million Readers.* New York: Dutton, 1941.

Gerard, J. R. *London and New York: Their Crime and Police.* New York: William C. Bryant, 1853.

Gilfoyle, Timothy J. *City of Eros: Prostitution in New York City.* New York: Norton, forthcoming.

Gilfoyle, Timothy J. "Strumpets and Misogynists: Brothel 'Riots' and the Transformation of Prostitution in Antelbellum New York City." *New York History* (January 1987), 68(1):45–65.

Gilfoyle, Timothy J. "The Urban Geography of Commercial Sex: Prostitution in New York City, 1790–1860." *Journal of Urban History* (August 1987), 13(4):371–93.

Gilje, Paul A. *The Road to Mobocracy: Popular Disorder in New York City, 1763–1864.* Chapel Hill: University of North Carolina Press, 1987.

Glaab, Charles N. "The Historian and the Urban Tradition." *Wisconsin Magazine of History* (Autumn 1963), 57(1):12–25.

Glad, Paul W. *McKinley, Bryan and the People.* Philadelphia: Lippincott, 1964.

Gordon, Lyman. "The Gibson Girl Goes to College: Popular Culture and Women's Higher Education in the Progressive Era, 1890–1920." *American Quarterly* (Summer 1982), 39(2):211–30.

Gordon, Michael, ed. *The American Family in Social-Historical Perspective.* New York: St. Martin's Press, 1973.

Gordon, Milton W. "Assimilation in America: Theory and Reality." *Daedalus* (Spring 1961), 90(2):263–85.

Gould, Louis D. *The Presidency of William McKinley.* Lawrence, Kans.: The Regents Press of Kansas, 1980.

Graham, Hugh D., and Ted R. Gurr, eds. *The History of Violence in America: Historical and Comparative Perspectives.* New York: Praeger, 1969.

Greeley, Horace. *Reflections of a Busy Life.* New York: J. B. Ford, 1868.

Griffith, Sally F. *Home Town News: William Allen White and the Emporia Gazette.* New York: Oxford University Press, 1989.

Gunther, John. *Inside USA.* New York: Harper & Row, 1951.

Hamilton, Thomas C. *Men and Manners in America*. Philadelphia: Carey, Lea and Blanchard, 1833.

Harris, Neil, ed. *The Land of Contrasts: 1880–1901*. New York: Braziller, 1970.

Hart, James D. *The Popular Book: A History of America's Literary Taste*. New York: Oxford University Press, 1950.

Hartman, Mary S. "The Hall-Mills Murder Case: The Most Fascinating Unsolved Murder Case in America." *Journal of the Rutgers Universities Libraries* (June 1984), 46(1):4–15.

Hays, Will H. *The Memoirs of Will H. Hays*. Indianapolis: Bobbs Merrill, 1955.

Heaton, John. *The Story of a Page*. New York: Harper & Row, 1913.

Hess, Stephen. "The Ungentlemanly Art." *Gannett Center Journal* (Spring 1989), 5(2):117–31.

Higham, John. *Send These to Me: Jews and Other Immigrants in Urban America*. New York: Atheneum, 1975.

Hoffman, Charles. *The Depression of the Nineties: An Economic History*. Westport, Conn.: Greenwood, 1970.

Hofstadter, Richard A. *The Age of Reform: From Bryan to FDR*. New York: Vintage Books, 1955.

Hofstadter, Richard A. *The Paranoid Style in American Politics and Other Essays*. New York: Knopf, 1966.

Hohenberg, John. *Foreign Correspondence: The Great Reporters and Their Times*. New York: Columbia University Press, 1964.

Hudson, Frederic. *Journalism in the United States, from 1600–1872*. New York: Harper, 1873.

Hughes, Helen M. *News and the Human Interest Story*. Chicago: University of Chicago Press, 1940.

Hugins, Walter. *Jacksonian Democracy and the Working Class: A Study of the New York Workingmen's Movement, 1829–1837*. Stanford: Stanford University Press, 1960.

Hynes, Teresa M. "The Portrayal of Women in Selected Magazines From 1911–1930." PhD dissertation, University of Wisconsin, 1975.

Irwin, Will. "The American Newspaper: A Study of Journalism in its Relation to the Public, Part 3" *Collier's* (February 18, 1911), 46(2):14–27.

Isenberg, Michael T. *John L. Sullivan and His America*. Urbana: University of Illinois Press, 1988.

Jackson, Holbrook. *The Eighteen-Nineties: A Review of Art and Ideas at the Close of the Nineteenth Century*. New York: Knopf, 1922.

Jackson, Kenneth T. *The Ku Klux Klan in the City, 1915–1930*. New York: Oxford University Press, 1967.

Jackson, Kenneth T., and Stanley K. Schultz, eds. *Cities in American History*. New York: Knopf, 1972.

Jasen, David A. *Tin Pan Alley: The Composers, the Songs, the Performers and Their Times*. New York: Donald I. Fine, 1988.

Jefferson, Thomas. *The Writings of Thomas Jefferson*. 20 vols. Washington, D.C.: Thomas Jefferson Memorial Association, 1907.

Johnston, Alva. "The Great Macfadden." *Saturday Evening Post* (June 28, 1941), 213(52):20–21, 90–92.

Juergens, George. *Joseph Pulitzer and the New York* World. Princeton: Princeton University Press, 1966.

Kandel, Aben. "A Tabloid a Day." *The Forum* (March 1927), 77(3):378–84.

Kasson, John F. *Civilizing the Machine: Technology and Republican Values in America, 1776–1900.* New York: Grossman, 1976.

King, Homer W. *Pulitzer's Prize Editor: A Biography of John A. Cockerill.* Durham, N.C.: Duke University Press, 1965.

Kirkland, Edward C. *Industry Comes of Age: Business, Labor and Public Policy, 1860–1897.* Chicago: Quadrangle, 1967.

Klurfeld, Herman. *Winchell: His Life and Times.* New York: Praeger, 1976.

Knightley, Phillip. *The First Casualty.* New York: Harcourt, Brace, Jovanovich, 1975.

Koenigsberg, Moses. *King News: An Autobiography.* Philadelphia: Stokes, 1941.

Korty, Jack. "What Makes Crime News?" *Media, Culture and Society* (January 1987), 9(1):47–75.

Kunstler, William M. *The Minister and the Choir Girl: The Hall-Mills Murder Case.* New York: William Morrow, 1964.

Kwiat, Joseph J., and Mary C. Turpie, eds. *Studies in American Culture: Dominant Ideas and Images.* Minneapolis: University of Minnesota Press, 1960.

Lee, James M. *History of American Journalism.* Boston: Houghton Mifflin, 1917.

Leonard, Thomas C. *Power of the Press: The Birth of American Political Reporting.* New York: Oxford University Press, 1986.

Lerner, Max. *America as a Civilization: Life and Thought of the United States Today.* New York: Simon & Schuster, 1957.

Lewis, Howard T. *The Motion Picture Industry.* New York: Van Nostrand, 1933.

"Life and Adventures of Editor Bombast, Alias James G–r–n B–n–n–t: A Scotch Pedlar's Tale." Philadelphia: n.d.

"Life and Writings of James Gordon Bennett." New York: n.p., 1844.

Lilly, W. S. "The Ethics of Journalism." *The Forum* (July 1889), 7(5):503–12.

Lippmann, Walter. *Public Opinion.* New York: Harcourt Brace, 1922.

Lipset, Seymour M., ed. *Harriet Martineau's Society in America.* New York: Doubleday Anchor, 1962.

Littlefield, Everett. *William Randolph Hearst: His Role in American Progressivism.* Lanham, Md.: University Press of America, 1980.

Lubove, Roy. *Community Planning in the 1920s: The Contribution of the Regional Planning Association of America.* Pittsburgh: University of Pittsburgh Press, 1963.

Luhan, Mabel D. *Movers and Shakers.* Albuquerque: University of New Mexico Press, 1936.

Lundberg, Ferdinand. *Imperial Hearst.* New York: Equinox, 1936.

Lyman, Susan E. *The Story of New York.* New York: Crown, 1964.

Lynn, Kenneth. "Only Yesterday." *American Scholar* (Autumn 1980), 49(4):513.

Mackey, Robert E. "Managing the Clerks: Office Management from the 1870s through the Great Depression." PhD dissertation, Boston University, 1985.

MacLean, Annie M. "Two Weeks in a Department Store." *American Journal of Sociology* (May 1899), 4(6):721–41.

MacLuhan, Marshall. *Understanding Media: The Extensions of Man.* New York: McGraw-Hill, 1964.

Marryatt, Frederick. *A Diary in America.* London: Longman, Orme, Brown, Green and Longmans, 1839.

May, Elaine T. *Great Expectations: Marriage and Divorce in Post-Victorian America.* Chicago: University of Chicago Press, 1980.

May, Henry F. "Shifting Perspectives on the 1920s." *Mississippi Valley Historical Review* (December 1956), 43(3):424–27.

McCullough, David G. *The Great Bridge.* New York: Simon & Schuster, 1972.

McGivena, Leo E. *The* News: *The First Fifty Years of New York's Picture Newspaper.* New York: News Syndicate Company, 1969.

McKenzie, R. D. *The Metropolitan Community.* New York: McGraw-Hill, 1933.

Miller, Michael. *The Bon Marche: Bourgeois Culture and the Department Store.* Princeton: Princeton University Press, 1981.

Milton, Joyce. *The Yellow Kids.* New York: Harper & Row, 1989.

Monmonier, Mark. *Maps With the News.* Chicago: University of Chicago Press, 1989.

Mooney, Edmund A. *A Catholic Runs For President.* New York: Ronald Press, 1956.

Mott, Frank L. *American Journalism: A History of Newspapers in the United States Through 250 Years.* 3d ed. New York: Macmillan, 1962.

Mowry, George E. *The Urban Nation, 1920–1960.* New York: Hill & Wang, 1965.

Mowry, George E. *The Twenties: Fords, Flappers and Fanatics.* New York: Prentice Hall, 1963.

Nathan, George J. "Clinical Notes: The Tabloids." *American Mercury* (March 1926), 7(27):363–64.

Nerone, John. "The Mythology of the Penny Press." *Critical Studies in Mass Communication* (1987), 4:376–404.

Newhall, Beaumont. *Photography, 1879–1937.* New York: Museum of Modern Art, 1937.

Nevins, Allan, ed. *The Diary of Phillip Hone.* New York: Dodd, Mead, 1927.

Nevins, Allan, and Milton H. Thomas, eds. *The Diary of George Templeton Strong.* 3 vols. New York: Macmillan, 1952.

Nilsson, Nils G. "The Origin of the Interview." *Journalism Quarterly* (Winter 1971), 48(4):707–13.

Nord, David Paul. "Teleology and News." Paper presented at Association for Education in Journalism and Mass Communication, 1987.

Nye, F. Ivan, and Felix M. Bernardo. *The Family: Its Structure and Interaction.* New York: Macmillan, 1973.

Nye, Russell. *Society and Culture in America.* New York: Harper Torchbooks, 1974.

O'Brien, Frank M. *The Story of the Sun.* New York: Appleton, 1928.

O'Connor, Richard. *The Scandalous Mr. Bennett.* Garden City, N.Y.: Doubleday, 1962.

Olasky, Marvin. "Advertising Abortion During the 1830s and 1840s: Madame Restelle Builds a Business." *Journalism History* (Summer 1986), 13(2):49–55.

Older, Mrs. Fremont. *William Randolph Hearst: American.* New York: Appleton, 1936.

Ostrander, Gilman. *American Civilization in the First Machine Age.* New York: Harper & Row, 1970.

Park, Robert E. *The City.* Chicago: University of Chicago Press, 1925.

Park, Robert E. "The Natural History of the Newspaper." *American Journal of Sociology* (November 1923), 29(3):273–89.

Park, Robert E. *The Immigrant Press and Its Control.* New York: Harper & Row, 1922.

Parmenter, William Q. "The News Control Explanation of News Making: The Case of William Randolph Hearst." PhD dissertation, University of Washington, 1979.

Payne, Darwin. *The Man of Only Yesterday: Frederick Lewis Allen.* New York: Harper & Row, 1975.

Pearson, Edmund L. *Masterpieces of Murder.* Boston: Little, Brown, 1963.

Perrett, Geoffrey. *America in the Twenties.* New York: Simon & Schuster, 1982.

Perry, Elisabeth. "Cleaning Up the Dance Halls." *History Today* (October 1989), 39(10):20–26.

Pessen, Edward. *Jacksonian America.* Urbana, Ill.: University of Illinois Press, 1985.

Peterson, Ted. "British Crime Pamphleteers: Forgotten Journalists." *Journalism Quarterly* (December 1945), 22(4):305–16.

Peterson, Ted. "James Catnach: Master of Street Literature." *Journalism Quarterly* (Spring 1950), 27(2):157–63.

Pickard, P. M. *I Could a Tale Untold: Of Violence, Horror and Sensationalism in Stories for Children.* London: Tavistock, 1961.

Plant, Marjorie. *The English Book Trade: Economic History of the Making and Sale of Books.* 2d ed. London: Allen & Unwin, 1965.

Potter, David M. *People of Plenty: Economic Abundance and the American Character.* Chicago: University of Chicago Press, 1954.

[Pray, Isaac C.] *Memoirs of James Gordon Bennett and His Times.* New York: Stringer & Townsend, 1855.

Pred, Allan R. *Urban Growth and the Circulation of Information: The American System of Cities, 1790–1840.* Cambridge: Harvard University Press, 1973.

President's Research Committee on Social Trends. *Recent Social Trends in the United States.* 2 vols. New York: McGraw-Hill, 1933.

Rammelkamp, Julian S. *Pulitzer's Post-Dispatch, 1878–1883.* Princeton: Princeton University Press, 1967.

Richardson, James A. *The New York Police: Colonial Times to 1901.* New York: Oxford University Press, 1970.

Rock, Howard B. *Artisans of the New Republic: The Tradesmen of New York City in the Age of Jefferson.* New York: New York University Press, 1979.

Rosebault, Charles T. *When Dana Was the* Sun: *A Story of Personal Journalism.* New York: Robert McBride, 1931.

Rosenwaike, Ira. *Population History of New York City.* Syracuse: Syracuse University Press, 1972.

Ross, Ishbel. *Ladies of the Press.* New York: Harper & Brothers, 1936.

Ross, Shelley. *Fall From Grace.* New York: Ballantine Books, 1988.

Rosse, James N. "The Decline of Direct Newspaper Competition." *Journal of Communication* (Spring 1980), 30(2):65–71.

Rudd, Arthur S. "The Development of Illustrated Tabloid Journalism in the United States." M.A. thesis, Columbia University, 1925.

Runyan, Damon. *Trials and Other Tribulations.* Philadelphia: Lippincott, 1947.

Samuels, Peggy and Harold. *Frederic Remington: A Biography.* Garden City, N.Y.: Doubleday, 1982.

Saxton, Alexander. "Problems of Class and Rank in the Origins of the Mass Circulation Press." *American Quarterly* (Summer 1984), 36(2):211–34.

Schama, Simon. *Citizens: A Chronicle of the French Revolution.* New York: Knopf, 1989.

Scheiber, Harry N., Harold G. Vatter, and Harold U. Faulkner. *American Economic History.* New York: Harper & Row, 1976.

Schiller, Dan, *Objectivity and the News: The Public and the Rise of Popular Journalism.* Philadelphia: University of Pennsylvania Press, 1981.

Schlesinger, Arthur M. *The Rise of the City, 1878–1898.* Chicago: Quadrangle, 1971.

Schudson, Michael. *Discovering the News: A Social History of American Newspapers.* New York: Basic Books, 1978.

Schudson, Michael. *Advertising, the Uneasy Persuader: Its Dubious Impact on American Society.* New York: Basic Books, 1984.

Schuneman, R. Smith. "Art or Photography: A Question for Newspaper Editors of the 1890s." *Journalism Quarterly* (Winter 1965), 42(1):43–53.

Schwarzlose, Richard A. *The Nation's Newsbrokers.* 2 vols. Evanston: Northwestern University Press, 1989.

Schwarzlose, Richard A. *The American Wire Services: A Study of Their Development as Social Institutions.* New York: Arno Press, 1979.

Seitz, Don C. *Joseph Pulitzer: His Life and Letters.* New York: Simon & Schuster, 1924.

Shannon, William V. *The American Irish.* New York: Macmillan, 1963.

Shaw, Arnold. *The Jazz Age: Popular Music in the 1920s.* New York: Oxford University Press, 1987.

Shaw, Donald L. "At the Crossroads: Change and Continuity in American Press News, 1820–1860." *Journalism History* (Summer 1981), 8(2):38–50.

Shenkman, Richard. *Legends, Lies and Cherished Myths of American History.* New York: William Morrow, 1988.

Shi, David E. "Advertising and the Literary Imagination." *Journal of American Culture* (Summer 1979), 2(2):167–75.

Siegel, Adrienne. *The Image of the American City in Popular Literature, 1820–1870.* Port Washington, N.Y.: Kennikat Press, 1981.

Slosson, Preston W. *The Great Crusade and After.* New York: Macmillan, 1930.

Smilor, Raymond W. "Cacophony at 34th and Sixth: The Noise Problem in America, 1900–1930." *American Studies* (Spring 1976), 18(1):23–37.

Smith, Anthony. *The Newspaper: An International History.* London: Thomas and Hudson, 1979.

Smythe, Ted C. "The Reporter, 1880–1900." *Journalism History* (Spring 1980), 7(1):2–8.

Soltow, Lee, and Edward Stevens. *The Rise of Literacy and the Common School in the United States.* Chicago: University of Chicago Press, 1981.

Soule, George. *Prosperity Decade: From War to Depression, 1917–1929.* New York: Rinehart, 1947.

Steffens, Lincoln. *The Autobiography of Lincoln Steffens.* New York: Harcourt Brace, 1931.

Steinbauer, Douglas. "Faking It With Pictures." *American Heritage* (October/November 1982), 33(6):52–57.

Steinberg, Allen R. "The Criminal Courts and the Transformation of Criminal Justice in Philadelphia, 1814–1874." PhD dissertation, Columbia University, 1983.

Stephens, Mitchell. *A History of News.* New York: Viking, 1988.

Stevens, John D. "Social Utility of Sensational News: Murder and Divorce in the 1920s." *Journalism Quarterly* (Spring 1985), 62(1):53–58.

Stevens, John D. "Media and Morality in the 20s." *History Today* (November 1989), 39(11):25–29.

Stevens, John D. "Sex as Entertainment: Social Hygiene Films Before 1930." *Film & History* (December 1983), 23(2):84–87.

Stewart, Kenneth, and John Tebbell. *Makers of Modern Journalism.* New York: Prentice-Hall, 1952.

Stewart, Robert K. "Jacksonians Discipline a Party Editor: Economic Leverage and Political Exile." *Journalism Quarterly* (Autumn 1989), 66(3):591–99.

Still, Bayard. *Mirror for Gotham: New York as Seen by Contemporaries from Dutch Days to the Present.* New York: New York University Press, 1956.

Surette, Ray, ed. *Justice and the Media: Issues and Research.* Springfield, Ill.: Charles C. Thomas, 1984.

Sutherland, Daniel E. *Americans and Their Servants: Domestic Service in the United States from 1880 to 1920.* Baton Rouge: Louisiana State University Press, 1981.

Swanberg, W. A. *Pulitzer.* New York: Scribner, 1967.

Swanberg, W. A. *Citizen Hearst.* New York: Scribner, 1961.

Switt, Edith E. "Comparative Analysis of Eight New York City Newspapers With Especial Reference to Anti-Social News." M.A. thesis, Columbia University, 1927.

Taft, William H. "Bernarr Macfadden: One of a Kind." *Journalism Quarterly* (Winter 1968), 45(4):627–33.

Taft, William H. "I Love Life: The Life of Bernarr Macfadden." Paper presented at Association for Education in Journalism and Mass Communication, 1967.

Talese, Gay. *The Kingdom and the Power.* New York: World, 1969.

Tarbell, Ida. "Ten Years of Women's Suffrage." *Literary Digest* (April 26, 1930), 105(4):11.

Taylor, Robert L. "Physical Culture." *New Yorker* (October 14–28, 1950) 26(33–35).

Thomas, Bob. *Winchell.* New York: Doubleday, 1971.

Thomas, M. Wayne. "Walt Whitman and Mannahatta-New York." *American Quarterly* (Fall 1983), 34(4):362–78.

Tocqueville, Alexis de. *Democracy in America.* New York: New American Library Mentor Edition, 1956.

Voigt, David Q. *America Through Baseball.* Chicago: Nelson-Hall, 1976.

Vigot, David Q. *American Baseball: From Gentlemen's Sport to the Commissioner System.* University Park, Pa.: Pennsylvania State University Press, 1983.

Walker, Stanley. *The Night Club Era.* New York: Frederick Stokes, 1933.

Walker, Stanley. *City Editor.* New York: Frederick Stokes, 1934.

Walkomir, Richard. "With Tabloids, 'Zip! You're in Another World." *Smithsonian* (October 1987), 18(7):240.

Ward, Julius. "The Future of Sunday Journalism." *The Forum* (June 1886), 2(3):389–98.

Weiner, Ed. *Let's Go to Press.* New York: Putnam, 1955.

Weisberger, Bernard. *The American Newspaperman.* Chicago: University of Chicago Press, 1961.

Welch, Richard E., Jr. *The Presidencies of Grover Cleveland.* Lawrence, Kansas: University Press of Kansas, 1986.

Welter, Barbara. "The Cult of True Womanhood: 1820–1860." *American Quarterly* (Summer 1966), 18(2):51–74.

Weyrauch, Martin. "The Why of the Tabloids." *The Forum* (April 1927), 78(4):499.

Whitcomb, Ian. *After the Ball: Pop Music From Rag to Rock.* New York: Simon & Schuster, 1972.

White, Morton and Lucia. *The Intellectual Versus the City: From Thomas Jefferson to Frank Lloyd Wright.* New York: New American Library, 1964.

Whiteaker, Larry H. "Moral Reform and Prostitution in New York City, 1830–1860." PhD dissertation, Princeton University, 1977.

Wiebe, Robert H. *The Search for Order, 1877–1920.* New York: Hill & Wang, 1967.

Wilcox, Delos F. "The American Newspaper: A Study in Social Psychology." *The Annals of the American Academy of Political and Social Sciences* (July 1900), 16:56–92.

Wiley, Louis. "The Making of a Newspaper." *University of Missouri Bulletin* (1923), 44(15):117–20.

Wilson, Colin and Donald Seaman. *An Encyclopedia of Scandal.* London: Grafton Books, 1987.

Winick, Charles, ed. *Deviance and Mass Media.* Beverly Hills, Calif.: Sage, 1978.

Winkler, John K. *William Randolph Hearst: A New Appraisal.* New York: Hastings House, 1955.

Wolling, George C. *Recollections of a New York Chief of Police.* New York: Caxton, 1888.

Index